ESSAYS ON FREE KNOWLEDGE

*The Origins of Wikipedia and
the New Politics of Knowledge*

ESSAYS ON FREE KNOWLEDGE

The Origins of Wikipedia and
the New Politics of Knowledge

By Larry Sanger

Sanger Press

CANAL WINCHESTER, OHIO

First published 2020 by Sanger Press.

International Standard Book Number: 978-1-7357954-1-6 (paper)
Library of Congress Control Number: 2020917842
PRINTED IN THE UNITED STATES OF AMERICA

To the volunteers

Contents

Part III: Freer Knowledge

Preface

FREE knowledge from an encyclopedia—that would be a glorious thing. It is a shame that it is impossible. Knowledge is something that exists in minds, not texts. Reading a text will give you some ground for belief; it will not, by itself, actually give you knowledge.

Still, we can speak loosely and say that encyclopedias contain what purports to be knowledge, and that is enough for me to love encyclopedias. I have always been greatly impressed by systematic catalogs of knowledge—and using the Internet to make new catalogs of knowledge has been the unplanned theme of the last twenty years of my career. Before that, I rarely left school or academia, where my specialization was the theory of knowledge.

The chapters of this book emerged out of my career. They began life as stand-alone articles for publication, speeches, and blog posts. I have edited and updated them all (except for Chapter 11) so that they represent authoritative editions and are readable in the context of this book, rather than a web page. I put link content into footnotes. I made stylistic improvements throughout. I have also added many footnotes containing more recent reactions to things I wrote 10 or 20 years ago. I hope these will add interest to the book.

I had well over twice the material that made it into this book to choose from. I limited myself to those essays I liked the best, which have proved to be popular, or which I thought were possibly of some lasting importance, for some reason. I deliberately avoided repetition where I could, as well as writings about projects of mine other than Wikipedia.

In my Internet career, I have thought a fair bit about two questions: What is the best way to catalog free knowledge? And what kind of project policies should we adopt? These two questions are of deep interest to people in many disciplines and professions: to computer scientists, for their technical implications; to Internet researchers, for the history, sociology, psychology, and politics of the Internet; to philosophers, for the deep theoretical aspects of a whole new form of life. All of these aspects are of interest to the field of communications.

These are hard, interdisciplinary questions. They are evergreen and can be expected to remain so. They have deep consequences. They ramify in many ways that have been vigorously debated in the last few decades.

I have collected some answers to these ramifying questions under three heads.

The first head is Wikipedia. What makes an open, online collaboration succeed? Do we need to have charters for collaborative projects? Should media, textbooks, and above all reference works aim to be neutral—or should they instead aim at what their editors claim is the objective truth? How should we organize people who are difficult to reconcile, who have different interests and agendas? How do we resolve disputes among anonymous people in open communities?

The second part concerns what I call the "new politics of knowledge." In an age of instant answers from collectively-built databases, should we care about accumulating individual knowledge, or are mere information and collective knowledge good enough? What sort of special role, if any, do experts deserve in declaring "what we all know"? Is individual knowledge, built from books and individual study, somehow outmoded? Is there not something anti-intellectual about saying so?

In the final part I include three recent essays bemoaning the fact that free knowledge is in dire straits, now that, like social media, Wikipedia has abandoned neutrality and is used as a tool for social manipulation. With the "Encyclosphere," I propose a free, decentralized encyclopedia network, open to contributions from all. I apply similar themes to the Internet generally in a "Declaration of Digital Independence." I conclude, in a brand new essay, that free information and knowledge on the Internet is under attack, and I ask how we can save it.

I hope this book will be of interest and use to Internet entrepreneurs, scholars, policymakers, and the broad public.

LARRY SANGER

Central Ohio
August 2020

Part I

HISTORY AND THEORY
OF WIKIPEDIA

<u>One</u>

The Early History of Nupedia and Wikipedia: A Memoir

An origin story and analysis, written in spring 2005 for Slashdot while memories were still relatively fresh. How did Wikipedia get started? How did such an unlikely-seeming idea actually work? This is one of the longer and most detailed accounts of the origin of Wikipedia, revised anew, with remarks from 2020 mostly relegated to footnotes and in this volume's concluding essay.

AN impassioned debate has been raging, particularly since the summer of 2004, about the merits of Wikipedia and the future of free online encyclopedias. This discussion has not benefitted by much detailed, accurate consideration of the origins of Wikipedia and of its parent project, Nupedia. But it seems to me that those origins are very important—crucial, even—to forming a proper judgment of the current state and best future direction of free encyclopedias.

Wikipedia as it stands is a fantastic project; it has produced enormous amounts of content, thousands of excellent articles, and now, after just four years, is getting high-profile, international recognition as a new way of obtaining at least a rough and ready idea about very many topics. Its surprising success may be attributed, briefly, to its free, open, and collaborative nature.

This has been my attitude toward Wikipedia practically since its founding. But a few months ago I wrote an article critical of certain aspects of the Wikipedia project, "Why Wikipedia Must Jettison Its Anti-Elitism,"[1] which occasioned much debate. I have also been quoted in many recent news articles about the project, making various other critical remarks. I am afraid I am getting an undeserved reputation as someone who is opposed to everything Wikipedia stands for. This is completely incorrect. In fact, I am one of Wikipedia's strongest supporters. I am partly responsible for bringing it into the world (as I will explain), and I still love it and want only the best for it. But if a better job can be done, a better job *should* be done. Wikipedia has shown fantastic potential, and it is open content—and so if the project has problems that will keep it from being the maximally authoritative, broad, and deep reference that I believe could exist, I firmly believe that the world has the right to, and should, improve upon it.

Wikipedia's predecessor, which I was also employed to organize, was Nupedia. Nupedia was to be a highly reliable, peer-reviewed resource that fully appreciated and employed the efforts of subject area experts as well as the general public. When the more free-wheeling Wikipedia took off, Nupedia was left to wither. It might appear to have died of its own weight and complexity. But, as I will explain, it could have been redesigned and adapted—it could have, as it were, "learned from its mistakes" and from Wikipedia's successes. Thousands of people who had signed up and who wanted to contribute to the Nupedia system were left disappointed. I believe this was unfortunate and unnecessary; I always wanted Nupedia and Wikipedia working together to be not only the

---

[1] Chapter 5 in this volume.

world's largest but also the world's most reliable encyclopedia. I hope that this memoir will help to justify this stance. Hopefully, too, I will manage to persuade some people that collaboration between an expert project and a public project is the correct approach to the overall project of creating open content encyclopedias.

I am not writing to request that Nupedia be resuscitated now, as nice as that would be. But I would like to tell the story of Nupedia and the first couple years of Wikipedia, as I remember it. A truly careful, unbiased, comprehensive, and scholarly history of the projects, as opposed to a memoir, would require study of the Nupedia and Wikipedia archives— if early archives of them still exist.[2] Interviews with many of those heavily involved in the projects would also help a great deal, so long as interviews were done of people on different sides of the disputes that helped to shape the project.

In July of 2001, while still working on both Wikipedia and Nupedia, I wrote, "if some other open source project proves to be more competitive, then it should and will take the lead in creating a body of free encyclopedic knowledge."[3] Since Wikipedia is open content and hence may be reproduced and improved upon by anyone, I have always been cognizant that it might not end up being the only or best version.[4] My personal devotion has always been to the ideal project as I have envisioned it, not necessarily to particular incarnations of Nupedia or Wikipedia; and I think this attitude is fully consistent with the (very positive) spirit of open source collaboration generally.

---

[2] Incomplete copies have come to light since this essay first appeared, on which one officially approved history has been written (Andrew Lih's *The Wikipedia Revolution*).

[3] In "Britannica or Nupedia?" in Chapter 2 in this volume.

[4] In other words, it is still possible, in 2020, that a fork of Wikipedia, like Everipedia.org, might one day emerge as more robust than Wikipedia itself.

This being said, let me also emphasize strongly that, throughout this discussion, I am not suggesting that Wikipedia needs to be replaced with something better.[5] I do, however, think that it needs to be supplemented by a broader, more ambitious, and more inclusive vision of the overall project.

Some Recent Press Reports

The following memoir seems all the more important to publish now because the early history of Nupedia and Wikipedia has been mischaracterized in the press. If there were only a few inaccuracies, which made no difference, I would be happy to leave well enough alone. But some of the mischaracterizations I have seen do make a difference, because they give the public the impression that Nupedia failed because it was run by snobbish experts whose standards were too high. As the following should make clear, that is not quite correct. One might also gather from some reports that the idea for Wikipedia sprang fully grown from Jimmy Wales' head. Jimmy, of course, deserves credit for investing in and guiding Wikipedia. But a more refined idea of how Wikipedia originated and evolved is crucial to have, if one wants to appreciate fully why it works now, and why it has the policies that it does have.

For example, reporter Brad Stone writes:

[Jimmy] Wales first tried to rewrite the rules of the reference-book business five years ago with a free online encyclopedia called Nupedia. Anyone could submit articles, but they were vetted in a seven-step review process. After investing thousands of his own dollars and publishing only 24 articles, Wales reconsidered. He

---

[5] By 2019, however, I had come to the view that Wikipedia is simply "broken." See Sharyl Attkisson, "'Wikipedia is...broken,' controlled by special interests and bad actors, says co-founder," *SharylAttkisson.com* (blog), May 25, 2019, https://bit.ly/39nZfdl.

scrapped the review process and began using a popular kind of online Web site called a "wiki," which allows its readers to change the content.[6]

This capsule history is, of course, very brief and so should not be expected to have every relevant detail. But some of the claims made here are not just vague, they are actually misleading, and so several clarifications are in order:

- The article makes it sound as if Jimmy were the only person making the relevant decisions. That is incorrect; the Nupedia system (indeed, seven steps) was established via negotiation with Nupedia's volunteer Advisory Board, mostly Ph.D. volunteers, who served as editors and reviewers. I articulated our decisions in Nupedia's "Editorial Policy Guidelines."[7] Jimmy started and broadly authorized it all, but as to the details, he really had little to do with them.

- Nupedia's Advisory Board might be surprised to learn that Jimmy (alone!) "scrapped the review process." Jimmy was certainly disappointed with the process (as were many people), and he did not actively support it after 2001 or so. But in fairness to the people actually working on Nupedia, the fact is that work on Nupedia gradually petered out in 2001-2. I in particular was stretched thin— in 2001, I was both chief organizer of Wikipedia and editor-in-chief of Nupedia—and my own slowing work on Nupedia was obvious to all active Nupedia contributors. It might be better to say that Nupedia withered due to neglect—which was largely due to a lack of sufficient funds for paid organizers—which was as much due to the bursting of the Internet bubble as anything else.

---

[6] *Newsweek*, "It's Like a Blog, But It's a Wiki," Nov. 1, 2004, https://bit.ly/32wDff2.

[7] As of 2020, still accessible via archive.org: https://bit.ly/2OFq6rO

- Also, to the best of my knowledge, the "thousands of his own dollars" invested in these projects were, if I am not mistaken, the dollars of Bomis.com, which is jointly owned by three partners, Jimmy, Tim Shell, and Michael Davis. (The money for Wikipedia now comes from donations.) But again, Jimmy was the prime motivating force within Bomis.

- Moreover, Nupedia had fewer than 24 articles when Wikipedia launched, being not quite a year old at that time. The idea of adapting wiki technology to the task of building an encyclopedia was mine, and my main job in 2001 was managing and developing the community and the rules according to which Wikipedia was run. Jimmy's role, at first, was one of broad vision and oversight; this was the management style he preferred, at least as long as I was involved. But, again, credit goes to Jimmy alone for getting Bomis to invest in the project, and for providing broad oversight of the fantastic and world-changing project of an open content, collaboratively-built encyclopedia. Credit also of course goes to him for overseeing its development after I left, and guiding it to the success that it is today.

An article by Daniel Pink also got a number of things wrong, despite being, in other respects, an excellent article:

With Sanger as editor in chief, Nupedia essentially replicated the One Best way model. He assembled a roster of academics to write articles. (Participants even had to fax in their degrees as proof of their expertise.) And he established a seven-stage process of editing, fact-checking, and peer review. "After 18 months and more than $250,000," Wales said, "we had 12 articles."

Then an employee told Wales about Wiki software. On January 15, 2001, they launched a Wiki-fied version and within a month, they had 200 articles. In a year, they had 18,000. ... Sanger left the project in 2002. "In the Nupedia mode, there was room for an editor in chief," Wales says. "The Wiki model is too distributed for that."[8]

This too needs clarifications.

- The "roster of academics" (the aforementioned Nupedia Advisory Board) was not limited to academics; they were experts in their fields, in any case. Moreover, they were editors and reviewers; the general public was able to propose and write articles on subjects about which they had some knowledge. (Consult the old assignment policy[9] if you are interested.)

- It is incorrect to say that participants had to fax their degrees as proof of their expertise; we did verify *bona fides* by matching the names and e-mail addresses of editors and reviewers with a web page—often, but not always, an academic web page. There was one, but only one, case that I recall in which I asked someone, who had no web page or any other easy way to prove who he was, to fax a degree. Verifying *bona fides* a bit seemed like a good idea especially when initially building what was to be an academically-respectable project.

- Again, I did not establish the editorial process alone; I had considerable assistance (for which I am still grateful) from Nupedia's excellent Advisory Board.

- The second paragraph begins, "Then an employee told Wales about Wiki software." I do not know how Jimmy first learned about wikis, but as I will explain below, I proposed to him and to the Nupedia community at large that we start a wiki-based encyclopedia.

- The context of the line "Sanger left the project in 2002"— particularly with Jimmy quoted as saying, "In the

---

[8] "The Book Stops Here," *Wired Magazine*, March 2005, https://bit.ly/2E9xQjY.

[9] See "Nupedia.com Editorial Policy Guidelines," Nupedia.com (archived), May 2000, https://bit.ly/3eGDBCk.

Nupedia mode there was room for an editor in chief"— makes it sound as if I were let go specifically because I was working only on Nupedia and that I was no longer needed for that. In fact, I was working on Wikipedia far more at the time than Nupedia, and the reason for my departure from both projects was that Bomis was, like virtually all dot-coms, losing money. They could not afford to pay me; I was told that I was the last of several newer Bomis employees to be laid off on account of the tech recession. But Wikipedia indeed was able to continue on without me, and I agreed even at the time that Wikipedia could survive without me, and that it had become essentially "unmanageable" (as I put it—the following memoir should make it clear what I meant by that).

In view of problematic reporting such as the above, considering the rather good chance that Wikipedia will become historically important (if it is not already), and considering that the planners of related projects might find some value in this, I want to tell my story as I remember it. This memoir covers only the first few years of the project. I personally would be very interested to read a memoir or history of the years that followed. But that is a job for someone else; I have followed the project fairly closely and with interest after my departure, but silently and from the sidelines.

Nupedia

I will begin with several paragraphs about Nupedia, because the origin of Wikipedia cannot be explained except in that context. Moreover, the Nupedia project itself was very worthwhile, and I think it *might* have been able to survive, as I will explain. Finally, some errors regarding Nupedia have been passed around, which are little better than unfounded rumors. It is unfortunate that the thousands of hours of excellent volunteer work done on Nupedia should be thus disrespected or grossly misunderstood. I personally will always be grateful

The Early History of Nupedia and Wikipedia: A Memoir

to those initial contributors who believed in the project and our management, worked hard for a completely unproven idea, and laid the groundwork for the growing institution of open content projects.

In 1999, Jimmy Wales wanted to start a free, collaborative encyclopedia. I knew him from several mailing lists back in the mid-90s, and in fact we had already met in person a couple of times. In January 2000, I e-mailed Jimmy and several other Internet acquaintances to get feedback on an idea for what was to be, essentially, a blog. (It was to be a successor to "Sanger and Shannon's Review of Y2K News Reports," a Y2K news summary that I first wrote and then supervised.) To my great surprise, Jimmy replied to my e-mail describing his idea of a free encyclopedia, and asking if I might be interested in leading the project. He was specifically interested in finding a philosopher, he said. He made it a condition of my employment that I would finish my philosophy Ph.D. quickly (whereupon I would get a raise)—which I did, in June 2000. I am still grateful for the extra incentive. I thought he would be a great boss.

To be clear, the original idea of an open source, collaborative encyclopedia was Jimmy's, not mine, and the funding was entirely by Bomis. I was an employee; I thought I was very lucky to have a job like that land in my lap. Of course, other people had had the idea; but it was Jimmy's foresight actually to invest in it. For this the world owes him a debt. The actual development of this encyclopedia was the task he gave me to work on: I executed the idea.

So I arrived in San Diego in early February, 2000, to get to work. One of the first things I asked Jimmy is how free a rein I had in designing the project. What were my constraints, and in what areas was I free to exercise my own creativity? He replied, as I clearly recall, that most of the decisions should be mine; and in most respects, as a manager, Jimmy was indeed very hands-off. Nevertheless, I always did consult with him about important decisions, and moreover, I wanted his advice. Now, Jimmy was quite clear that he wanted the project to be

11

in principle open to everyone to develop, just as open source software is (to an extent). Beyond this, however, I believe I was given a pretty free rein. So I spent the first month or so thinking very broadly about different possibilities. I wrote quite a bit (that writing is now all lost in a hard drive crash) and discussed quite a bit with both Jimmy and one of the other Bomis partners, Tim Shell.

I maintained from the start that something really could not be a credible encyclopedia without oversight by experts. I reasoned that, if the project is open to all, it would require both management by experts and an unusually rigorous process. I now think I was right about the former requirement, but wrong about the latter, which was redundant; I think that the subsequent development of Wikipedia has borne out this assessment. But I fully realize that all this is a matter of debate. Some will claim that the experience of Wikipedia refuted my original judgment that expert oversight is necessary for a very credible encyclopedia; but I disagree with them. More on this below.

Also, I am fairly sure that one of the first policies that Jimmy and I agreed upon was a "nonbias" or neutrality policy. I know I insisted on it strongly from the beginning, because neutrality has been a hobby-horse of mine for a very long time. Neutrality, we agreed, required that articles should not represent any one point of view on controversial subjects, but instead fairly represent all sides. We also agreed in rejecting an alternative that (for a time) Tim and some early Nupedians plugged for: the development, for each encyclopedia topic, of a series of different articles, each written from a different point of view.

I believed, moreover, that a strongly collaborative and open project could not survive if its contributors were not "personally invested" in the project, and that this required some input and management by its users. So I think it was very early on that I decided that Nupedia should have an Advisory Board—editors and reviewers who would together agree on project policy—and that the public should have a say in the formulation of policy.

An early incarnation of Nupedia's Advisory Board was in place by summer of 2000 or so. It was made up of the project's highly-qualified editors and reviewers, mostly Ph.D. professors but also a good many other highly-experienced professionals. Eventually the Advisory Board agreed to an extremely rigorous seven-step system. A lot of the details of the Nupedia policy and processes were, I think, *proposed* by me, but then tweaked and elaborated by others, and the policy was not published as project policy until we had a quorum of editors and reviewers who could fully discuss and approve of a policy document. But I do not think that we discussed the proposal well enough, and further initial discussion could have made a difference, because, as it turned out, a clear mistake we made was to assume that such a complicated system would be navigated patiently by many volunteers, even if they had clear-enough instructions. That is a mistake I doubt anyone designing volunteer content creation systems will make again; I certainly would not make it again.

I spent a huge amount of time recruiting people for Nupedia, e-mailing new arrivals, posting to mailing lists, giving interviews, etc. I had had some experience publicizing Internet projects when I worked on several philosophy discussion groups as a grad student in the 1990s (I had started an "Association for Systematic Philosophy" as well as a group devoted to a "Tutorial Manifesto"), and I knew that getting many willing and active participants was difficult but important. I even had an administrative assistant for six months in 2000 and 2001, Liz Campeau, whose sole job was to recruit people to work on Nupedia and then Wikipedia. A large part of the reason Wikipedia got off the ground so quickly and so well is that it was started by Nupedians, who were then a very large base of people who wanted to work on an encyclopedia, and who had many definite ideas about how it should be done. So Nupedia was not a waste of time, for that reason at least. Around 2,500 Nupedia members were subscribed to the general announcement list in January of 2001, when Wikipedia launched, as an old project news page indicates.[10]

We operated the system initially using e-mail and mailing lists, while planning and finalizing process details. That lasted from spring through fall 2000. I think our first article ("atonality" by Christoph Hust), that made it entirely through the system, was published in June or July of 2000. To move the system to a completely web-based one, there was, of course, a great deal of design and programming to do. So in fall of 2000 I worked a lot with a specifically-hired programmer (Toan Vo) and the Bomis sysadmin (Jason Richey) to transfer the system from a clunky mailing list system to the web. But by the time the web-based system was ready—I think December of 2000, just a month before Wikipedia got started—it had become obvious to Jimmy and me that the seven-step editorial process would move too slowly, even when managed on the web.[11]

Some institutional traditions begin easily but die hard. So, in 2001, it was only after many months and uncomfortable comparison of Nupedia with the thriving, younger Wikipedia, that Nupedia's Advisory Board was willing to consider a simpler system seriously. That was because Nupedia editors and reviewers had a very strong commitment to rigor and reliability, as did I. Moreover, as Wikipedia became increasingly successful in 2001, Jimmy asked me to spend more and more time on it, which I did; Nupedia suffered from neglect. But by the summer of 2001, I was able to propose, get accepted (with very lukewarm support), and install something we called the Nupedia Chalkboard, a wiki which was to be closely managed by Nupedia's staff. It was to be both a simpler

[10] See "Nupedia News," Nupedia.com (now archived), Dec. 15, 2000, https://bit.ly/2WAeU4a.

[11] Magnus Manske later, in 2001, made some very nice additions to the Nupedia system.

way to develop encyclopedia articles for Nupedia, and a way to import articles from Wikipedia. No doubt due to lingering disdain for the wiki idea—which at the time was still very much unproven—the Chalkboard went largely unused. The general public simply used Wikipedia if they wanted to write articles in a wiki format, while perhaps most Nupedia editors and reviewers were not persuaded that the Chalkboard was necessary or useful.

By early winter, 2001, Nupedia had published approved versions of only about 25 articles, although there were many more (I vaguely recall over 150 drafts) at various stages in process. I was finally able to persuade the Advisory Board to move the system to a much simpler two-step process, virtually identical to that used to run many academic journals: articles would be submitted to an editor; the editor would, if the article seemed good enough, forward it to a reviewer for acceptance or rejection; if accepted, the article would be posted. We also were thinking of various ways of allowing public comment on or moderated editing of posted articles. I believe this new, simpler system would have produced thousands of articles for Nupedia very quickly. The general public on Nupedia was certainly interested and motivated, and I think it was finally becoming generally accepted by the Advisory Board that the complexity of the system was the main reason that they were not starting articles and getting them through the system.

But, unfortunately, Nupedia's new system was never adopted when it should have been—the winter of 2001-2—because at the same time, Wikipedia was demanding as much attention as I could give it, and I had little time to implement the new Nupedia system. I am quite sure we could have started the new Nupedia system in early 2002, if we had made the time. But Bomis lost the ability to pay me and, newly unemployed, I did not have the time to lead Nupedia as a volunteer. I did not entirely lose hope on Nupedia, however, as I will explain below.

The Origins of Wikipedia

In the fall of 2000, Jimmy and I were very well agreed that Nupedia's slow productivity was probably going to be an ongoing problem and that there needed to be a way, moreover, in which ordinary, uncredentialed people could participate more easily. Uncredentialed people could and did participate in Nupedia, particularly as writers and copyeditors, but it was pretty painful for most of them to get articles through the elaborate system. So there seemed to be a huge fund of talent, motivated to work on an encyclopedia but not motivated enough to work on Nupedia, going to waste.

It was my job to solve these problems. I wrote multiple detailed proposals for a simpler, more open editing system—two or three, at least—and I ran them by Jimmy, and I think his reply to each one was that it would require too much programming and he could not afford to pay more high-priced programmers (and we already had Toan and Jason working quite a bit on Nupedia's new web-based system). Now, of course, I fully realize that we could have found a way to enlist volunteers to develop the system. Jimmy and I both probably knew that at the time; I am not sure why we did not pursue it.

So it was while I was thinking hard about how to create a more open system, that would require minimal programming to set up, that I had dinner with an old Internet friend of mine, Ben Kovitz. Ben had moved to town for a new job and we were out at a Pacific Beach Mexican restaurant on January 2, 2001, talking about jobs, techie stuff, and philosophy, no doubt. (Ben, Jimmy, and I were all active on those philosophy mailing lists in the mid-90s, and we all knew each other.) So Ben explained the idea of Ward Cunningham's WikiWikiWeb[12] to me. Instantly I was considering whether wiki would work as a more open and simple editorial system

---

[12] See http://www.c2.com/cgi/wiki?WelcomeVisitors. As I edit this in 2020, the site appears largely as it did back then.

for a free, collaborative encyclopedia, and it seemed exactly right. And the more I thought about it, without even having seen a wiki, the more it seemed obviously right. So I am sure it was that very evening or the following morning that I wrote a proposal—unfortunately, lost now—in which I said that this might solve the problem and that we ought to try it. After he had nixed my several earlier proposals, and given that setting up a wiki would be very simple and require hiring no programmer, Jimmy could scarcely refuse. I vaguely recall that he liked the idea but was initially skeptical—properly so, as I was also, to a lesser extent, despite my excitement.

Wiki advocates often used to point out[13] (and I am sure some still do) that Wikipedia is nonstandard as a wiki. This is partly because we began just with the very basic wiki concept and not so much of the culture. Wiki culture is very distinctive. I cannot hope to explain even the highlights briefly, so I will not try; I will simply give a few notions. Wiki pages can be started and edited by anyone, but, in "Thread Mode"[14] (as in "the thread of this discussion") the dialogue can become complex. In that case, or when consensus is reached, or when positions have hardened, it is considered a good idea to "refactor"[15] pages (a term borrowed from programming), i.e., to rewrite them, but honestly, taking into account the highlights of the dialogue. Then the dialogue might be represented as in "Document Mode."[16] Opinions are very welcome on a typical

---

[13] For example, at "WikiPediaIsNotTypical," MeatballWiki.org, accessed July 2020, https://bit.ly/3fO90E8. This and the next few footnotes are from wikis that predate Wikipedia.

[14] See http://wiki.c2.com/?ThreadMode. As of 2020, the information referred to in the discussion in this section can still be found on these wiki pages—which ought to give you an idea of how stable wiki pages can be.

[15] See http://www.c2.com/cgi/wiki?WhatIsRefactoring.

[16] See http://www.c2.com/cgi/wiki?DocumentMode.

wiki. There are many other collective habits that make up typical wiki culture; these are only a few.

But I denied the necessity of organizing Wikipedia according to these precise principles. To be sure, a few other participants wanted Wikipedia to adopt wiki culture wholesale, so that it would be "just another wiki," and they had some small influence over the direction of the project; but speaking for myself, I viewed wiki software as simply a tool, a way to organize people who want to collaborate. I saw no necessity whatsoever of partaking in all aspects of the idiosyncratic culture that happened to be associated with the advent of this very generally-applicable tool, since we were engaged in a very specific sort of project, with very specific requirements. This caused some consternation among some wiki advocates, who appeared to think that Wikipedia should, or inevitably would, become just another wiki, somehow *necessarily* partaking of typical wiki culture. Ward Cunningham's prediction, when Jimmy asked him whether wiki software "could successfully generate a useful encyclopedia," was: "Yes, but in the end it would not be an encyclopedia. It would be a wiki." [17] As I said in reply: "Wikipedia has a totally different culture from this wiki, because it is pretty single-mindedly aimed at creating an encyclopedia. It is already rather useful as an encyclopedia, and we expect it will only get better."

Typical wiki culture aside, wiki software does encourage, but does not strictly require, extreme openness and decentralization. It encourages openness since (as the software is typically designed) page changes are logged and publicly viewable, and (again, only typically) pages may be further changed by anyone. It encourages decentralization because in order for work to be done, there is no need for a person or body to assign work, but rather, work can proceed as and when people want to do it. Wiki software also discourages (or

---

[17] Comment by Ward Cunningham, "Wiki Pedia," *WikiWikiWeb*, accessed July 2020, http://www.c2.com/cgi/wiki?WikiPedia.

at least does not facilitate) the exercise of authority, since work proceeds at will on any page, and on any large, active wiki it would be too much work for any single overseer or limited group of overseers to keep up. These all became features of Wikipedia.

My initial idea was that the wiki would be set up as part of Nupedia; it was to be a way for the public to develop a stream of content that could be fed into the Nupedia process. I think I got some of the basic pages written—how wikis work, what our general plan was, and so forth—over the next few days. I wrote a general proposal for the Nupedia community, and the Nupedia wiki went live January 10. The first encyclopedia articles for what was to become Wikipedia were written then. It turned out, however, that a clear majority of the Nupedia Advisory Board wanted to have nothing to do with a wiki. Again, their commitment was to rigor and reliability, a concern I shared with them and continue to have. Still, perhaps some of those people are kicking themselves now. They (some of them) evidently thought that a wiki *could* not resemble an encyclopedia at all, that it would be too informal and unstructured, as the original WikiWikiWeb was (and is), to be associated with Nupedia. They of course were perfectly reasonable to doubt that it would turn into the fantastic source of content that it did. Who could reasonably guess that it would work? But it did work, to an extent, and now the world knows better.

Wikipedia's First Few Months

So we decided to relaunch the wiki under its own domain name. I came up with the name "Wikipedia," a silly name for what was at first a very silly project, and the newly independent project was launched at Wikipedia.com on January 15, 2001. It was a ".com" at first because, at the time, we were contemplating selling ads to pay for me, programmers, and servers. It was easy to replace ".com" with ".org" in 2002, as Jimmy did once he was able to assure users that Wikipedia would *never* (at least I think he said, or clearly implied, "never") run ads to support the project.

I took it to be one of my main jobs to promote Wikipedia, and this resulted in a steady influx of new participants. I wrote on the Wikipedia announcement page on January 24, "Wikipedia has definitely taken [on] a life of its own; new people are arriving every day and the project seems to be getting only more popular. Long live Wikipedia!" By the end of January we reportedly[18] and approximately had 600 articles; there were 1,300 in March, 2,300 in April, and 3,900 in May. Not only was the project growing steadily, the growth rate was increasing. It continued to increase.

Wikipedia started with a handful of people, many from Nupedia. The influence of Nupedians was, I think, pretty important early on; I think, especially, of the tireless Magnus Manske (who worked on the software for both projects), our resident stickler Ruth Ifcher, and the very smart poker-playing programmer Lee Daniel Crocker—to name a few. All of these people, and several other Nupedia borrowings, had a good understanding of the requirements of good encyclopedia articles, and they were good, intelligent writers. The direction that Wikipedia ought to have gone in seemed obvious to me and to them, in terms of what sort of content we wanted. But how the community should be organized was an issue we did not have it worked out in advance, and, not surprisingly, that turned out to be the thorniest problem. But the facts that the project started with these good people, and that we were able to adopt, explain, and promote good habits and policies to newer people, does help account for why the project was able to develop a robust, functional community at all, and eventually to succeed. As to project leadership or management, we began with me, Jimmy, and Tim Shell; but Tim stopped participating so much after the first few months.

---

[18] "Wikipedia:Size of Wikipedia," Wikipedia.com, revision saved November 7, 2001, https://bit.ly/2OJkVHw.

But the many rank-and-file users did the heavy lifting, and if there had not been a reasonable consensus among them about what the project should look like, it just would not have happened. In any collaborative project, it is the contributors who are responsible for the outcome. Those early adopters should feel proud of themselves, because they were absolutely instrumental in shaping a useful thing.

I recall saying casually and repeatedly in the project's first nine months or so that experts should be given some particular respect when writing in their areas of expertise. They should be deferred to, I thought, unless there were some clear evidence of bias. So, in those first months, deference to expertise was a policy that at least *I* usually insisted upon, but not strongly or clearly enough. It was nearly a year after the project began that I finally articulated this view reasonably clearly as a policy to consider.[19] Perhaps this was because, indeed, most users did make a practice of deferring to experts up to that time. "This is just common sense," as I wrote, "but sometimes common sense needs to be spelled out!" What I now think is that that point of common sense needed to be spelled out quite a bit sooner and more forcefully, because in the long run, it was not adopted as official project policy, as it could have been.

Some questions have been raised about the origin of Wikipedia policies. The tale is interesting and instructive, and one of the main themes of this memoir. We began with no (or few) policies in particular and said that the community would determine—through a sort of vague consensus, based on its experience working together—what the policies would be. The very first entry on a "rules to consider" page[20] was the "Ignore All Rules" rule (to wit: "If rules make you nervous and depressed, and not desirous of participating in the wiki,

---

[19] "Deferring to the Experts," January 3, 2002, meta.wikipedia.org, http://meta.wikimedia.org/wiki/Deferring_to_the_experts.
[20] The April 2, 2001 version: https://bit.ly/2CN07vV.

then ignore them entirely and go about your business"). This is a "rule" that, current Wikipedians might be surprised to learn, I personally proposed. The reason was that I thought we needed experience with how wikis should work, and even more importantly at that point, we needed participants more than we needed rules. As the project grew and the requirements of its success became increasingly obvious, I became ambivalent about this particular "rule" and then rejected it altogether. As one participant later commented, "this rule is the essence of Wikipedia." That was certainly never my view; I always thought of the rule as being a temporary, humorous injunction to participants to add content rather than be distracted by (then) relatively inconsequential issues about how exactly articles should be formatted, etc. In a similar spirit, I proposed that contributors be bold in updating pages.[21]

I also, for similar reasons, specifically disavowed any title; I was organizing the project but I did not want to present myself as editor-in-chief. I wanted people to feel comfortable adding information without having to consult anything like an editor. Participation was more important, I felt. Others referred to me, later, as Wikipedia's editor; I always rejected that title.

As we set it up, Wikipedia did have some minimal wiki cultural features: it was wide open, extremely decentralized, and (provisionally anyway) featured very little attempt to exercise authority. Insofar as I was able to organize it at all, I guided the project through force of personality and what "moral authority" I had as co-founder of the project. Jimmy and I agreed early on that, at least in the beginning, we should not eject anyone from the project except perhaps in the most extreme cases. Our first forcible expulsion (which Jimmy

---

[21] "Be bold in updating pages," Wikipedia.com, October 29, 2001, https://bit.ly/2OI78kc. This particular "rule" really was, for many years, more correctly celebrated as the essence of all things wiki. As Wikipedia came to be locked down.

performed) did not occur for many months, despite the presence of difficult characters from nearly the beginning of the project. Again, we were learning: we wished to tolerate all sorts of contributors in order to be well-situated to adopt the wisest policies. But—and in hindsight this should have seemed perfectly predictable—this provisional "hands off" management policy had the effect of creating a difficult-to-change tradition, the tradition of making the project extremely tolerant of disruptive (uncooperative, "trolling") behavior. And as it turned out, particularly with the large waves of new contributors from the summer and fall of 2001,[22] the project became very resistant to any changes in this policy. I suspect that the cultures of online communities generally are established pretty quickly and then become resistant to any abrupt change, because they are self-selecting; that was certainly the case with Wikipedia, anyway.

So I could only attempt to shame any troublemakers into compliance; without recourse to any genuine punitive action, that was the most I could do. In about the first eight months of the project, this was usually sufficient for me to do my job. After that, however, my job got increasingly difficult, as I will explain.

So Wikipedia began as a good-natured anarchy, a sort of Rousseauian state of digital nature. I always took Wikipedia's anarchy to be provisional—purely for purposes of determining what the best rules and the nature of authority on the wiki should be. What I, and other Wikipedians, failed to realize is that our initial anarchy would be taken by the next waves of contributors as the very essence of the project—how Wikipedia was "meant" to be—even though Wikipedia could have become anything we the contributors chose to make it.

---

[22] Reactions to the two "Slashdottings" (massive influxes of traffic from Slashdot.org) that resulted from the two articles in this volume's Chapter 2.

This point bears some emphasis: Wikipedia became what it is today because, having been seeded with great people with a fairly clear idea of what they wanted to achieve, we proceeded to make a series of free decisions that determined the policy of the project and culture of its supporting community. Wikipedia's system is neither the only way to run a wiki nor the only way to run an open content encyclopedia. Its particular conjunction of policies is in no way natural, "organic," or necessary. It is instead artificial, a result of a series of free choices, and we could have chosen differently in many cases; and choosing differently on some issues might have led to a project better than the one that exists today.

Though it began as an anarchy, there were quite a few policies that were settled upon, more or less, within the first six months or so. This required some struggle, especially on my part, particularly because, since the project was a wiki, some participants thought that there should be literally no rules at all. Enforceable rules were regarded as "anti-wiki," which was supposed to be a bad thing. But it was made clear from the beginning that we intended Wikipedia to be an *encyclopedia,* and so we were able to plug for at least those rules that would help define and sustain the project as an encyclopedia.

For instance, throughout the early months, people added various content that seemed less than encyclopedic in various ways. Many people seemed to confuse encyclopedia articles with dictionary entries, and eventually I wrote a page called "Wikipedia is not a dictionary." As people found new ways not to write encyclopedia articles, I started "What Wikipedia is not": I and others would note on an article's discussion page that some certain content did not belong in an encyclopedia, and then underscored the point by adding an entry to the "What Wikipedia is not" page. To take another example, Wikipedia was not to be a place for publishing original research. In fact, this is a policy that had been settled upon and even enforced in Nupedia days; enforcing it actually led to the departure of Nupedia's erstwhile Classics editor sometime in 2001.

Many of our first controversies were over these restrictions. At the time, I had enough influence within the community to get these policies generally accepted. If we had not decided on these restrictions, Wikipedia might well have ended up, like many wikis, as nothing in particular. Frankly, if it had not been for my own personal perfectionism and prickly editorial habits, Wikipedia would have spluttered into an unserious collection of essays (like some other, similar projects) and failed. But since we insisted that it was an encyclopedia, even though it was just a blank digital bulletin board and a group of people to begin with, it became an encyclopedia. Perhaps there is something profound in that. I also like to think that we helped to show the world the potential that wikis, and radical collaboration more generally, have.

Another policy that was instituted early on was the nonbias or neutrality policy. This was borrowed from the Nupedia project[23] and made a "Rule to Consider"—in a very early version, I put the policy this way:

Avoid bias: Since this is an encyclopedia, after a fashion, it would be best if you represented your controversial views either (1) not at all, (2) on *Debate, *Talk, or *Discussion pages linked from the bottom of the page that you are tempted to grace, or (3) represented in a fact-stating fashion, i.e., which attributes a particular opinion to a particular person or group, rather than asserting the opinion as fact. (3) is strongly preferred. See the NeutralPointOfView page for elaboration.[24]

Jimmy then started a specialized policy page he called "Neutral Point of View," which I greatly elaborated in line

---

[23] "Nupedia.com Editorial Policy Guidelines," Nupedia.com (archived), November 16, 2000, https://bit.ly/2ZJLK4B.

[24] "RulesToConsider," Wikipedia.com, April 2, 2001, https://bit.ly/3hgJA2c.

with the Nupedia policy.[25] I did not like this name as a name for the policy, because it implies that to write neutrally is actually to express a *point of view*, and, as the definite article is used, a single point of view at that. "Neutrality" is a better descriptor. But the acronym "NPOV" came to be used, by Wikipedians wanting to seem hip, and then the unfortunate "POV" came to be used when the perfectly good English word "biased" would do.

In addition to these, I recall suggesting a number of other rules—no doubt most matters of historical fact, along these lines, can be verified in archives. I believe I am responsible for many of the original formulations of a lot of the article naming conventions, as well as the conventions of bolding the title of the article, starting articles with full sentences, making article titles uncapitalized, and much else. I think these policies were just a matter of common sense for anyone who understood what a good encyclopedia should be like. Of course I was not the only person proposing conventions. Moreover, actual project policy, or community habits, succeeded in being established only by being followed and supported by a majority of participants. It was then, we said, that there was a "rough consensus" in favor of a policy. Consensus, we said, is required for a policy actually to be considered project policy. For our purposes, a "consensus" appeared to consist of (1) widespread common practice, (2) many vocal defenders, and (3) virtually no detractors.

But that way of settling upon policy proposals—viz., by alleged consensus—did not scale. After about nine months or so, there were so many contributors, and especially brand new contributors, that nothing like a consensus could be reached, for the simple reason that condition (3) above was never achievable: there would after that always be somebody who insisted on expressing disagreement. There was, then, a non-scaling policy adoption procedure, and a crying need to

---

[25] My own final version is reproduced in Chapter 3 in this volume.

continue to adopt sensible policies—and ultimately just as important, to make sensible, stable, and fair decisions about how articles should read. This led to some pretty serious problems in the community, which I will relate below. But first, something more positive.

Why Wikipedia Started Working

This is a good place to explain why Wikipedia actually got started and why it came to work reasonably well for many years. The explanation I offer combines quite a few factors, some borrowed from the open source movement, some from wiki software and culture, and some more idiosyncratic:

- *Open content license.* We promised contributors that their work would always remain free for others to read. This, as is well known, motivates people to work for the good of the world—and for the many people who would like to teach the whole world, that is a pretty strong motivation.

- *Focus on the encyclopedia.* We said that we were creating an encyclopedia, not a dictionary, etc., and we encouraged people to stick to creating the encyclopedia and not use the project as a debate forum.

- *Openness.* Anyone could contribute. Everyone was specifically made to feel welcome. (E.g., we encouraged the habit of writing on new contributors' user pages, "Welcome to Wikipedia!" etc.) There was no sense that someone would be turned away for not being bright enough, or not being a good enough writer, or whatever.

- *Ease of editing.* Wikis are pretty easy for most people to figure out. In other collaborative systems (like Nupedia), you have to learn all about the system first. Wikipedia had an almost flat learning curve.

- *Collaborate radically; do not sign articles.* Radical collaboration, in which (in principle) anyone can edit any part of anyone else's work,[26] is one of the great innovations of the open source software movement. On Wikipedia, radical collaboration made it possible for work to move forward on all fronts at the same time, to avoid the big bottleneck that is the individual author, and to burnish articles on popular topics to a fine luster.

- *Offer unedited, unapproved content for further development.* This is required if one wishes to collaborate radically. We encouraged putting up unfinished drafts—as long as they were at least roughly correct—with the idea that they can only improve if others collaborate. This is a classic principle of open source software. It helped get Wikipedia started and helped keep it moving. This is why so many original drafts of Wikipedia articles were basically garbage (no offense to anyone—some of my own drafts were sometimes garbage), and also why it was surprising to the uninitiated that many articles turned out very well indeed.

- *Neutrality.* A firm neutrality policy made it possible for people of widely divergent opinions to work together, without constantly fighting. It is a way to keep the peace.

- *Start with a core of good people.* I think it was essential that we began the project with a core group of intelligent good writers who understood what an encyclopedia should look like, and who were basically decent human beings.

- *Enjoy the Google effect.* We had little to do with this, but had Google not sent us an increasing amount of traffic each time they spidered the growing website, we would not have grown nearly as fast as we did. (See below.)

---

[26] Somewhat similar in meaning to the later-coined "crowdsourcing." For discussion of the concept, see my "Why Collaborative Free Works Should Be Protected by the Law," in Adam Moore, ed., *Information Ethics: Privacy, Property, and Power* (University of Washington Press, 2005).

That is pretty much it. The focus on the encyclopedia provided the task and the open content license provided a natural motivation: people work hard if they believe they are teaching the world stuff. Openness and ease of editing made it easy for new people to join in and get to work. Collaboration helped move work forward quickly and efficiently, and posting unedited drafts made collaboration possible. The fact that we started with a core of good people from Nupedia meant that the project could develop a functional, cooperative community. Neutrality made it easy for people to work together with relatively little conflict. Finally, the Google effect provided a steady supply of "fresh blood"—who in turn supplied increasing amounts of content.

Probably, all or nearly all other project rules were either optional, or straightforward applications of these principles. The project probably would still have succeeded nicely even if it had moderated or tweaked some of the above principles. For instance, radical openness, that is, being open even to those who brazenly flouted and disrespected the project's mission, might not have been necessary; after all, without them, the project would have been more welcoming to the many people who felt they could not work with such difficult people. And if we had required people to sign in, that would not have made very much difference (although it probably would have made some in the beginning; the project would not have grown as fast). Of course we did not have to use the GNU FDL for the license, and later Wikipedia adopted a dual-licensing scheme, including a Creative Commons license. Certainly, we did not need to set the community up initially as an anarchy governed by some vague consensus: instead, we could have adopted a charter from the very start. The project could have been managed quite differently; there could have been specially-designated and well-qualified editors. The project could have officially encouraged and deferred to experts. An article approval process could have been adopted without threatening the principle of posting unedited content for collaboration. Certainly, many of the later bells and whistles—the arbitration committee, a three-revert rule, having administrators with the particular configuration of rights they have, etc.—were not absolutely necessary to adopt in the precise forms they took. These differences would not have threatened the basic principles that made the project work, listed above.

So the basic principles that explain why Wikipedia could start working—and still does work—are relatively simple, few in number, and above all general. The more specific principles that Wikipedia wound up with was a matter of historical accident. There was a great deal of "wiggle room." Those intent on studying or replicating the Wikipedia model would do well to bear that in mind.

A Series of Controversies

So much for the very early history of Wikipedia; the next phase involved rapid growth and some serious internal controversies over policy and authority. If Wikipedia's basic policy was settled upon in the first nine months, its culture was solidified into something closer to its present form in the next nine.

The project continued to grow. We had 6,000 articles by July 8; 8,000 by August 7; 11,200 by September 9; and 13,000 by October 4. Consulting the website logs, we noted a "Google effect": each time Google spidered the website, more pages would be indexed; the greater the number of pages indexed, the more people arrived at the project; the more people involved in the project, the more pages there were to index. In addition to this source of new contributors, Wikipedia was Slashdotted a few times in 2001, and had large influxes of new users particularly after two articles I wrote for Kuro5hin were posted on Slashdot.[27]

This growth brought difficult challenges, challenges that perhaps I did not sufficiently anticipate and plan for. Some of

---

[27] Again, see Chapter 2 in this volume.

our earliest contributors, Nupedia recruits, were academics and other highly-qualified people, and it seems to me that they were slowly worn down and driven away by having to deal with difficult people on the project. I hope they will not mind that I mention their names, but the two that stick in my mind are J. Hoffman Kemp and Michael Tinkler, a couple of Ph.D. historians. They helped to set what I think was a good precedent for the project in that they wrote about their own areas of expertise, and they contributed under their own, real names. The latter has the salutary effect of making the contributor more serious and more apt to take responsibility for his or her contributions. They are also very nice people, but did not suffer fools gladly. Consequently, they wound up in some pretty silly disputes that would have driven less patient people away instantly. So there was a growing problem: persistent and difficult contributors tended to drive away many more skilled contributors who were ultimately more valuable to the effort; Kemp and Tinkler were only two of many examples. Many quietly came and quietly left. Short of removing the problem contributors altogether—which we did only in the very worst cases—there was no easy solution, under the system as we had set it up. And I am sorry to have to admit that those aspects of the system that led to this problem were as much my responsibility as anyone else's. Obviously, I would not design the system the same way if given the chance again.

As a result, I grew both more protective of the project and increasingly sensitive to abuse of the system. As I tried to exercise what little authority I claimed, as a corrective to such abuse, many newer arrivals on the scene made great sport of challenging my authority. One of the earliest challenges happened in late summer, 2001. The front page of Wikipedia—then open to anyone to edit, like any other page on the project—was occasionally vandalized with infantile graffiti. Someone then tried to make an archive of the vandalism that had been done to the front page of Wikipedia, despite the undisputable fact that the vandalism was just that, and had absolutely no merit. I maintained that to make such an archive would be to encourage such vandalism, so I deleted the archive. The archiver debated this. Then a user made the archive a "subpage" of his own user page—and user pages were generally held to be the bailiwick of the user. Consequently I deleted that subpage, which occasioned a further hue and cry; perhaps, they suggested, I was abusing my authority. The vandalism-preserving user in question proceeded to create a "deleted pages" page, on which the deleted vandalism archives were listed, as if to accuse me of trying to act without public scrutiny; but this was, of course, perfectly acceptable to me. At the time, I thought that this controversy was just as silly as it will sound to most people reading this. I thought that I needed only to "put my foot down" a little harder and, as had happened for the first six months of the project, participants would fall into line. What I did not realize was that this was to be only the first in a long series of controversies, the ultimate upshot of which was to undermine my own moral authority over the project and to make the project as comfortable as possible for the most abusive and contentious contributors.

Throughout this and other early controversies, much of the debate about project policy was conducted on the wiki itself. Other debates were conducted on mailing lists, Wikipedia-l and then later, for the English language project, WikiEN-l. In addition, people had taken to putting their own essays on Wikipedia, as subpages of their user pages. These too were occasioning controversy. It seemed to me, and many other contributors, that this debate was distracting the community from our main goal: to create an encyclopedia. Consequently I proposed[28] that we move the debate to another wiki that was to be created specifically for that purpose—what became known as the "meta wiki." This proposal was widely supported, so we set it up.

---

[28] "Moving commentary out of Wikipedia," meta.wikipedia.org, November 3, 2001, https://bit.ly/2WyFjiK.

As it happened, the meta-wiki became even more uncontrolled than Wikipedia itself, and for many months was continually infested with contributions by people that can only be called "cranks" and "trolls." The latter epithet came to be discouraged, however, for reasons soon to be explained. The existence of trolls was a problem we felt we should tolerate—and deal with only *verbally*, not with harsh penalties—for the sake of encouraging the broadest amount of participation. In the first years, only the worst trolls were ever expelled from the project.[29] I do not know whether this policy was changed as a result of the operation of the much-later installed Arbitration Committee.

The reasons the meta-wiki became (at least temporarily) more uncontrolled are not far to seek. First, it had no specific purpose, other than to host project debate and essays that do not belong on the main wiki—which was not enough to make anyone care very much about it. Second, because many people did not care what happened on the meta-wiki, they did not do the very necessary weeding that takes place on Wikipedia; besides, as the meta-wiki was a repository of opinion, people felt less comfortable editing or deleting what was, after all, only opinion.

What happened was that project policy discussions moved almost exclusively to the project mailing lists. There is a reason why this was a superior solution to having much debate on an uncontrolled, "unmoderated" wiki. On a wiki, contributions exist in perpetuity, as it were, or until they are deleted or radically changed; consequently, anyone new to a discussion sees the first contribution first. So whoever starts a new page

---

[29] Some twenty years later, I now think this was definitely and rather obviously a mistake. Fairness and due process are important, but tolerance for deliberately disruptive behavior in a collaborative knowledge project (as distinguished from social media, which might well be different) is extremely damaging to the morale of more decent people.

for discussion also, to a great extent, sets the tone and agenda of the discussion. Moreover, nasty, heated exchanges live on forever on a wiki, festering like an open wound, unless deliberately toned down afterwards; if the same exchange takes place on a mailing list, it slips mercifully and quietly into the archives.

At about the same time that we decided to start the meta-wiki, and soon after the vandalism archive affair, I was thinking a great deal about Wikipedia's apparent anarchy, and I wrote an essay titled, "Is Wikipedia an experiment in anarchy?"[30] This and the discussion that ensued tended to ossify positions with regard to the authority issue: I and a few others agreed that Jimmy and I should have special authority within the system, to settle policy issues that needed settling. Jimmy was relatively quiet about this issue; this, I think, was probably because his authority as co-owner was generally not in question. But mine was, because I was "in the trenches" and continuing to encourage good habits and solidify policy positions.

By November or December of 2001, Wikipedia was growing so fast and the subject of regular news reporting, even by the likes of *The New York Times* and MIT's *Technology Review*; after the Slashdottings earlier in the year, we knew that large influxes of members could have a tendency to change the nature of the project, and not necessarily for the better. If there were some major news coverage—an evening news story in the U.S., for example—there might be many new people who would need to be taught about Wikipedia's standards and positive cultural aspects. So I proposed what I thought was a humorously-named "Wikipedia Militia" which would manage new (and very welcome) "invasions" by new contributors. By this time, however, there was a small core group of people who were constantly on the watch for anything that smacked the

---

[30] "Is Wikipedia an experiment in anarchy?" meta.wikipedia.org, November 1, 2001.

least bit of authoritarianism; consequently, the name, and various aspects of how the proposal was presented, were vigorously debated. Eventually, we switched to "The Wikipedia Welcoming Committee" and finally, the "Volunteer Fire Department"—which eventually, it seems, fell into disuse.

The Governance Challenge

After the September Slashdotting, I composed a page originally called "Our Replies to Our Critics" (later called "Replies to Common Objections"), in which I addressed the problem that "cranks and partisans" might abuse the system:

> Moreover—and this is something that you might not be able to understand very well if you have not actually experienced it—there is a fair bit of (mostly friendly) peer pressure, and community standards are constantly being reinforced. The cranks and partisans, etc., are not simply outgunned. They also receive considerable opprobrium if they abuse the system.[31]

This reflects very well the conception I had in September 2001 of Wikipedia's culture; the reply above was as much hopeful and prescriptive as descriptive. But it turned out to be only partly true.[32] As difficult users began to have more of a "run of the place," in late 2001 and 2002, opprobrium was in fact meted out only piecemeal and inconsistently. It seemed that participation in the community was becoming, increasingly, a struggle over principles, rather than a shared effort toward shared goals. Any attempt to enforce what should have already been set policy—neutrality, no original research, and no wholesale deletion without explanation—was

---

[31] See my version of "Wikipedia/Our Replies to Our Critics," October 11, 2001, https://bit.ly/2OBBs00.

[32] And a decade later, it was simply false. The partisans had taken over. Today, in 2020, they are absolutely dominant.

frequently if not usually met with resistance. It was difficult to claim the high ground in a dispute, because the basic project principles were constantly coming under attack. Consequently, Wikipedia's environment was not cooperative but instead competitive, and the competition often concerned what sort of community Wikipedia should be: radically anarchical and uncontrolled, or instead more single-mindedly devoted to building an encyclopedia. Sadly, few among those who would love to work on Wikipedia could thrive in such a protean environment.

It is one thing to lack any equivalent to police and courts that can quickly and effectively eliminate abuse; such enforcement systems were rarely entertained in Wikipedia's first two early years, because according to the wiki ideal, users can effectively police each other. It is another thing altogether to lack a community ethos that is unified in its commitment to basic ideals, so that the community's champions could claim a moral high ground at all. So why was there no such unified community ethos and no uncontroversial "high ground"? I think it was a simple consequence of the fact that the community was to be largely self-organizing and to set its own policy by consensus. Any loud minority, even a persistent minority of one person, can remove the appearance of consensus. In fact, I recall that (in October 2002, after I resigned) I felt compelled by ongoing controversies to request[33] that Jimmy declare that certain policies were in fact non-negotiable, which he did.[34] Unfortunately, this declaration was too little, too late, in my opinion.

By late 2001, I had gained both friends and detractors. I think I had become, within the project, a symbol of opposition to anarchism, of the enforcement of standards, and

[33] "What we need," message on the WikiEN-l mailing list, November 20, 2001, https://bit.ly/2ORGMwB.

[34] Response to the foregoing by Jimmy Wales, November 21, 2001, https://bit.ly/3hhAOBe.

consequently of the exercise of authority in a radically open project. But I was still trying to manage the project as I always had—by force of personality and moral authority. So when people arrived who clearly and openly disrespected established policy, I was, in my frustration, short with them; and when the project continued to try to establish new policies, my role in articulating those policies and actually establishing them (attempting to express a "consensus") was challenged. This undermined what moral authority I had. I felt my job was on the line, and the project continued in turmoil day in and day out; from my point of view, fires were spreading everywhere, and as I had become a somewhat controversial figure, I did not have quite enough allies to help me put them out. Consequently I was rather too peremptory and short with some users—or perhaps we were in fact too tolerant. This attempt to walk a fine line between tolerance and enforcement of reasonable standards, however, exacerbated the problem in an open community increasingly dominated by anarchist types, because the attitude could not be backed up by punishment. Harsh words from a leader are empty threats if unenforceable. I thereby handed my anti-authoritarian "wiki-anarchist" opponents an advantage, because—ironically—they were able to portray me as dictatorial, when I was anything but. I came to the view, finally and belatedly, that it would be better to "ignore the trolls." But as it turns out, this is particularly hard to do as leader of a wiki, because, again, unlike on an e-mail list, trollish contributions do not just disappear into the archives; they sit out in the open, as available as the first day they appeared, and "festering." Attempts to delete or radically edit such contributions were often met by reposting the earlier, rules-violating version: the ability to do that is a necessary feature of collaboration. Persistent trolls could, thus, be a serious problem, particularly if they were able to draw a sympathetic audience (or to invent an audience of dummy accounts they control). And there was often an audience of sympathizers: contributors who philosophically were opposed to nearly any exercise of authority, but who were not trolls themselves.

It is ironic that I initially embraced the idea that there should be no enforceable rules in the community, as if collaboration would magically solve all problems. Some legal theorists would maintain that a community that lacks enforceable rules lacks any "law" at all. In retrospect it is clear that there was a fundamental problem with my role in the system: to have real authority, I needed both to be able to enforce the rules and, for both fairness and the perception of fairness, there needed to be clear rules from the beginning. But, by my own design, I had very early on rejected the label "editor-in-chief" and much real enforcement authority; a year into the game, it would have been difficult if not impossible to claim enforcement authority over active but problem users. Moreover, I was the author of the "ignore all rules" rule. My early rejection of any enforcement authority, my attempt to portray myself and behave as just another user who happened to have some special moral authority in the project, and my rejection of rules—these were all clearly mistakes on my part. These stances did, I think, help the project get off the ground; but I really needed a more subtle and forward-looking understanding of how an extremely open, decentralized project might work.

In retrospect, I wish I had taken Teddy Roosevelt's advice: "Speak softly and carry a big stick." I suppose I felt compelled to "speak loudly," which I regret. (This was not such a problem, by the way, on Nupedia; partly, that was because there were not nearly as many problem users on Nupedia, but partly it was because there *was* clear enforcement authority.) As it turns out, it was Jimmy who spoke softly and carried the big stick; he first exercised "enforcement authority." Since he was relatively silent throughout these controversies, he was the "good cop," and I was the "bad cop": that, in fact, is precisely how he (privately) described our relationship. Eventually, I became sick of this arrangement. Because Jimmy had remained mostly in the background in the early days of the project, and showed that he was willing to exercise enforcement authority upon occasion, he was never so ripe for attack as I was.

Perhaps the root cause of the governance problem was that we did not realize well enough that a community would form, nor did we think carefully about what this entailed. For months I even denied that Wikipedia was a community at all, claiming that it was, instead, only an encyclopedia project, and that there should not be any serious governance problems if people would simply stick to the task of making an encyclopedia. This was strictly wishful thinking. In fact, Wikipedia was from the beginning and is both a community and an encyclopedia project. And for a community attempting to achieve something, to be serious, effective, and fair, a charter seems necessary. In short, a collaborative community would do well to think of itself as a polity with everything that that entails: a representative legislative, a competent and fair judiciary, and an effective executive, all defined in advance by a charter. There are special requirements of nearly every serious community, however, best served by playing specific roles. I think a prominent role for the relevant experts should be written into such a charter.[35] I would recommend adopting a community charter—not just legal terms of service—to anyone launching an online knowledge community. But in January 2001, we were in both "uncharted" and "unchartered" territory. The world, I hope, will eventually be able to benefit from this and our other initial mistakes.

But in fairness to ourselves, it was a good idea to allow the community to decide by experience and consensus what article content rules to endorse. This allowed us to generate a very sensible set of article content rules. But it was not such a good idea to apply the same thinking to the organization of the community itself; we should have acknowledged that a community would form, that it would have certain persistent

---

[35] I started just such an alternative community in 2006 with Citizendium.org, which still exists in 2020.

and difficult issues that would need to be solved, and that a lack of any effective founding community charter might result in chaos. But chaos did result, and it never went away.

My Final Months with the Project

Throughout the governance controversy, I was preparing for my wedding, which happened in December 2001. A few days after I arrived back from my honeymoon, I was informed that I should probably start looking for another job, because Bomis was having to lay off most of its workers; they had 10-12 workers at the end of 2000, and by the beginning of 2002 they were back to their original 4-5. My salary was reduced in December and then halved in January. This seemed inevitable because Wikipedia was not bringing in any money at all for Bomis, even if Wikipedia was becoming even more of a publicly-recognized, if still modest, success. Our first anniversary came just before we announced having 20,000 articles, and I was invited to talk about the project at Stanford in January.[36]

I was officially laid off at the beginning of February, which I announced a few weeks later.[37] I had continued on as a volunteer; Wikipedia and Nupedia were, after all, volunteer projects. But I was laboring in the aftermath of the governance controversies of the previous fall and winter, which promised to make the job of a volunteer project leader even more

---

[36] "Wikipedia and why it matters," speech delivered to the Stanford University Computer Systems Laboratory Colloquium, January 16, 2002, https://bit.ly/2Wz95UL; you might notice that in early 2002, I was still plugging the notion of using Nupedia to vet Wikipedia articles, as an answer to the objection that Wikipedia articles are unreliable.

[37] "Announcement about my involvement in Wikipedia and Nupedia," meta.wikimedia.org, February 13, 2002, https://bit.ly/39bAd0S.

difficult. Moreover, I had to look for a real job. So throughout the month of February I considered resigning altogether.

But Jimmy had told me the previous December that Bomis would start trying to sell ads on Wikipedia in order to pay for my job.[38] Even in that horrible market for Internet advertising, there were already enough pageviews on Wikipedia that advertising proceeds might have provided me a very meager living. We knew that this would be controversial, because some vocal people who are involved in open source and open content projects hated the idea of advertising on the web pages of free projects, even to support project organizers. In fact, when this advertising plan was announced, in late February of 2002, the Spanish Wikipedia was forked (something I urged them not to do[39]).

Bomis was not successful in selling any ads for Wikipedia anyway—early 2002 was at about the very bottom of the market for Internet advertising. I also had some hope that we might, finally, set up the project's managing nonprofit, which we had discussed doing for a long time, and which eventually did come into being: the Wikimedia Foundation. The job of setting up the nonprofit was left to me, but ongoing controversies seemed to eat up any time I had for Wikipedia, and frankly I had no idea where to begin. So, after a month without pay, I announced my general resignation[40]; I completely stayed away from the project for a few months.

By the way, Wikipedia's offshoot projects—a dictionary, a textbook project, a quotation project, a public domain book

---

[38] As I did not know (when I drafted this memoir), and as I was told later by a Bomis co-worker, this was a lie Jimmy Wales told me, apparently to keep me quiet, i.e., no one there actually tried to sell any ads for Wikipedia.

[39] "Statement by Larry Sanger about the Spanish wiki encyclopedia fork," es.wikipedia.org, February 2002, https://bit.ly/3hgy4UK.

[40] "My resignation—Larry Sanger," meta.wikipedia.org, March 1, 2002, https://bit.ly/3jdwy7s.

repository, etc.—were all started in 2002 or later, and I cannot claim any credit for them. I did supply the name "Wiktionary"[41] in April 2001, more or less on a whim. I quickly disavowed[42] any responsibility for leading any such project, and it seems the Wiktionary project did not start up for another year and a half (December 12, 2002). My view now is that ordinary dictionaries and the OED are quite good enough as far as English dictionaries go. There will always be excellent free dictionaries in every language online. To try to develop a dictionary by collaboration among random Internet users, particularly in a completely uncontrolled wiki format, now strikes me as a nonstarter. I confess I am now puzzled why I did not think so instantly; it was no doubt because I simply was throwing out ideas as they occurred to me, and also because we had too many dictionary definition-type entries in Wikipedia.[43] But Jimmy's first reaction was properly skeptical regarding the use of wikis[44] and Ruth Ifcher made a stronger criticism very nicely.[45] Dictionaries, even more than encyclopedias, must be extremely reliable to be even minimally usable; without direct oversight by linguists, a public dictionary project seems pointless.

As to the other projects, they are mostly conducted using wikis and according to some of the basic founding principles of Wikipedia. But other sorts of project—for example, textbook projects, quotation repositories, and archives—necessarily require quite different specifications from those of an

---

[41] See "Wiktionary," message on the Wikipedia-l mailing list, April 17, 2001, https://bit.ly/2WMLLD6.

[42] Response in same thread, April 19, 2001, https://bit.ly/3jy9mAW.

[43] So why not give people a place to put their dictionary definitions?—Perhaps that is what I was thinking, but it hardly seems like a good justification for starting a project.

[44] Response in the same thread, April 17, 2001, https://bit.ly/39d4H2K.

[45] *Ibid.*, https://bit.ly/2CShBqB.

encyclopedia. For example, the fact that the wiki format works for encyclopedia development hardly means that it is appropriate for the hosting of public domain books. Since the same texts are available in many other places online, such as the wonderful Project Gutenberg, why would anyone get the text of *The Iliad* for any serious purpose from a wiki, which could have been carelessly edited or subtly changed by any random passer-by, without any oversight by someone who had access to and ability to use an authoritative text? There is a fact about the way the text actually reads (and supportable variants), according to the source material; so is editing via wiki software more apt to increase or reduce the number of errors over other systems, such as Project Gutenberg's? I do not mean to dismiss any such efforts. I simply think that considerable thought needs to be put into exactly how those other projects should be organized: the wiki format is not a magic pill that somehow makes all problems go away. Wiki is just one software paradigm, which must be adapted, supplemented, changed, or replaced in order to solve the unique set of problems a project faces.

In the spring, a controversy erupted. Caring as I did—and still do—about the future of free encyclopedias, I felt compelled to get involved. The controversy featured a troll who was putting up huge numbers of screeds on the "meta-wiki" and on Wikipedia as well. The controversy began with a discussion of what to do about, and how to react to, this particular troll. I maintained that one should not "feed the troll," and that the troll should be "outed" (it was an anonymous user, but it was not hard to use Google to determine the identity of the troll) and shamed.

There resulted a broader controversy about how to treat problem users generally. There were, as I recall, two main schools of thought. One, to which I adhered and still adhere, was that bona fide trolls should be "named and shamed" and, if they were unresponsive to shaming, they should be removed from the project (by a fair process) sooner rather than later. We held that a collaborative project requires commitment to ethical standards which are—as all ethical standards ultimately are—socially established by pointing out violations of those standards. Hence naming and shaming.

A second school of thought held that all Wikipedia contributors, even the most difficult, should be treated respectfully and with so-called WikiLove. Hence trolls were not to be identified as such (since "troll" is a term of abuse), and were to be removed from the project only after a long (and painfully depressing) public discussion. For the latter school, which I do not think was really sincere,[46] the only egregious faux pas one could commit in the project was to suggest that there were objective standards that could be enforced via this sort of shaming.

I felt at the time that the prevalence of the second school entailed rejection of both objective standards and rules-based authority. It is impossible to explain why one is removing some partisan screeds from the wiki without, in some way, identifying it as a partisan screed, and pointing out that such productions are inconsistent with the neutrality policy. This was necessarily received as less than respectful and "loving," especially if one must engage the troll himself in a long, drawn-out dispute. In a very long dispute with any trollish type, it is only a matter of time before some epithet gets bandied about, since they are so descriptive, and darned useful, when applied to trolls.

More generally, the very application of rules, or laws, entails a moral judgment, or what for its effectiveness must have the force of a moral judgment. I suppose I agree with those legal theorists who say that there is necessarily, in its core, a moral component to the law. Consequently, such a new policy of "WikiLove" would hand trolls and other difficult users a potent weapon for combating anyone who attempted to enforce a rule against them. After all, any forthright

---

[46] It now, in 2020, strikes me as a rather clear example of gaslighting by a gang of ideologues.

declaration that a user is doing something that is clearly against established conventions—posting screeds, falsehoods, nonsense, personal opinion, deleting perfectly good text, etc.— is nearly always going to appear disrespectful, because such a declaration involves a moral accusation. The only way to avoid such an appearance of disrespect, perhaps, is to step very lightly and use much flattery and qualifications: "Now do not get me wrong, I think you are doing a good job overall, but it seems to me that in this particular case, your contribution is slightly inconsistent with the neutrality policy." Suppose the offender replies: "So what? I disagree with the neutrality policy." Or: "I disagree. What I wrote is perfectly neutral. Who do you think you are, anyway?" It is a very rare person who can practice "WikiLove" when confronted with people who ignore rules while demanding that you follow them. In Wikipedia's developing culture, if anyone reacted out of frustration, or merely attempted to apply the law as a moral instrument, as laws typically are applied, *he* would become the problem, and a much more serious problem, than mere violations of the neutrality policy, say. The result is that, on pain of becoming *persona non grata* in the community, one had to treat brazen, self-conscious violators of basic policy with particular respect. It was a perfect coup for the resident wiki-anarchists. I again left the project for several months.

In fall of 2002, I had started teaching at a local community college, and with some extra time on my hands, I started editing Wikipedia a little and engaging in mailing list discussions. I think my first new post to Wikipedia-l, from September 1, 2002, was "Why the free encyclopedia movement needs to be more like the free software movement."[47] In it I argued that the free software movement is led and dominated by highly-qualified programmers, and that the "free encyclopedia movement"—that is, Wikipedia, Nupedia, and other newer projects—needs to move in that direction. I

---

[47] See https://bit.ly/39inDNx.

suggested that Nupedia be redesigned to release "approved" versions of Wikipedia articles; Wikipedia itself was not to be touched by this approval project.[48] This proposal met with a very cool reception. After a few months of discussion, Jimmy himself said he was "intending to revive Nupedia in the near future" and "thinking very much along the lines of what is being discussed here."[49] Unfortunately, this never happened.

Soon, I had proposed and Magnus Manske had very helpfully coded an expert-controlled approval process for Wikipedia that was in fact to be independent of both Nupedia and Wikipedia.[50] It would not have affected the Wikipedia editorial process. It would have lived in a separate namespace or domain, as an independent add-on project for Wikipedia. Expert reviewers, the recruitment of which I would have organized, would examine Wikipedia articles and approve or disapprove of particular versions of those articles. We set up a mailing list, Sifter-l,[51] which for several weeks discussed policy issues.

There was not a great deal of support for the proposal on Wikipedia-l. There was little or no excitement that the new project might bring a fresh crop of subject area specialists into Wikipedia. But that was fine as far as I was concerned, since the project was to operate independently of Wikipedia. Still, I had the very distinct sense that any specialists arriving on the scene would not necessarily be met with open arms in Wikipedia—particularly if before approving an article they wished to make whatever changes to articles that they felt necessary. There were even a few Wikipedians who made it

---

[48] I elaborated this proposal in "Wikipedia subset proposal," message in Wikipedia-l, October 20, 2002, https://bit.ly/3htDMm7.

[49] Jimmy Wales, response to "Wikipedia subset proposal," Wikipedia-l, November 4, 2002, https://bit.ly/3eJGLoX.

[50] Magnus Manske, response to "Wikipedia subset proposal," Wikipedia-l, November 4, 2002, https://bit.ly/3eCOwNi.

[51] Archives no longer online, apparently.

clear that experts should not expect to be treated any differently than anyone else, even when writing about their areas of expertise.

I then considered whether the interaction between Wikipedians and the new reviewers might be a problem after all. Surely, I thought, most specialists would want to edit even very good articles before approving them (in the independent system). This would require that the reviewers interact quite a bit with Wikipedians. Wikipedia's culture had become twisted and perverse, so that disrespect of expertise was tolerated, while trolls were merely warned, but very politely (in keeping with the policy of WikiLove), that they please ought to stop their destructive behavior. Trolls would certainly find ripe targets in expert reviewers, I thought. I recalled that patient, well-educated Wikipedians like J. Hoffmann Kemp and Michael Tinkler had been driven off the project not only by trolls but by some of the more abrasive and disrespectful regulars. I then considered: could I in good conscience really ask academics, who are very busy, to engage in this activity that would probably annoy most of them and do nothing to contribute to their academic careers? Recruiting for Nupedia was very easy by comparison, and caused me no such pangs of conscience.

I believe it was this problem that finally prompted me, in I believe January of 2003, to inform Jimmy as follows[52]: I was breaking with the project altogether; the only way he could prevent this, I told him, was that he both personally crack down on problem users and make the project more officially welcoming to experts. I also told him that I did not expect this information to change his mind and that I did not mean to issue an ultimatum. But, in retrospect, it is easy to see that it *was* an ultimatum. Indeed, our exchange did not change his mind. I concluded that we had a fundamental disagreement

---

[52] By private e-mail, lost now.

about how the project should be run. That is where matters ended, and it was then that I broke with Wikipedia altogether.

Some Final Attempts to Save Nupedia

Nevertheless, I was interested in pursuing Nupedia's development. It still seemed possible to rescue.

I recall two incidents in which I tried to have Nupedia revived, in 2002 or 2003, but I do not recall exactly. First, I approached Jimmy with the offer to try to find a buyer/managing organization for Nupedia. The suggestion was that, since Bomis did not have enough money to support it, and since Jimmy did not appear to have any specific intentions with the project other than to let it run on the system set up in 2000-1, I might be able to find a university or other organization that would take on the responsibility. I do not recall the details, and we did not pursue this possibility. Second, and later, I offered to buy Nupedia myself—that is, the domain name, the membership list, and whatever other proprietary material Bomis might have controlled. I wanted to start it up again as a simpler, more streamlined, but still fully peer-reviewed project; I thought, moreover, that if I owned it I might be able to give it to a suitable sponsoring educational or nonprofit institution. Jimmy seemed cool to the idea and did not ask for any specific offers.

Perhaps it is, therefore, not entirely accurate to say that Nupedia died due to the inefficiency of its system. To some extent it was also allowed to die, even after it was clear that its former editor-in-chief expressed an interest in continuing the project under a different system. The result was that, without an organization that could support its mission, Nupedia died a slow death. The server it lived on had some trouble in 2003, and as a result the website went offline. For whatever reason, the website was never brought up again after that.

I obviously cannot speak for Jimmy, but I will say that, *if* he was worried that Nupedia would essentially fork Wikipedia—again, I do not claim that he actually had that concern—then it seems to me that such a concern would not have justified letting Nupedia wither untended. The projects, Wikipedia and Nupedia, were naturally complementary parts of a single, symbiotic whole. That at least is how I always regarded them, indeed, from the very founding of Wikipedia. From the founding of Wikipedia, I always thought Wikipedia without Nupedia would have been unreliable, and that Nupedia without Wikipedia would have been unproductive. Together they were to be an "unstoppable high-quality article-creation juggernaut."[53]

It is still disappointing to me, that we made plans and promises to thousands of Nupedians, including hundreds of extremely well-qualified people, some of them leaders in their fields. We spent many thousands of person-hours, all told, on the project. I apologize to those people, and I can only hope that they will find some future open content encyclopedias worthy of their participation, which will show the world the potential that Nupedia had.

Conclusions

I have some advice for anyone who would like to start new projects on the model of Wikipedia.

You can learn from Wikipedia's success. First and most importantly, see above ("Why Wikipedia Started Working") for considerations about why Wikipedia works.

But you can also learn from our mistakes. The following primarily concerns project governance, because governance issues are, in my opinion, the primary failing of Wikipedia. Bear in mind, also, that these are only rough guidelines, for those who are starting projects that have enough resemblance to Wikipedia. These are not perfectly general rules:

- If you create a large, open, collaborative project, establish early on that there will be some non-negotiable policy.

---

[53] "Britannica or Nupedia?", Chapter 2.

Wikis and collaborative projects necessarily build communities, and once a community becomes large enough, it absolutely must have rules to keep order and to keep people at work on the mission of the project. "Force of personality" might be enough to make a small group of people hang together; for better or worse, however, clearly enunciated rules are needed to make larger groups of people hang together.

- There is some policy that, with forethought, it can be predicted will be necessary. Articulate this policy as soon as possible. Indeed, consider making a tentative project charter to make it clear from the beginning what the basic principles governing the project will be. This will help the community to run more smoothly and allow participants to self-select correctly.

- Establish any necessary authority early and clearly. This is necessary to keep an open project from being dominated by ideologues, as Wikipedia was. Managers should not be afraid to enforce the project charter by removing people from the project; as soon as it becomes necessary, it should be done. Standards that are not enforced in any way do not exist in any robust sense. Do not tolerate deliberate disruption from those who oppose your aims; tell them to start their own project. After all, there is a potentially infinite amount of cyberspace.

- As any disagreements among project managers are apt to be publicly visible in a collaborative project, and as this is apt to undermine the (very important) moral authority of at least one manager, make sure management is on the same page from the beginning—preferably before launch. This requires a great deal of frank discussion.

- In open knowledge-creation projects, make special roles for experts from the beginning; do not attempt to add those roles later, as an afterthought. Specialists are one of your most important resources, and it is irrational not to use them as much as you can. Preferably, design the charter so that they are included and encouraged. Moreover, make the volunteer project *management* a meritocracy, and not based on longevity but based on the ability to lead and contribute to the project; that is the only condition under which very many of the best-qualified people will want to participate.

Another point needs more in-depth development.

Radical and untried new ideas require constant refinement and adaptation in order to succeed; the first proposal is very rarely the best, and project designers must learn from their mistakes and constantly redesign better projects. Nupedia's Advisory Board failed to admit to inherent flaws in its system, and its delay in admission shut the window of opportunity to its improvement. It seems to me that the Wikipedia community fell into a mistake by thinking that just one or two features—the wiki feature, the neutrality policy, and a few other things—explained Wikipedia's success, and that those features can thus be applied with no significant changes to new projects. But there is no substitute for constant creativity and problem-solving—nor for honesty about what problems need solving. The honesty to recognize problems and creativity in solving them are, after all, what made Wikipedia succeed in the first place.

This is a crucial point: if you use a tool or model from another project, think through very carefully how that tool or model should be adapted. Do not assume that you need to use every feature, or every aspect of the surrounding culture, that you are borrowing. Wikipedia borrowed rather too much from (1) the culture of wikis, (2) unmoderated online discussions, and (3) free-wheeling online culture generally. To be sure, Wikipedia is also a product of those cultures, and works as well as it does largely because of what it borrowed from those cultures. I would not dream of denying that. But it also shares some of its more serious flaws of such cultures. Those planning new projects, or wanting to overhaul old ones, might well bear in mind that a certain cultural context, including the context that has grown up around a tool, just might not be right for that project. Let me elaborate.

(1) Consider first the culture of wikis. On the one hand, I said we wanted to determine the best rules, and experience would help us determine that; so we had no rules to begin with. On the other hand, one might add that another reason we began without rules was that we were partaking in the extremely uncontrolled, free-wheeling nature of "traditional" wikis. I think that is right. But there is an excellent reason why an encyclopedia project should not partake in that extremely uncontrolled nature of wiki culture, and why it should adopt actually enforceable rules: unlike traditional wikis, encyclopedia projects have a very specific aim, with very specific constraints, and efficient work toward that aim, within those constraints, practically requires the adoption of enforceable rules. The mere fact that most wikis, when Wikipedia was created, did not have enforceable rules hardly meant that one could not innovate further, and create one that did have rules.[54]

(2) Moreover, Jimmy and I and most of the first participants on Wikipedia were veterans of unmoderated Internet discussion groups. Naturally, we could appreciate the advantages of letting a virtual community develop in the absence of any real (enforced) authority. In unmoderated forums there is often found a sense, among some participants, that any attempt to oust a particularly troublesome user amounts to unjustifiable censorship. The result is that the existence of many unmoderated forums online has created a small army of people militantly opposed to the slightest restriction on speech, who feel that they do and should have a right to say whatever they like, wherever they like, online. Any

---

[54] I stand behind this point, but it is possible to take it too far. In the end, especially after 2010 or so, Wikipedia's devotion to its own rules became so strict as to be cult-like; rules came to be treated like totems of a cargo cult.

attempt to create and enforce rules for Internet projects, when that small army is ready to cry "censorship," will seem daring or even outrageous in many contexts online.[55] But there is an excellent reason why such anarchy is inappropriate for many projects, including encyclopedia projects, even one that is self-policing like a wiki: there simply must be a way to enforce rules in order for rules to be effective. Given that encyclopedia project development happens almost entirely using words, nearly any rules will also be restrictions on speech. Anyone who advocates many enforceable rules on a collaborative project, in the cultural context of an Internet filled with so many unmoderated discussion groups, can be made to seem reactionary.[56] But this is only a result of that cultural context; in any other context, the existence of rules would be perfectly natural and unobjectionable.

(3) Finally, and generally speaking, the Internet is a great leveler. Since social interaction can proceed among complete strangers who cannot so much as see each other, things that used to matter in many "meatspace" discussions, such as age, social status, and level of education, are often dismissed as unimportant online. Much of social media as well as chat, old-fashioned forums, and blogs are populated by people who are identified by only a username, and any suggestion that

---

[55] The preceding sentences, written in 2005, is apt to strike some as ironic 15 years later, considering that many of those same ideologues are, today, cracking down on free speech.

[56] Again, in 2020, this is apt to strike some as ironic, because restrictions of online speech are now regarded as the province of progressive ideologues, while defense of free speech rights is associated with the right. However that might be, my own views have not changed: I both was and still am a free speech zealot, but that does not mean anyone should be able to say anything they want in any forum online. The point here is not ideological, but a matter of practical common sense: different forums need different kinds of rules, and you should not expect to be able to say just whatever you want in an open knowledge project.

communication should be restricted or in any way altered in accordance with "expertise" or "authority" is likely to be met with outrage, in most forums.[57] But there are several excellent and obvious reasons why expertise *does* need special consideration in an encyclopedia project, and in other collaborative knowledge projects. First, while there are many topics that any intelligent person can write about credibly, there are also many topics on which dilettantes cannot. I, for example, could not write very credibly about astronomy or speleology, but I have a passing interest in both. If I am working only with other dilettantes, our articles are apt to remain amateurish at best; we can fill in the gaps in each other's knowledge, and do research, but the results will remain unimpressive until someone with more knowledge of the subject contributes. Second, in most academic and professional fields, there are many highly specialized subjects about which no one but experts has any significant knowledge (or interest) at all. Third, on many topics, it is only the opinions of experts that should be trusted by most of the public as authoritative in determining whether an article is generally reliable or not. Moreover, the standards of public credibility are not likely to be changed by the widespread use of Wikipedia or by online debate about the reliability of Wikipedia.[58] Like them or hate them, those are the facts. But if one points these facts out online, culturally "leveled" as it is, particularly in forums or projects like Wikipedia which go out of their way to ignore individual differences among people, one finds a frosty reception at best.

Consider, if you will, that it was *because* Wikipedia was started in the context of the ingrained cultures of wikis, of

---

[57] Societal expertise on this, clearly, have changed since 2005, largely owing to gradually increasing speech restrictions by social media companies.

[58] The experience of the last 20 years on Wikipedia bears this claim out very well, I find.

unmoderated discussion forums, and of the leveling, anti-elitist influence of the Internet at large, that it was very difficult for us to exercise the maximal amount of creativity that a maximally successful project would require. In establishing a new cultural context, we were deeply constrained by the old. Now, to be sure, I have said above and many times elsewhere that Wikipedia did not have to adopt the particular conjunction of policies that it did. But it is not surprising that it did adopt its particular conjunction of policies, considering the conjunction of influences on its development.

It would have required much more explanation and persuasion, and indeed, much more struggle, for us to, for example, have persuaded potential participants that some persons, in a wiki environment, should have special rights that others do not.[59] The influence of cultural context is powerful. There are quite a few people whose lack of imagination is such that they believe that—ironically—I must not understand why the project I started works, if I am willing to suggest that it does not have to work in precisely the way it does work. Constantly-reinforced cultural habits die very hard indeed, and place very strong constraints upon what can be imagined, and what bare possibilities seem even worth thinking about.

But it was our willingness to exercise our creativity and follow our imagination, and create what is, to some extent, a new kind of culture, that led to Wikipedia's success. For the overall project of creating open content encyclopedias—and indeed, for the fantastic collaborative Internet that has yet to be created—to reach its full potential, the process of identifying mistakes honestly and creatively seeking solutions must be ramped up and continued unabated.

---

[59] Yet this is the basis on which I started the Citizendium.org project eighteen months after first writing this memoir.

Two

Two Early Articles
about Wikipedia

These two pieces appeared in the blog Kuro5hin.org in Wikipedia's first year (in July and in September, 2001), reflecting how we promoted and thought about the developing projects at the time. The edits made for this volume are mostly stylistic.

I. Britannica or Nupedia? The Future of Free Encyclopedias

BRITANNICA recently announced that it was going to require payment to view anything beyond the first few paragraphs of their articles. It was predictable that it would do so, eventually, particularly after the technology stock bubble burst. "The economics of the all-free model has changed," said *Britannica* spokesman Tom Panelas says in the AP story. Gone are the halcyon days of free content.

Au contraire—that is only what *Britannica* wants you to think. The grandest days of free content have not yet begun. *Britannica* and other proprietary encyclopedias will be hopelessly obsolete within ten years—small, out-of-date, and generally irrelevant—by comparison with Nupedia, Wikipedia, and the many other non-proprietary reference works that are being and will be developed. This is a dramatic claim, but an interesting and surprising case can be made for it.

How to Keep High-Quality Encyclopedic Content Free

It is now hackneyed, but still perfectly sound, to argue that good content online will always be free. Even a small number of producers of excellent content will satisfy most of the demand, due to the ease of Internet distribution. So the price of content will stay low, if the law of supply and demand is to be trusted. In other words, if someone charges others for premium content, then users, not being stupid, will look elsewhere for comparable content. In all likelihood, they will find it, simply because the number of Internet content-producers is huge. An academic, hobbyist, amateur journalist, or some other person will want to educate the public. Like everyone, they have a natural desire to communicate and teach.

One might plausibly object that the argument does not apply to the present case. An encyclopedia is a special kind of content. Making an encyclopedia requires focused effort, which people are not apt to make without financial incentive. So the supply of free encyclopedic content will not be there.

This is where Nupedia and Wikipedia come into the picture. They are open content encyclopedias, or free encyclopedias (in Richard Stallman's sense of "free"—in fact, Nupedia has Stallman's explicit support). This means, as you no doubt already know, that anyone may use their content, for nonprofit or for-profit purposes, provided they link back to the content's source. It also means that the content can be developed further by other parties. Someone who releases an article under an open content license does so in order to guarantee that the article remains free to the public. This guarantee of freedom is a strong motivation to work on a free encyclopedia.

Moreover, if scholars concentrate their forces in building an open content encyclopedia, they will be fired by a further motive: there is considerable value in the collaboration that can be found in a general encyclopedia project and in the uniformity and high quality of the results. This value cannot be found in as high a degree in the activities of each writer posting content independently.

1. Nupedia's Experience So Far

"This theorizing is all fine and well," a critic might say, "but Nupedia's experience itself illustrates that it is mistaken. Nupedia has just over 20 articles now, and the project has been in existence for eighteen months. It seems that the rigorous system it has in place—which does seem to be necessary in order for a body of volunteers to generate really high-quality content—is so arduous that most volunteers do not feel their time is well-spent on it. If someone were to pay them, they would work more quickly, and you might produce something to make *Britannica* nervous; if you do not, you are not apt to motivate people to work much. But you cannot afford to pay them using an open content model, because you will have no content to sell. Nor would donations to a nonprofit supporting organization generate enough money to support a really enormous open content encyclopedia."

I think this reasoning is weak, because it is short-sighted. There are many possible improvements that Nupedia can try (and is in the process of trying). But for the sake of argument, let us temporarily concede the point. After all, one might well come to the conclusion that a less rigorous project, much easier to contribute to, would have some value as a project complementary to Nupedia. In January 2001, Nupedia's leaders discovered WikiWiki software, or "wiki" for short, and immediately saw that it could be used to create an encyclopedia, which we called Wikipedia.

On a wiki website, anyone can view and edit any page. The edits to pages are tracked in a "Recent Changes" log; the participants in the wiki are constantly watching that log, and if any vandal happens along and ruins a page, it is immediately changed back (back copies of previous versions of pages are kept and are easily accessible).

So Nupedia's principals created a wiki-based encyclopedia last January, and what happened was astonishing. A small number of mostly undistinguished regulars (just a few dozen people) together with a constant flow of random article-inputters managed to create over 6,000 articles in the first six months of Wikipedia's existence. Moreover, the quality of the articles and the average expertise of the participants has increased as well. All in all, Wikipedia is a roaring success and just keeps plowing along, creating more and more good articles.

The reason for this, in retrospect, is clear: contributing articles to Wikipedia is easy, as is editing other people's articles. There is naturally little motivation to make substantive edits to articles on subjects about which one knows nothing, and mistakes are often caught and made a public spectacle. So experts are respected and deferred to, which encourages and motivates the experts—thus the increasing level of expertise on the website. Moreover, Wikipedians edit each other's stuff, so they feel a sense of collective purpose, responsibility, and camaraderie, which is yet another motivation to participate.

Having observed the success of Wikipedia, just a few weeks ago Nupedia set up its own supplementary, experimental article-development wiki, called the Nupedia Chalkboard. It differs from Wikipedia in that it is managed by Nupedia's editors and reviewers, and its purpose is to create high-quality articles to input into Nupedia's system. The idea is that Chalkboard articles can get through the rigorous Nupedia system more quickly because they will have already been vetted by Nupedia's experts. Moreover, articles can be easily transferred from the relatively wild-and-woolly, yet extremely productive Wikipedia project to the Chalkboard, which can act as a sort of staging area. In this way, the slow but powerful Nupedia system can indirectly benefit from the activity of Wikipedia. More on this point below.

Now let us return to the argument. A critic was made to say that a volunteer-only project could not generate high-quality content quickly enough to make *Britannica* nervous. This is an empirical prediction about totally novel phenomena, the proper evaluation of which requires data. And surely, Wikipedia's success in sheer numbers—1,000 articles per month—is an important datum. Wikipedia is a volunteer project that has produced huge amounts of content.

2. Can an Open Project Produce High-Quality Content?

My critic is unlikely to be impressed: "Sure, like on all the rest of the web, the content is cheap and plentiful, but the quality of the content is nowhere near what the professionals associated with *Britannica* can produce. They were paid to produce high quality. On Wikipedia, you get what you pay for. The point remains that a body of volunteers lacks the required economic incentive in order to produce really good quality."

This looks like a good argument, but there are three excellent ways to reply to it.

First, in fact, experience shows that the conclusion is actually false. Nupedia articles, while arriving at a stately clip, are uniformly superb. It is even more important, for purposes of replying to the critic, to note that many Wikipedia articles so far are of surprisingly high quality. There is a page on Wikipedia called "brilliant prose" in which Wikipedia members praise each other for really superlative work. The articles on that page—and that is only a selection of the best work, not all of it—are at or near the level of quality that you would find in an proprietary encyclopedia. Out of the thousands of Wikipedia articles, there are hundreds of articles that are of this level of quality. All of the articles tend to grow in level of quality, as well—to paraphrase Linus Torvalds, "Given enough eyeballs, all typos, factual errors, and other errors of content are shallow."

Second, Wikipedia articles can be vetted further by Nupedia. As explained above, Nupedia's principals are, even now, setting up a system whereby the best content from Wikipedia can undergo Nupedia's rigorous review process. Time will tell, but the combination of Nupedia and Wikipedia, together with the new Chalkboard, seems to be an unstoppable high-quality article-creation juggernaut. Many articles will begin life on Wikipedia as mediocre, short items, where they will be expanded and cleaned up; the best of these will move to the Chalkboard, where Nupedia's experts will further hammer them into shape; then, by the time they enter Nupedia's system, there will be almost no work to be done on them, and they will slip through the system very quickly. This too is a prediction, but it seems reasonable enough.

Third, time and creativity will take care of the rest. It is worth remembering that Nupedia has been in existence for 18 months, and Wikipedia for just six. Because these are public projects with thousands of supporters, and because they are open content, it is quite reasonable to think that they will be around—perhaps changing management, perhaps not—for many more years to come. So, whatever they are called and whatever their exact form, open content encyclopedias are natural institutions—they are not going to go away.[1] This is, above all, what should have *Britannica* quaking in their boots.

3. A Few Speculations about a Perhaps Amazing Future

Suppose that, as is perfectly possible, Wikipedia continues producing articles at a rate of 1,000 per month. In seven years, it would have 84,000 articles. This is entirely possible;

---

[1] I still believe this is true. Whatever the ultimate fate of the Wikipedia.org website and the Wikimedia Foundation, the content it has developed will live on, managed by some organizations.

Everything2, which uses wiki-like software, reached 1,000,000 "nodes" recently. If Wikipedia does not do it, some other website will (and perhaps many of them will).

Wikipedia's content is useful, and so people are starting to link to it. Google and other search engines have already discovered Wikipedia and the daily traffic they send to the project produces a steady stream of new readers and participants. The greater the number of Wikipedia articles, the greater the number of links to them, and therefore the higher the rankings and numbers of listings on Google. As they say, "the rich get richer." So it is far from inconceivable that the rate of article-production will actually increase over the coming years—in fact, this seems rather likely.

Wikipedia articles are getting constantly better as people go back again and again to old articles to add to them, reword misleading statements, correct factual errors, etc. This means that the quality of Wikipedia articles is ever-improving. An improvement in quality will be noticeable to experts. A shoddy article about topic T in 2001 will be a great article about topic T in 2002.

So, whereas, in 2001, an expert on T would be so disgusted by the article that he would not think of participating in Wikipedia, in 2002 he might be so impressed by the article, and therefore also by Wikipedia's collaborative article-creation process, that he becomes a Wikipedian on the spot. It does not take many experts, thus inspired, to create a lot of good articles. Therefore, as Wikipedia articles improve, the project will surely attract more and more experts. Wikipedia participants in the beginning were limited mainly to hobbyists, students, and generalists, and a few experts; but it now has the attention of a lot more graduate students and professionals. In a few years, the project will have attracted the attention of very many more experts.

Nupedia will certainly not be left in the dust, however. Indeed, here is where things might get even more interesting. Nupedia will directly benefit from Wikipedia's productivity, whatever else happens. As the projects become better and better known, and as more examples of the excellent results Nupedia's rigorous review process appear, it is only natural that it should become a more widely-recognized academic honor to be associated with Nupedia. It is reasonable to expect that, at some point in the coming years, the floodgates will open: academics, seeing the increasing value of being associated with the project, will pour into the project and begin the long, hard, but rewarding work of hammering original, Wikipedia-sourced, and other-sourced articles into professional-level articles. After all, MIT's online course notes program—not open content, but free of charge to read—demonstrates a very encouraging willingness on the part of distinguished academics to associate themselves with imparting free knowledge.

Moreover, these projects will not be the only open source references to be created, nor should they be. There is much that Wikipedia and Nupedia cannot do at present, or that it cannot do well, such as making free multimedia—and if some other open source project proves to be more competitive, then it should and will take the lead in creating a body of free encyclopedic knowledge.

Already, cnet's encyclopedia metasearch engine is searching Wikipedia and returning results alongside *Britannica*'s. But since Nupedia and Wikipedia, and other references to come, are open content, commercial enterprises can opt not just to return such references among search results; they will be able to reproduce the latest content free of charge. Thus, when commercial enterprises like Yahoo! start using Nupedia's approved, peer-reviewed content, and when people start publishing dirt-cheap paper copies of the encyclopedia on newsprint, *Britannica* and all the other commercial references will be officially finished.

It will be a new and glorious day.

II. Wikipedia is wide open. Why is it growing so fast? Why isn't it full of nonsense?

AFTER the July 25 K5 article I wrote about Wikipedia was Slashdotted,[1] the free encyclopedia project has broken the 10,000 article barrier, and it has been the focus of stories in MIT's *Technology Review* as well as in *The New York Times*. The most recent development is that free software guru Richard Stallman has endorsed the Wikipedia project alongside his endorsement of Nupedia. Stallman described Wikipedia's successes to me as "really exciting news."

This growth and attention is paradoxical. Why should anyone care about it? After all, Wikipedia is a wide-open project—anyone can write for it. Moreover, the wiki software that runs the project allows anyone to edit any page, instantly. So, it must be full of a bunch of crank submissions, vandalism, and plain old sophomoric stupidity. But it is not. It is not half bad. In places, it is of very high quality, and its overall quality is growing. And that is even more paradoxical.

(Full disclosure: I am, with Jimmy Wales, the co-founder of Wikipedia and its only full-time paid participant. I feel very uncomfortable calling myself its "editor-in-chief." The participants would rebel at that title, which would be "anti-wiki"—"anti-wiki" is bad, in case you did not know.)

Among Wikipedia's active contributors are Axel Boldt, mathematics professor at Metropolitan State University in Saint Paul, Minnesota; Michael Tinkler, a professor of art history; Ruth Ifcher, a professor in both ESL and mathematics at Columbia U. and CUNY; and well over a dozen other Ph.D.'s, M.D.'s, and highly-educated people from around the world. In addition, there are many extremely bright, articulate graduate students and undergraduates involved. There are also dozens of computer programmers who are constantly

---

[1] I.e., the essay just above, section I in this chapter.

displaying their knowledge both within and outside the bounds of computer science. Everyone is welcome and their work is judged on its own merits.

But why all this activity and interest? Surely that is puzzling. Wiki software must be the most promiscuous form of publishing there is—Wikipedia will take anything from anybody. So how is it possible that so many otherwise upstanding intellectuals love Wikipedia (some, secretly) and spend so much time on it? Why are we not writing for academic journals, or something?

It is fun, first of all. But it can be fun for intellectually serious people only if we know that we are creating something of quality. And how do we know that? The basic outlines of the answer ought to be fairly obvious to anyone who has read Eric S. Raymond's famous essay on the open source movement, "The Cathedral and the Bazaar."[2] Remember, if we can edit any page, then we can edit each other's work. Given enough eyeballs, all errors are shallow. We catch each other's mistakes and enjoy correcting them.

So we are constantly monitoring Wikipedia's Recent Changes page. When—as happens rarely—some eejit shows up and vandalizes a page, it is fixed nearly instantly. (We save back copies of all pages, and these are easily accessible.) We participants work on a lot of different pages, and I think most of us feel some collective responsibility for how the whole thing looks. We are constantly cleaning up after each other and new people.

In the process, a camaraderie—a politeness and collegiality not found on many online discussion forums—has developed. We have got to respect each other, because we are each other's editors, and we all have more or less the same goal: to create a

---

[2] Free online, reprinted in Eric S. Raymond, *The Cathedral and the Bazaar: Musings on Linux and Open Source by an Accidental Revolutionary*, Revised & Expanded edition (O'Reilly, 2001).

huge, high-quality free encyclopedia. The way I see it, we are having fun creating a thing of beauty.

Perhaps this does not explain something, though. Why should highly-qualified people get involved with Wikipedia? It is not peer-reviewed. So, surely it is lightweight. Why should any serious researcher care about it? Why should anyone rely on it?

This is a common first reaction. The attitude appeared, gently expressed, in the *Technology Review* article:

Walter Bender, executive director of MIT's Media Laboratory, believes that what makes *Britannica* a valuable resource is the scope and depth of its editing, and free Web-based encyclopedias such as Wikipedia will probably never be able to compete with that.[3]

As well as the *New York Times* article:

But even if Wikipedia does not become a popular resource it may survive, even thrive, because of what it offers to those working on it.

That is the view of James J. O'Donnell, a professor of classical studies and vice provost for information systems at the University of Pennsylvania...

"The thing and the experience may be much more valuable for those who are creating it than it is for somebody who just walks in saying, 'So when is the Second Punic War and which one was that?'" Mr. O'Donnell said. "A community that finds a way to talk in this way is creating education and online discourse at a higher level."[4]

The implication is that Wikipedia has a nice community, but it does not have much breadth, depth, or reliability; so if you want serious information, go to *Britannica*.

---

[3] Judy Heim, "Free the Encyclopedias!" *MIT Technology Review*, September 4, 2001, https://bit.ly/2OSXnzR.

[4] Peter Meyers, "Fact-Driven? Collegial? This Site Wants You," *The New York Times*, September 20, 2001, https://nyti.ms/3jAZl68.

If Wikipedians believed that, we would bag the whole thing. We think we are—gradually, and sometimes from very rough first drafts—developing a reliable resource. So what answer can I offer to the above concerns?

Part of the answer is already given above: Wikipedia's self-correction process (Wikipedia co-founder Jimmy Wales calls it "self-healing") is very robust. There is considerable value created by the public review process that is continually ongoing on Wikipedia—value that is very easy to underestimate, for those who have not experienced it adequately.

Another part of the answer is that, of course, we have been around since just last January, 2001. (*Britannica*'s had a few centuries' head start.) Significantly, Wikipedia's rate of growth has been steadily increasing—in terms of article numbers and quality, traffic to the website, and attracting more highly-qualified contributors. So it seems very reasonable to think that within a few years the project will surpass *Britannica* in both breadth and depth. At our current rate of growth, we will have over 100,000 articles by 2005[5]; articles begun this year will be, in all likelihood, fleshed out to great detail. Not a few articles already have been.

But what about reliability? That is a third part of the answer. It seems very likely that, in coming months, Wikipedia will set up some sort of approval process,[6] whereby certain versions of articles receive the stamp of approval of some body of Wikipedia reviewers. There have been two main proposals about how to set up a review process. Whatever the shape of the process, it would act entirely independently of article generation. (We certainly do not want to kill the goose that lays the golden eggs.) But after it is in place, we will be able to present a set of genuine expert-approved articles that

---

[5] This milestone was actually reached January 21, 2003: "Milestones 2003," Wikipedia.org, https://bit.ly/2CARSDD.

[6] Never actually done, for reasons explained in Chapter 1.

can favorably compare with articles from any general encyclopedia, *Britannica* included.

Admittedly, Wikipedia is not on the verge of world domination—yet. But it is growing beyond anyone's expectations. The rate of growth continues to increase. Once an approval process is installed, in short order Wikipedia will—I think—be able to boast a breadth, depth, and reliability to compare to any general encyclopedia you please.[7]

Then we will try to get to the depth and reliability of a whole reference library full of specialized encyclopedias—something no general encyclopedia has ever done.

---

[7] Notice that I made the chances of Wikipedia's future excellence depend on there being an approval process. I stand by this today, in 2020. It is worth asking why Wikipedia continues to refuse to adopt such a process, or even a rating feature that is open to outside, credible, identified reviewers.

Three

Wikipedia's Original
Neutrality Policy[1]

This version of a Wikipedia policy document was the last I edited. It was official policy for years, and it served as one focus of the broader media debate over neutrality. I originally drafted, and thoroughly edited, all of it. The version below was only lightly copyedited.

WIKIPEDIA has an important policy: roughly stated, you should write articles without bias, representing all views fairly. This is easily misunderstood. The policy does not assume that it is possible to write an article from just one point of view, which would be *the* one neutral (unbiased, "objective") point of view. The Wikipedia policy is that we should fairly represent all sides of a dispute, and not make an article state, imply, or insinuate that any one side is correct.

---

[1] "Wikipedia: Neutral point of view," January 5, 2002; licensed under the Creative Commons Attribution-Share-Alike License 3.0. Readable at https://bit.ly/32quwJR.

It is crucial that we work together to make articles unbiased. It is one of the things that makes Wikipedia work so well.

Writing unbiased text is an art that requires practice.

The following essay explains this policy in depth, and is the result of much discussion. We strongly encourage you to read it, comment on it, if necessary edit it, and generally come to grips with it.

Introduction: the Basic Concept of Neutrality and Why Wikipedia Must Be Unbiased

A key Wikipedia policy is that articles should be "unbiased," or written from a "neutral point of view." We use these terms in a precise way that is different from the common understanding. It is crucial to grasp what it means to be neutral (in this sense)—a careful reading of this page will help.

Basically, to write without bias (from a neutral point of view) is to write so that articles do not advocate any specific points of view; instead, the different viewpoints in a controversy are all described fairly. This is a simplistic definition and we will add nuance later. But for now, we can say just that to write articles without bias is to try to describe debates rather than taking one definite stand.

Why should Wikipedia be unbiased?

Wikipedia is a general encyclopedia, which means it is a representation of human knowledge at some level of generality. But we (humans) disagree about specific cases; for any topic on which there are competing views, each view represents a different theory of what the truth is, and insofar as that view contradicts other views, its adherents believe that the other views are false, and therefore not knowledge. Where there is disagreement about what is true, there is disagreement about what constitutes knowledge. Wikipedia works because it is a collaborative effort; but, whilst collaborating, how can we solve the problem of endless "edit wars" in which one person asserts that p, whereupon the next person changes the text so that it asserts that *not-p*?

70

A solution is that we accept, for purposes of working on Wikipedia, that "human knowledge" includes all different (significant, published) theories on all different topics. So we are committed to the goal of representing human knowledge in that sense. Something like this is surely a well-established sense of the word "knowledge"; in this sense, what is "known" changes constantly with the passage of time, and when we use the word "know" in this sense, we often use so-called scare quotes. In the Middle Ages, we "knew" that the Earth was at the center of the universe.[2] We now "know" otherwise.

We could sum up human knowledge (in this sense) in a biased way: we would state a series of theories about topic T, and then claim that the truth about T is such-and-such. But again, consider that Wikipedia is an international, collaborative project. Probably, as we grow, nearly every view on every subject will (eventually) be found among our authors and readership. To avoid endless edit wars, we can agree to present each of these views fairly, and not make our articles assert any one of them as correct. And that is what makes an article "unbiased" or "neutral" in the sense we are presenting here. To write from a neutral point of view, one presents controversial views without asserting them; to do that, it generally suffices to present competing views in a way that is more or less acceptable to their adherents, and also to attribute the views to their adherents.

To sum up the primary reason for this policy: Wikipedia is an encyclopedia, a compilation of human knowledge. But since Wikipedia is a community-built, international resource, we surely cannot expect our collaborators to agree in all cases, or even in many cases, on what constitutes human knowledge in a strict sense. We can, therefore, adopt the looser sense of "human knowledge" according to which a wide variety of

---

[2] I had it here as "flat." This was, of course, a sloppy mischaracterization of the more common medieval view, which was that the Earth was a sphere at the center of the universe.

conflicting theories constitute what we call "human knowledge." We should, both individually and collectively, make an effort to present these conflicting theories fairly, without advocating any one of them.

There is another reason to commit ourselves to a nonbias policy. Namely, when it is clear to readers that we do not expect them to adopt any particular opinion, this is conducive to our readers' feeling free to make up their own minds for themselves, and thus to encourage in them intellectual independence. So totalitarian governments and dogmatic institutions everywhere might find reason to be opposed to Wikipedia, if we succeed in adhering to our nonbias policy: the presentation of many competing theories on a wide variety of subjects suggests that we, the creators of Wikipedia, trust readers' competence to form their own opinions themselves. Texts that present the merits of multiple viewpoints fairly, without demanding that the reader accept any one of them, are liberating. Neutrality subverts dogmatism. This is something that nearly everyone working on Wikipedia can agree is a good thing.

1. What Is the Neutral Point of View?

What we mean is not obvious, and is easily misunderstood.

There are many other possible valid understandings of what "unbiased," "neutral," etc., mean. The notion of "unbiased writing" that informs Wikipedia's policy is "presenting controversial views without asserting them." This needs further clarification, as follows.

First, and most importantly, consider what it means to say that unbiased writing presents controversial views without asserting them. Unbiased writing does not present *only* the most popular view; it does not assert the most popular view as being correct after presenting all views; it does not assert that some sort of intermediate view among the different views is the correct one (as if the intermediate view were "the neutral point of view"). Presenting all points of view says, more or less, that *p*-ists believe that *p*, and *q*-ists believe that *q*, and that is where the debate stands at present. Ideally, presenting all points of view also gives a great deal of background on who believes that *p* and *q* and why, and which view is more popular (being careful, here, not to word the statement so as to imply that popularity implies correctness). Detailed articles might also contain the mutual evaluations of the *p*-ists and the *q*-ists, allowing each side to give its "best shot" at the other, but studiously refraining from saying who won the exchange.

A point here bears elaboration. We said that the neutral point of view is not, contrary to the seeming implication of the phrase, some actual point of view on a controversial issue that is "neutral," or "intermediate," among the different positions. That represents a particular understanding of what "neutral point of view" means. The prevailing Wikipedia understanding is that the neutral point of view is not a *point of view* at all; according to our understanding, when one writes neutrally, one is very careful not to state (or imply or insinuate or carefully but subtly massage the reader into believing) that any particular view at all is correct.

Another point bears elaboration as well. Writing without bias can be conceived very well as representing disputes, characterizing them, rather than engaging in them. One can think of unbiased writing as the cold, fair, analytical description of debates. Of course, one might well doubt that this can be done at all without somehow subtly implying or insinuating that one position is correct. But experienced academics, polemical writers, and rhetoricians are well-attuned to bias, both their own and others', so that they can usually spot a description of a debate that tends to favor one side. If they so choose, with some creativity, they can usually remove that bias.

Now an important qualification. Articles that compare views need not give minority views as much or as detailed a description as more popular views. We should not attempt to represent a dispute as if a view held by only a small minority of people deserved as much attention as a very popular view. That may be misleading as to the shape of the dispute. If we are to represent the dispute fairly, we should present various competing views in proportion to their representation among experts on the subject, or among the concerned parties.

None of this, however, is to say that minority views cannot receive as much attention as we can possibly give them on pages specifically devoted to those views. There is no size limit to Wikipedia. But even on such pages, though the content of a view is spelled out possibly in great detail, we still make sure that the view is not represented as the truth.

Bias *per se* need not be conscious or particularly partisan. For example, beginners in a field often fail to realize that what sounds like uncontroversial common sense is actually biased in favor of one controversial view. (So not infrequently we need an expert in order to render the article entirely unbiased.) To take another example, writers can, without intending it, propagate "geographical" bias, by for example describing a dispute as it is conducted in the United States (or some other country) without stating so or knowing that the dispute is framed differently elsewhere.

2. Assert Facts about Opinions

We sometimes give an alternative formulation of the nonbias policy: assert facts, including facts about opinions, but do not assert opinions themselves.

By "fact," on the one hand, we mean "a piece of information about which there is no serious dispute." In this sense, that a survey produced a certain published result is a fact. That Mars is a planet is a fact. That 2+2=4 is a fact. That Socrates was a philosopher is a fact. No one seriously disputes any of these things. So Wikipedians can feel free to assert as many of them as we can. By "opinion," on the other hand, we mean "a piece of information about which there is some serious dispute."

There are bound to be borderline cases where we are not sure if we should take a particular dispute seriously; but there are many propositions that very clearly express opinions. That God exists is an opinion. That the Beatles were the greatest rock and roll group is an opinion. That intuitionistic logic is superior to ordinary logic is an opinion. That the United States was wrong to drop the atomic bomb over Hiroshima and Nagasaki is an opinion.

For determining whether something is fact or opinion in this sense, it does not matter what the actual truth is; there can at least in theory be false "facts" (things that everybody agrees upon, but which are, in fact, false), and there are very often true "opinions," though necessarily, it seems, there are more false ones.

Wikipedia is devoted to stating facts and only facts, in this sense. Where we might want to state opinions, we convert that opinion into a fact by attributing the opinion to someone. So, rather than asserting, "God exists," which is an opinion, we can say, "Most Americans believe that God exists," which is a fact, or "Thomas Aquinas believed that God exists," which is also a fact. In the first instance we assert an opinion; in the second and third instances we convert that opinion into a fact by attributing it to someone. In presenting an opinion, moreover, it is important that we bear in mind that there are sometimes even disagreements about how opinions might be best stated. Sometimes, it will be necessary to qualify the description of an opinion or to present several formulations, simply to arrive at an overall characterization that fairly represents all the leading views of the situation.

But it is not enough, to express the Wikipedia nonbias policy, just to say that we should state facts and not opinions. When asserting a fact about an opinion, it is important also to assert facts about competing opinions, and to do so without implying that any one of the opinions is correct. It is also generally important to give the facts about the reasons behind the opinions, and to make it clear who holds them. (It is often best to cite a prominent representative of the view.)

3. Fairness and Sympathetic Tone

If we are going to characterize disputes fairly, we should present competing views with a consistently positive, sympathetic tone. A lot of articles end up as partisan commentary even while presenting both points of view; this is wrong. Even when a topic is presented in terms of facts rather than opinion, an article can still radiate an implied stance through either selection of which facts to present, or more subtly their organization—for instance, refuting opposing views as one goes along tends to make them look a lot worse than collecting them in an opinions-of-opponents section.

We should, instead, write articles with the tone that all positions presented are at least plausible. Let us present all competing views sympathetically. We can write with the attitude that such-and-such is a good idea, except that, on the view of some detractors, the supporters of said view overlooked such-and-such a detail. If we cannot do that, we will probably write stuff with so much contempt that subsequent edits are going to have a hard time doing anything but veiling it.

4. Characterizing Aesthetic Opinions

A special case is the expression of aesthetic opinions. Some Wikipedia articles about art, artists, and other creative topics (e.g., musicians, actors, books, video games, etc.) have tended toward the effusive. This is, we can agree, out of place in an encyclopedia; we might not all be able to agree that so-and-so is the greatest bass guitar player in history. But it is very important information indeed how some artist or some work has been received by the general public, by reviewers, or by some very prominent experts. Providing an overview of the common interpretations of a creative work, preferably with citations or references to notable individuals holding that interpretation, is appropriate. For instance, that Shakespeare is one of the greatest authors of the English language is an important bit of knowledge a schoolchild might need to learn from an encyclopedia. Notice, determining how some artist or work has been received publicly or critically might require research; but that reception, unlike the idiosyncratic opinion of the Wikipedia article writer, is an opinion that really matters, for purposes of an encyclopedia.

5. Writing for the Enemy

Those who constantly attempt to advocate their own views on politically charged topics (for example), who seem not to care at all about whether other points of view are represented fairly, are violating the nonbias policy. That is, the policy entails that it is our job to speak for the other side, and not just represent our own views. If we do not commit ourselves to doing that, Wikipedia will be much, much weaker for it. We should all be engaged in explaining each other's points of view as sympathetically as possible.

In saying this, we are explicitly spelling out what might have been obvious to some people from an initial reading of the policy. If each of us individually is permitted to make totally biased contributions, then how is it possible that the policy is ever violated? The policy says, "Write without bias." If that does not mean that each of us individually should fairly represent views with which we disagree, then what does it mean? Maybe you think it means, "Represent your own view fairly, and please allow others to have a say." Maybe that makes a bit of sense as an interpretation—not a lot, but a bit. But consider, if we each take responsibility for the entire article when we hit that "save" button, then when we make a change to an article that represents our own views but not contrary views, or represents contrary views unfairly or incompletely (etc.), surely we are adding bias to Wikipedia.

Does it really ever make sense *not* to take responsibility for the entire article? Does it make sense to prise out some sentences and say, "These are mine, those are yours"? Perhaps, but in the context of a project that is so strongly and explicitly committed to collaboration, that sort of attitude seems totally out of place.

The other side might very well find your attempts to characterize their views substandard, but that can be fixed; it is the thought that counts. In resolving disputes over neutrality issues, it is far better that we acknowledge that all sides must be presented fairly, and make at least a college try at presenting the other sides fairly. That will be appreciated much more than not trying at all.

"Writing for the enemy" might make it seem as if we were adding deliberately flawed arguments to Wikipedia, which would be a very strange thing to do. But it is better to view this otherwise puzzling behavior as adding the best (published) arguments of the opposition, preferably citing some prominent person who has actually made the argument in the form in which you present it, stating them as sympathetically as possible. Academics, e.g., philosophers, do this all the time.

6. An Example

It might help to consider an example of a biased text and how Wikipedians have rendered it at least relatively unbiased.

On the abortion page, early in 2001, some advocates had used the page to exchange rhetorical barbs, being unable to agree about what arguments should be on the page and how the competing positions should be represented. What was needed—and what was added—was an in-depth discussion of the different positions about the moral and legal viability of abortion at different times. This discussion of the positions was carefully crafted so as not to favor any one of the positions outlined. This made it rather easier to organize and understand the competing arguments surrounding the topic of abortion, which were each then presented sympathetically, each with its strengths and weaknesses.

There are numerous other "success stories" of articles that began life as virtual partisan screeds but were nicely cleaned up by people who concerned themselves with representing all views clearly and sympathetically.

Objections and Clarifications

What follows is a list of common objections, or questions, regarding Wikipedia's nonbias policy, followed by replies.

Question. There is no such thing as objectivity. Everybody with any philosophical sophistication knows that. So how can we take the "neutrality" policy seriously? Neutrality, or lack of bias, is not possible.

Answer. This is probably the most common objection to the neutrality policy. It also reflects the most common misunderstanding of the policy. The misunderstanding is that the policy says something controversial about the possibility of objectivity. It simply does not. In particular, the policy does not say that there even is such a thing as objectivity, a "view from nowhere"[3]—such that articles written from that point of view are consequently objectively true. That is not the policy and it is not our aim. Rather, we employ a different understanding of "neutral" and "unbiased" than many of us might be used to. The policy is simply that we should do our best to characterize disputes rather than engage in them. To say this is not to say anything contentious, from a philosophical point of view; indeed, this is something that philosophers are doing all the time, even strongly relativist philosophers. They are virtually required to be able to first characterize their opponents' views fairly, in order to avoid being accused of setting up straw men to knock down. Sophisticated relativists will immediately recognize that the policy is perfectly consistent with their relativism.

If there is anything possibly contentious about the policy along these lines, it is the implication that it is possible to characterize disputes fairly, so that all the major participants will be able to look at the resulting text, agreeing that their views are presented sympathetically and as completely as possible (within the context of the discussion). It is an empirical question, not a philosophical one, whether this is possible; but that such a thing is indeed possible is evident simply by observing that such texts are being written daily by the most capable academics, encyclopedists, textbook writers, and journalists.

---

[3] In Thomas Nagel's phrase. See *The View from Nowhere*, Revised edition (Oxford, 1989).

Question. How are we to write articles about pseudoscientific topics, about which majority scientific opinion is that the pseudoscientific opinion is not credible and does not even really deserve serious mention?

Answer. If we are going to represent the sum total of "human knowledge"—of what we believe we know, essentially—then we must concede that we will be describing views repugnant to us without asserting that they are false. Things are not, however, as bad as that sounds. The task before us is not to describe disputes fairly, on some bogus view of fairness that would have us describe pseudoscience as if were on a par with science; rather, the task is to represent the majority (scientific) view as the majority view and the minority (sometimes pseudoscientific) view as the minority view, and, moreover, to explain how scientists have received pseudoscientific theories. This is all in the purview of the task of describing a dispute fairly.

There is a minority of Wikipedians who feel so strongly about this problem, however, that they believe Wikipedia should adopt a "scientific point of view" rather than a "neutral point of view." What these people have failed to establish, however, is that there really is a need for such a policy, given that the scientists' view of pseudoscience can be clearly, fully, and fairly explained to those who might be misled by pseudoscience.

Question. What about views that are morally offensive to most Westerners, such as racism, sexism, and Holocaust denial, that some people actually have? Surely we are not to be neutral about them?

Answer. We can certainly include long discussions that present our moral repugnance to such things; in doing so, we can maintain a healthy, consistent support for the neutral point of view by attributing the view to some prominent representatives or to some group of people. Others will be able to make up their own minds and, being reasonable, surely come around to our view. Those who harbor racism, sexism, etc., will surely not be convinced to change their views based on a biased article, which only puts them on the defensive; on the other hand, if we make a concerted effort to apply our nonbias policy consistently, we might give those with morally repugnant beliefs insight that will change those views.

Question. But wait. I find the optimism about science vs. pseudoscience to be baseless. History has shown that pseudoscience can beat out facts, as those who rely on pseudoscience use lies, slander, innuendo and numerical majorities of its followers to force their views on anyone they can. If this project gives equal validity to those who literally claim that the Earth is flat or that the Holocaust never occurred, the result is that it will (inadvertently) legitimize and help promote that which can only be termed evil.

Answer. Please be clear on one thing: the Wikipedia neutrality policy certainly does not state, or imply, that we must "give equal validity" to completely repugnant views. It does state that we must not take a stand on them *qua* encyclopedia writers; but that does not stop us from representing the majority views as such; from fairly explaining the strong arguments against the repugnant views; from describing the strong moral repugnance that many decent people feel toward them; and so forth.

Hence, on the one hand, Wikipedia does not officially take a stand even on such obvious issues, but on the other, it will not look as though we (the authors of Wikipedia) had accorded equal credibility to morally repugnant views. Given that the authors of Wikipedia represent a rough cross-section of the educated public, our readers can expect us to have a similar cross-section of opinion about extremism: most of us abhor it.

Question. Wikipedia seems to have an American point of view. Is this not contrary to the neutral point of view?

Answer. Yes, it certainly is, and it has no defenders on Wikipedia. The presence of articles written from a point of view associated exclusively with the United States is merely a reflection of the fact that there are many Americans working on the project, which in turn is merely a reflection of the fact that the (English language) project is being conducted in English and that so many Americans are online.

This is an ongoing problem that can be corrected by active collaboration from people outside of the U.S., of whom there are many.

Question. The neutrality policy is used sometimes as an excuse to delete texts that are perceived as biased. Is this not a problem?

Answer. In many cases, yes. Most of us believe that the mere fact that some text is biased is not enough, by itself, to delete the text outright. If it contains perfectly valid information, the text should simply be edited accordingly, and certainly not deleted.

There is sometimes trouble determining whether some claim is true or useful, particularly when there are few people on board who know about the topic. In such a case, it is a good idea to raise objections on a talk page; if one has some reason to believe that the author of the biased material will not be induced to change it, we have sometimes taken to removing the text to the talk page itself (but certainly not deleting it entirely). But the latter should be done more or less as a last resort, never merely as a way of punishing people who have written something biased.

Question. I agree with the nonbias policy, but there are some here who seem completely, irremediably biased. I have to go around and clean up after them. What do I do?

Answer. This is difficult.

Unless the case is really egregious, maybe the best thing is to call attention to the problem publicly, pointing the perpetrators to this page (but politely—one catches more flies with honey) and asking others to help. If the problem is really serious, Larry Sanger might be enlisted to beat the person over the head (so to speak) and, in the most recalcitrant cases, ask them to leave the project. There must surely be a point beyond which our very strong interest in being a completely open project is trumped by the interest the vast majority of our writers have, in being able to get work done without constantly having to fix the intrusions of people who do not respect our policy.

Question. How can we avoid constant and endless warfare over neutrality issues?

Answer. Would that people asked this question more often. We should never debate about how Wikipedia should be biased. It should not be biased at all.

The best way to avoid warfare over bias is to remember that we are all reasonably intelligent, articulate people here, or we would not be working on an encyclopedia and caring so much about it. We have to make it our goal to understand each others' perspectives and to work hard to make sure that those other perspectives are fairly represented. When any dispute arises as to what the article "should" say or what is "true," we must not adopt an adversarial stance; we must do our best to step back and ask ourselves, "How can this dispute be fairly characterized?" This has to be asked repeatedly as each new controversial point is stated.

It is not our job to edit Wikipedia so that it reflects our own idiosyncratic views and then defend those edits against all comers; it is our job to work together, mainly adding new content, but also, when necessary, coming to a compromise about how a controversy should be described, so that it is fair to all sides.

Question. What about the case where, in order to write any of a long series of articles on some general subject, we must make some controversial assumptions? That is the case, e.g., in writing about evolution. Surely we will not have to hash out the evolution-vs.-creationism debate on every such page?

Answer. No, surely not. There are virtually no topics that could not proceed without making some assumptions that someone would find controversial. This is true not only in evolutionary biology, but also philosophy, history, physics, etc.

It is difficult to draw up general principles on which to rule in specific cases, but the following might help: there is probably not a good reason to discuss some assumption on a given page, if an assumption is best discussed in depth on some other page. Some brief, unobtrusive pointer might be apropos, however. For example, in an article about the evolutionary development of horses, we might have one brief sentence to the effect that some creationists do not believe that horses (or any other animals) underwent any evolution, and point the reader to the relevant article. If there is much specific creationist argumentation on some particular point, it might be placed on a special page of its own.

Question. I am not convinced by what you say about "writing for the enemy." I do not want to write for the enemy. Most of them rely on stating as fact many things which are demonstrably false. Are you saying that, to be neutral in writing an article, I must lie, in order to faithfully represent the view I disagree with?

Answer. This is a misunderstanding of what the neutrality policy says. *You* are not claiming anything, except to say, "So-and-so argues that such-and-such." This can be done with a straight face, with no moral compunctions, because you are attributing the claim to someone else. That is the important thing here. If we are summing up human knowledge on a subject, in the sense above-defined, then you are leaving out important information when you omit so-and-so's argument.

It is worth observing that, at least in the humanities, scholars are trained so that, even when trying to prove a point, one must bring forth counter-arguments that seem to disprove one's thesis, so that one can explain why the counter-arguments fail. Such scholarly training also gives one a better knowledge of source material and what may have been rejected over the years. Something very much like the neutral point of view is just an assumption (more or less) among scholars—if it is not adhered to, or if only those facts that prove a particular point are used, one might lose one's position and reputation.[4]

---

[4] This point was much more plausible in 2002. It might no longer be true today.

Four

Why Neutrality?

We are naturally incensed by bias, and for good reason. The importance of neutrality as a topic—what it is, and why certain texts should be neutral—is greatly underestimated, in my opinion. The topic greatly repays careful study, not just in the fields of communication, publishing, and journalism, but also in social philosophy and civics more generally. While working on Wikipedia, I regret that I never found the time to craft a suitably lengthy formal defense of neutrality as a policy. In fall of 2015, Ballotpedia asked me to do so, and it is reproduced here in an updated version.

AS a teenager, I often scanned encyclopedias, newspapers, and textbooks angrily, on the lookout for bias. I had discovered, to my frequent irritation, that writers of authoritative texts would present only one side of a dispute, as if the truth were all on that side and there were no controversy at all. Honest and important debates were treated as if they did not exist. An encyclopedia writer was supposed to be an objective source, imparting facts. Where a dispute existed, the writer was supposed to represent a broad range of opinions fairly, and anything controversial should have been left up to me to decide for myself. Instead, these writers were indoctrinating me, or trying to. What an abuse of a position of authority! How infuriating!

Later in life, given the opportunity to start an encyclopedia, I was a zealot for neutrality. My teenage ire at shamefully biased writers and editors found expression in Nupedia's neutrality policy, which in turn became Wikipedia's. I defended these policies at length against criticisms, but I never carefully articulated or defended my views on neutrality in a paper. I finally have an opportunity to do so.

In this essay, I will defend neutrality as the preferred policy for some, but only some, types of writing. I will define neutral writing, lay out four arguments in favor of a policy of neutrality, and refute some common criticisms. I will conclude by suggesting that publishers adopt both neutrality guidelines and editorial processes to make sure that the guidelines are followed.

Criticisms are lurking in the background throughout this essay, and let me tip my hat slightly at them before I dive in.

I concede that neutrality is a headache. It is so difficult to achieve that bias is the norm, and it will continue to be the norm wherever it is not deliberately eradicated.

Neutrality, even if it is a writer's aim, can be very hard to achieve. Neutral writers have to have mastered their subject and then be extremely careful and fair-minded. Otherwise, they are almost sure to display bias. In my experience, neutrality does not come easily to any of us; it is a discipline that must be practiced. Some of us do not even seem to have the concept, or rather we confuse it with objectivity or being scientific or describing a middle ground or taking the most mainstream position. Even if we understand the ideal of neutrality—understanding it does make it easier to achieve—and our writing is successfully unbiased, others may misunderstand what we have achieved. Partisans might think we are soft on "the other side" (meaning the one they are opposed to) or even biased in its favor. Neutral writers are accused, perversely I think, of "false balance." So, as difficult as it is, a neutrality policy might seem more trouble than it is worth.

Besides, not everyone is on board with neutrality. Bias (in the sense of tendentious, one-sided communication) has its apologists. Some claim that neutrality is not just difficult but actually impossible. We are each hopelessly biased and we simply cannot keep our biases from coming out, they say. Some go further to claim that neutrality is simply wrong or unreasonable in many cases. Some points of view do not deserve any expression. Where the truth is known, they say, it is wrong to pretend it is not.

I disagree. What if I were to tell you that, if you write biased encyclopedia and newspaper articles, you are doing a *moral* wrong, and what you are doing is on a par with propaganda? Ridiculous, you say? But it is true, and I will lay out strong arguments to think it is true.

What Is Neutrality?

1. Defining "Neutrality"

First, let us define neutrality.

Here is the basic idea: if you are neutral, you do not take a position. You present all sides fairly and let your reader decide which is correct.

A disputed topic is treated neutrally if each viewpoint about it is not asserted but rather presented (1) as sympathetically as possible, bearing in mind that other, competing views must be represented as well, and (2) with an equitable amount of space being allotted to each, whatever that might be.

On this account, neutrality is a concept dealing specifically with disputed topics, and it has three basic requirements.

First, if an issue that is mentioned in the text is disputed, the text takes no position on the issue. Neutrality is not some midpoint in between competing options. A political moderate's positions are not "the neutral positions": they are positions as well. Neutral writing takes no position, left, right, or middle.

Second, there is the requirement of tone, or the strength of the case made for a viewpoint. Basically, if you are going to be neutral, you have to represent all the main views about the topic, *and* you have to represent them all sympathetically, i.e., according to their best, most convincing arguments, evidence, and representatives.

Third, there is the question of how much space it is fair or equitable to spend in a text on the different sides. Prima facie, it would seem that spending a numerically equal amount of space on both (or all) sides is fair, but it does not always work out that way. Exactly how to apportion limited space is a complex question I will address further down.

Basically, to write neutrally is to lay out all sides of any disputed question, without asserting, implying, or insinuating that any one side is correct. If a debated point is mentioned, you represent the state of the debate rather than taking a stand.

As I will explain below, it is practically impossible to achieve perfect neutrality, in all probability, if that were understood to mean neutrality with respect to all cultures and all historical eras. I will also mention the notion of a "good enough" neutrality. One observer noticed that these concessions seem to commit me to the proposition that neutrality comes in gradations or aspects—which is something I happily admit. What I advocate might be described as a strict or professional standard of neutrality.

2. Some Principles of Neutrality

Here are some general principles that are more or less implied by this definition. I do not claim that these principles have no exceptions but only that they give a fairly good idea of what neutrality entails.

It is impossible to tell reliably what side of a disputed issue the author of the text is on, if the text is neutral with respect to that issue. The text avoids word quantity, choice, and tone that favors one side over another. Both or all sides agree that their side is fairly represented. Barring that, the text will tend to anger or dissatisfy everyone equally, although for different reasons. Generally, there is a focus on or preference for agreed-upon "facts." If an opinion is included, it is attributed to a source. The debate is not engaged but rather described and characterized, including information about proportions of people on the different sides, where available. Controversial claims—i.e., claims that a party to a dispute might want to take issue with—are all attributed to specific sources. The author does not personally assert such claims. Biased sources are either eschewed or used in approximately equal numbers on both or all sides throughout a document. A document that uses many biased sources on only one side looks biased itself. When there is a "significant" (this word admittedly glosses over an important problem) ongoing debate and a source implies a definite stand on it in an article that is not about that debate, at the very least there must be some acknowledgment in the text that a disagreement exists. When it makes no sense for articles to be individually neutral, reporting and publications that are neutral with respect to a debate, or a field, will publish in equal amounts on both or all sides of an issue. If a publication favors one side because more papers are received on that side, or because more of the research community embraces that side, that might appear fair and reasonable, but it is not neutral and equally balanced: it will tend to make one side look better than the other.

3. Neutrality Distinguished from Objectivity

Let us get clear about one thing: neutrality is different from being rational, scientific, or objective. People often use these terms as if they were synonyms. For example, at least one journalist[1] has argued that "'neutral' journalism cannot die fast enough," but only by glossing over the distinction between neutrality and objectivity, and his piece simply did not consider the notion of neutrality discussed in this paper.

---

[1] Ned Resnikoff, "'Neutral' journalism cannot die fast enough," *Salon*, June 29, 2010, https://bit.ly/2WCNpqy.

Rationality means (roughly) following the rules of logic and careful observation and proportioning belief to the amount and quality of the evidence. Being scientific (also roughly) means following the scientific method and, again, not believing a hypothesis unless it has been well established by the canons of science. Objectivity means deciding what to believe (or write) not based on mere feelings or prejudice, but strictly based on substantive considerations of evidence that are supposedly independent of our personal views.

Rationality, scientific method, and objectivity all concern epistemology or methodology, i.e., they are standards of knowledge, or else methods we use to determine our beliefs in an attempt to arrive at knowledge. Neutrality is in a different category altogether: it is a standard of exposition, of expression. If I write neutrally, I am simply refusing to take a position. As I am neither evaluating or staking out a claim, the rationality, scientific merit, and objectivity of my claim are not at issue. It is true that in writing neutrally, I might help others to be objective. But neutrality is a style of writing, while objectivity is a state of mind. Expression is neutral; people and their mental states are (ideally) objective.

Neutrality and those other qualities are orthogonal. You can have one without the other. In fact, if you have written much in a neutral way, then you have probably represented views fairly that you believe to be irrational, unscientific, or subjective. You have simply not taken a position. Similarly, you can write a perfectly rational, scientific, and objective treatment of a topic—which takes one particular position in a hotly-debated dispute.

For example, suppose in a piece of writing, you discuss the measles vaccination controversy. If you are going to write in accordance with the canons of science (and also rationality and objectivity, no doubt), then in my opinion, you will support the view that children should be vaccinated by vaccines that science has proven to be safe. But if what you write is going to be neutral with respect to current American society, you will have to withhold any such forthright claim. Rather, you will report that while a very large majority of doctors and scientists strongly advise vaccination, still something like 9%[2] of the population thinks that the measles vaccine is unsafe. You, the writer, will not take or project any stand one way or another, although, to be fair to the vast majority of the public in favor of measles vaccination, in some kinds of articles you might spend only about 9% of the article on the anti-vaccination position.

4. Equitable Division of Space

You might well disagree with the latter sentence. Even if it is a minority view, why should the anti-vaccination position get only 9% of a news article (say)? It does not seem obvious that that is fair. If we are trying to help people make up their minds, why is 50% not fair and neutral? If neutrality means, ultimately, that the reader cannot guess your position as the writer, then a case can be made for 9%, and a case can be made for 50%.

I suggest that it depends on the type of writing. Consider two examples.

First, science journalism: each time a science news service reports a new study on a scientific controversy, neutrality does not require that the journalist give equal space to all competing theories. That would be unreasonable. Neutrality, in that case, is not an article-level concept but a service-level concept. For example, the news service might have a rule to the effect that major studies supporting competing theories should be covered in proportion to how often they appear in major journals. Perhaps the journalist is obligated to acknowledge briefly that there are one or more competing theories, and if there happens to be a debate or disagreement about the study itself, that debate should be covered neutrally.

Second, articles introducing policy debates: surely we do expect an encyclopedia or debate website article on the

---

[2] Aaron Blake, "Here's how many Americans are actually anti-vaxxers," *Washington Post*, February 9, 2015, https://wapo.st/399IXog.

vaccination issue to be scrupulously even-handed, and perhaps that really does mean giving approximately equal time to both or all sides. But why? Why should a description of the debate give 50% of the space to the anti-vaccination side if only 9% of the public (and probably less than 1% of doctors and medical researchers) are on that side? Why *not* give something like 9% to the anti-vaccination side? Would that not be fair? Why *should* the minority position be dignified to that extent?

I think the answer stems from the premise that the major purpose of reporting on a controversy is to enable people to come to their own conclusions about it. In that case, devoting more space to one side, even if it is the majority side, would suggest that that side is correct. This in turn would interfere with the mission of supporting readers in deciding the issue for themselves. Scrupulously presenting both or all sides in approximately equal proportions, and with the best available arguments, etc., gives readers no clues as to "the right" answer, requiring them to fall back on their own critical thinking skills. In other words, covering the debate in a strictly even-handed way enables readers to be more rational.

Advocacy journalism, I am well aware, rejects my premise that the purpose of reporting on a controversy is to enable people to come to their own conclusions about it, though. Still, that ought to clarify at least somewhat better what I mean by the third part, on fair apportionment of space, of my definition of "neutrality." It gets more complicated, as I will explain in sections toward the end of this paper.

5. Traditionally Neutral Texts

There are at least three categories of text that are traditionally neutral: encyclopedia and reference writing, straight news writing, and basic textbooks. These are not always neutral, of course, but they are generally expected to be. Why? Why should they be expected to be neutral when opinion pieces, art, documentaries, scholarly papers and monographs, various other forms are not? The present essay, for instance, is rather strongly biased in favor of neutrality.

Why Neutrality?

Lower-level textbooks (through the junior high school level, say) are expected to impart facts and avoid controversy in order to give a student a basic foundation of knowledge. If an elementary school textbook is full of opinion, theory, and controversy, it is less likely to be used, because students are expected to begin their studies with commonly known facts, which are more than enough to learn. At higher levels, a range of opinions and controversial theories may and indeed should be included, but even then, if they are not neutrally presented, the text runs the risk of alienating students and their parents. By making textbooks neutral, we make them satisfactory for everyone in a diverse society. Of course, there are biased texts—especially at the high school and college levels. Thoroughly biased texts, which inculcate only one political or religious view, are used especially by highly ideological teachers and professors, at religious schools, and in home schools; but such texts and teaching generally earn the contempt of many of us because the students who emerge will not be so well prepared for life in a more intellectually diverse society. Besides all that, texts that are biased are more likely to get the facts wrong, as I will argue with respect to journalism.

Not all journalism is or is expected to be neutral, of course. We think of journalism as straight reporting, but it also includes outright opinion pieces, advocacy journalism, and opinion and debate broadcasts. These biased forms have become dominant in 21st century society, especially on cable news shows, opinion websites, blogs, most news magazines, and talk radio. Yet even in our modern, cynical news consumption societies, "straight news" is still a fairly well-understood category and is generally expected to be neutral, even if it comes to partisan networks like CNN and Fox News. In a straight news story, the journalist's opinion is irrelevant and distracting. Partly this is because there is typically a lot of news to report and reader time is quite limited as well. In addition, there are a lot of people—I am one—who simply do not like any opinion mixed with their straight facts.

But a deeper reason is that ideologues seem to get the facts wrong so often when reporting the news. Reporting the straight facts speedily and readably with a maximum of accuracy and relevance is surprisingly difficult—a fact of which many news consumers are simply ignorant. Seeing the world always through red- or blue-colored lenses makes writing easier, but the hard job of accuracy on a deadline harder: it tends to blind writers to facts that sit poorly with their filters. So we naturally and rightly distrust the factual claims contained in reporting that strikes us as biased (cf. the "backfire effect"[3]).

Finally, the function of encyclopedias and other reference material is to serve as highly relevant compendia of searchable facts. They are expected to be neutral for similar reasons to the foregoing. On the one hand, mixing opinion with straight factual writing wastes our time and distracts us from what we are using reference materials for: learning the basic facts of what is known and believed about a topic. On the other hand, again, we do not trust a reference to catalog complex facts reliably if it is also trying to persuade us of a particular point of view. Getting the facts right is hard enough as it is.

So, for the rest of this essay, I will refer to "traditionally neutral texts," meaning encyclopedias, straight news, and textbooks.

By the way, there have been societies in which the news, encyclopedias, and textbooks were, all three, expected to reflect a single point of view, as if none other were possible: totalitarian societies are like that. The old Soviet Union is perhaps the most famous historical example, with its *Pravda* newspaper serving as the voice of the Communist Party, its *Great Soviet Encyclopedia* the source of state-approved facts, and its notoriously propaganda-laden textbooks. Such openly,

---

[3] Brendan Nyhan and Jason Reifler, "When Corrections Fail: The persistence of political misperceptions," *Political Behavior* 32, no. 2 (2010): 303-330. https://bit.ly/39mROmZ.

complacently biased publications strike us in the 21st century West as deeply problematic subversions of their traditional forms, serving as especially pungent illustrations of why totalitarian societies are so problematic.

That journalism, Wikipedia, and education are becoming so ideologically charged, as they are today, does not bode well.

Four Arguments for Neutrality

6. Neutrality Respects Personal Autonomy

So, why neutrality?

I have attempted to outline some pragmatic reasons why, traditionally, we have expected certain categories of text to be neutral. Next, I will advance four arguments for neutrality as a general policy, arguments that apply equally to all of these traditionally neutral categories of text.

My first argument is the longest and most important, and it will take several sections to go through.

Consider some examples of neutrality and objectivity:

- a science textbook fairly explaining competing theories
- a detailed encyclopedia article breaking down competing narratives and explanations of the Great Depression, and you cannot tell what side the author is on
- a scrupulously balanced news article clarifying the latest drug legalization policy debate, with all sides fully and sympathetically presented

I admire such approaches. Probably, you do too. But why do we?

It is because neutral writing respects the reader. It shows the author is treating us like adults who wish to make up our minds rationally, using reason, logic, and evidence. If somebody is being conspicuously neutral, it gives us confidence that we are getting the facts, all the relevant facts, with emotion-driven rhetoric left out. We are being left to decide the matter for ourselves, rationally.

Someone who writes neutrally supports our natural desire to be rational and thus puts us on the road to truth. The choice of belief is left entirely up to us.

Neutrality, I will argue, respects our personal autonomy. Autonomy can be roughly defined as the capacity to govern oneself freely, independently of other influences generally (*metaphysical* autonomy), of the moral dictates of others (*moral* autonomy), of law and government control (*political* autonomy), of religious dictates or restrictions on religion (*religious* autonomy), and of the pressure and indoctrination of authorities such as educators (*intellectual* autonomy).

It is our intellectual autonomy that neutral encyclopedists, journalists, and educators respect. They leave us free to make up our own minds for ourselves. Naturally, we appreciate that—assuming we value our autonomy, as we should and typically do.

Propagandists, by contrast, sometimes insist that neutrality is impossible or wrong, and they use such assertions as an excuse for taking definite, controversial positions in traditionally neutral forms. Political hacks use journalism, especially, to try to control their readers. They do not want to leave them free to make up their own minds. They do not respect their autonomy. Propagandists are not interested in giving readers the tools they need to decide rationally, for themselves; they want to indoctrinate or trick them into believing precisely the way they believe.

7. Independence, Deliberation, and Autonomy

In my mind, autonomy is bound up with two good things: free will and the Enlightenment.

Autonomy is essentially the same as freedom—as in the freedom of the will—and therefore it is deeply important to morality. My view[4] is that to act with free will is simply to act

---

[4] Larry Sanger, "Why There Is Free Will," *LarrySanger.org* (blog), January 12, 2014, https://bit.ly/2BjltOM.

with an unencumbered, mature ability to think our decisions through. Our ability to deliberate rationally on what we ought to do is what gives us our freedom, or autonomy. It is also what gives us our dignity as individuals. It is our own intellects—our independent, reflective minds and our ability to make them up for ourselves in a mature, adult fashion—that command that basic level of respect we call dignity.

Now, as philosophers often observe, our beliefs themselves are frequently out of our immediate or direct control. For example, if I am an atheist, I cannot simply up and decide, "Today I am going to believe in God." But we can control the inputs of our beliefs. We can control whether our beliefs are informed by facts and reasoning, or instead by emotion and rhetoric. We can control how long and how carefully we think a view through, before we accept it or that we are committed to it.

If we carefully think through the issues, especially if we consider all sides and all the evidence, then we embrace, as genuinely our own, whatever conclusion we come to. That we have reasoned our way to a conclusion means we accepted it freely. By contrast, if we simply find ourselves with an opinion after idly, passively receiving messages from mass media or from friends, we are less likely to take responsibility for that view. It seems to be less "our own" and easier to reconsider.

If that is true, then the more independently deliberative we are, over the course of our lives, the freer we are. This is the conclusion that Spinoza came to, famously, in his *Ethics*.[5] The more that we guide our beliefs by our own careful reasoning and observation, the more freedom or autonomy we have.

Intellectual autonomy was naturally a key feature of the Enlightenment, and it remains robust and important to this day; we are still encouraged to think for ourselves far more than we were in the Middle Ages. Immanuel Kant opened his essay, "What is Enlightenment?" with these ringing words:

---

[5] See, e.g., Baruch Spinoza, *Ethics*, Book IV, Prop. X.

Enlightenment is man's emergence from his self-imposed nonage [immaturity]. Nonage is the inability to use one's own understanding without another's guidance. This nonage is self-imposed if its cause lies not in lack of understanding but in indecision and lack of courage to use one's own mind without another's guidance. Dare to know! (*Sapere aude.*) "Have the courage to use your own understanding," is therefore the motto of the enlightenment.[6]

We like and admire neutral writing because it fosters our personal enlightenment. Bias, by contrast, treats us like immature children—who are in "nonage"—who cannot be trusted to arrive independently at the beliefs some authority wishes us to have.

8. Neutrality Fosters Autonomy

I say neutrality respects autonomy. It also fosters autonomy. So, how does it, exactly?

Neutrality has at least two features: (1) it involves presenting competing positions, and (2) it presents them sympathetically, according to their strongest arguments. Let us take these in turn.

(1) If *various* competing views are presented, then we must naturally fall back on our own resources in deciding between them. Neutral writing removes the crutch of simply accepting the single view that the author informs us of. If we are simply "told the One Truth" about a topic, then we do not engage our own brains or curiosity, and we become dependent on the author and less autonomous or free in how we think about the topic. By contrast, if we are given several options, our natural curiosity and desire to settle upon the truth will impel us to reflect on those different options. That is just what intellectual autonomy requires of us.

---

[6] Immanuel Kant, "Answering the Question: What Is Enlightenment?" trans. Mary C. Smith, originally published in *Berlinische Monatsschrift*, December 1783, https://bit.ly/30q6SMl.

(2) Moreover, if the competing views are all presented sympathetically, in their strongest forms, we will be given the best data, evidence, and arguments—the tools needed to make up our minds rationally. Armed with those tools, we will be more likely to deliberate rationally in an attempt to arrive at the truth.

This, again, is exactly what intellectual autonomy requires of us: fully adult, intellectual freedom is not simply a matter of choosing a view by whim, emotion, or social pressure, but only after carefully examining and comparing the competing arguments and evidence for ourselves.

Bias, by contrast, frequently encourages us simply to leap to a view based on our prejudices, on emotional and social appeals, without thinking the matter through. Even when one side is presented in great rational detail and the other is not mentioned, the lack of mention itself implies without argument that the view is not worth spending any time on. In any event, we are made dependent on whoever propagates a single view. To the extent that we are subject to emotional manipulation or other kinds of fallacy, we are less autonomous or free in how we think about the topic. In short, bias is a tool of control, especially but not only emotional control.

Bias more generally dulls the brain. In an educational setting, it actually discourages people from forming, and exercising, the habits that *constitute* intellectual autonomy. In civil society generally, it dulls the practice of individual reason, encourages groupthink, and devalues the coin of rational debate.

To sum up both points and to put it metaphorically, neutrality does not give us a free ride. It throws us into the issues and requires us to swim through them under our own power. This can be difficult and frightening (thus Kant's injunction, *sapere aude*) but it also makes us feel empowered to decide for ourselves. Neutrality supports us both intellectually and emotionally in the act of exercising autonomous judgment by presenting us with all the options and providing us the tools to judge among them for ourselves.

9. Bias Makes Us Less Morally Responsible

A case can be made, though I cannot make it here, that there is no more to autonomy than doxastic, or belief-related, autonomy. In other words, the only real sort of free will we have stems from our ability to deliberate, to think things through for ourselves. That is what Spinoza argued in the *Ethics*, and (after long reflection, of course) I agree with him. But free will is what makes us morally responsible; if we are not free when we act, we are not responsible for what we do. If that is true, a surprising consequence follows: biased writing, which just tells us what to think, has a tendency to make us less morally responsible. The more that we are simply instructed of the truth, the less our beliefs are our own, and the less morally responsible we are for our own actions.

Perhaps that just sounds strange. But on reflection, we can see that it is true. Consider the infamous Milgram experiment, in which a browbeating scientist presented his subjects with exactly one option: to deliver what they believed to be (but in fact were not) painful electric shocks to other subjects. There was a doubly shocking bias at work—in favor of continuing the experiment. Think of any number of cults in which the leadership, possessing ultimate religious, moral, and intellectual authority, issues not-to-be-questioned rules and commands, impelling members to do things they would otherwise never dream of doing. The leaders' injunctions were presented in a thoroughly biased fashion. Reflect on how powerful Nazi and Communist propaganda campaigns made it possible for the hapless citizenry to demonize the "enemies of the state," dissociate themselves from their own appalling behavior, and act as informants and tools of the state. These are all particularly appalling examples of bias.

If bias can have such horrifying effects on our moral autonomy, then our obligation to strive for neutrality is very strong, indeed. Neutral writing makes us more reflective and therefore more capable of taking moral responsibility for our commitments.

10. Bias as a Moral Failing

If I am right, neutrality is not just being kind and respectful to readers; it is a positive obligation. When we write neutrally, we help others to be free, and so neutrality is a virtue. Bias, by contrast, is revealed as a moral failing.

Perhaps it should not be surprising that Kant—champion of the Enlightenment—also believed we have a fundamental obligation to respect others' dignity, their basic, irreducible value as human beings. We should treat others as ends in themselves, Kant famously wrote in his *Foundations of the Metaphysics of Morals*, not as mere means to our own ends. And what is it that gives us our dignity as human beings? Again, I, like Kant and other philosophers, maintain that it is our autonomy or free will, our ability to deliberate rationally, as adults should, that gives us this basic value, this right to be considered not as a mere means to others' ends.[7]

When you write with bias, you are treating your readers as your pawns, as mere means to your ends. You are not treating them as autonomous agents, capable of making up their own minds rationally. You are not respecting their dignity.

This is especially the case when you are writing in a traditionally neutral form, one in which people expect to learn the whole story or debate. Admittedly, if you are writing an opinion piece, it is up to the reader to find alternative points of view; while you should still be fair-minded, it is not necessarily your job to make your opponents' case for them. But if you are writing in a traditionally neutral form, then your audience expects you to lay out everything relevant. If there is some dispute in the relevant community, and you take sides, you are putting one over on your audience, for your own purposes. I say—though it might sound like hyperbole—that is morally wrong.

---

[7] Cf. the Second and Third Formulations of the Categorical Imperative in Kant's *Foundations of the Metaphysics of Morals*.

I mean it. But let me clarify. When I say you are treating your readers as pawns or as mere means to your ends, I do not mean that you think that way consciously. Maybe what I am suggesting never occurred to you. But the fact of the matter is that, if you are writing in a traditionally neutral form, and if you give your readers just one out of various possible views to consider, or only one is presented sympathetically or with all the most convincing evidence and argument, then you are in fact treating your readers fraudulently: you are falsely portraying a controversial issue as if there were only one view that an uninformed person would want to be fully and fairly informed about. Neutrality respects people as autonomous individuals, capable of hearing all sides and judging the evidence fairly for themselves.

Encyclopedists, journalists, and textbook writers should all take note: neutrality is the best policy for free people.

11. Neutrality as Adversarial, Bias as Inquisitorial

The phraseology "hearing all sides and judging the evidence fairly" suggests an analogy: an encyclopedist acts as a fair and impartial judge, enabling the dueling sides to call their witnesses and present their cases as forcefully as possible. Presented with a full airing of all evidence that both sides deem relevant, the jury will, we hope, arrive at a just verdict.

In an analogy with neutral writing, the judge, who organizes and oversees the proceedings, is the author. The counsel are the partisans on the sides of some issue discussed, the witnesses are experts and eyewitnesses, and the evidence and arguments are precisely analogous in both cases. The jury is the reader; the jury's verdict, the reader's judgment of the truth. The analogy, then, is that just as we trust that a fair presentation of both sides will result in a fair verdict in a court case, so also we may trust that a neutral account of a dispute will maximize the reader's chances of believing something true.

What, then, is the analogy to biased text? I propose that it is the elimination of an adversarial jury trial altogether. In the inquisitorial system, the judge leads the trial, never engages a jury, and determines the verdict from the bench, speaking from authority. And this is essentially what biased texts do: the ultimate judging role of the individual reader is dismissed. How justice plays out depends on the abilities of the judge, but generally, the details of a position are not covered if the judge deems that position implausible. Perhaps justice, or the truth, will be arrived at. However that might be, the judge, or author, decides for us all, thereby infantilizing us and failing to respect our autonomy and dignity as free people.

12. Totalitarian Propaganda as Extreme Bias

There is yet another way into the same argument.

We agree that totalitarian propaganda is wrong. We resent totalitarian personality cults and indoctrination in schools and mass media. The Nazi propaganda minister, Joseph Goebbels, is generally thought to have been among the worst of the worst Nazis. There is surely something deeply alarming and oppressive about being expected not only to say certain things but also to believe a certain way, on pain of punishment by the authorities.

We in the liberal West regard these episodes with horror. Their horror is not just a reflection of the horror of mass killing and the threat of concentration camps. There is something soul-killing about the propaganda, the cults, the indoctrination itself.

I think the Goebbelses of the world, the puppet masters who perpetrate totalitarian propaganda, have tremendous contempt for our right to make up our minds for ourselves. The propagandists do not want us to think for ourselves; they want to do our thinking for us. An independent mind—an enlightened one, in Kant's sense—threatens the regime.

Totalitarian propaganda seems obviously bad; but why is it?

The answer, my arguments suggest, is that propaganda offends against human dignity because it does not respect our intellectual autonomy. If it is an essential part of human nature to be able to deliberate and reach our own conclusions, if that gives us our freedom, our dignity as human beings, then totalitarian propaganda is a deliberate and systematic attempt to totally deny us our dignity and our full humanity.

But if this is correct, then the error of more ordinary bias— journalistic, encyclopedic, and pedagogical—is no different, except in degree, from the crime of totalitarian propaganda. Nazi propaganda strikes horror in us because, in treating us as mindless drones, its offends against human dignity. If so, should we not be horrified, albeit to a smaller degree, when a journalist comes out in favor of a certain proposal, repeating only one side's most persuasive talking points and failing to interview anyone on the other side?

13. Neutrality's democratic consequences

There is one last variant on the theme of autonomy: it is that neutrality fosters democracy, a system in which power is ultimately vested in individual citizens. The consequences of neutrality are not just epistemological and moral, but also social and political.

Journalists have the franchise like everyone, and naturally they individually favor one party or another. Fully and fairly stating the evidence and arguments of all political parties, not just their own, doubtless harms their own party's chances in an election. Still, the practice of neutrality is very important, for it has deeper and more important consequences than the temporary victory of this party or that.

I want to maintain that the robust practice of neutrality by the fourth estate strengthens democracy itself. It keeps power more firmly in the hands of independent, individual citizens, and out of the hands of an elite. It does so in remarkably many and diverse ways.

Neutrality requires that political journalists give a fair and colorful account of the drama of policy debates. This practice informs voters, allowing them to make fairer choices. It makes voters more anxious, as they should be, about the necessity of actually being informed when they do vote. It calls attention to and raises interest in substantive policy debate, causing more of such debate to occur. It calls attention to the details of policy and the evidence for and against positions and thus, one hopes, improves everyone's quality of reasoning. It causes voters to reflect on that substance and not just react to slogans and personalities. It raises expectations that politicians ought to be serious thinkers and not just empty suits. It causes us to take our leaders and our fellow voters more seriously.

Last but certainly not least, it makes the practice of politics more intellectually complex, making us better appreciate the sort of critical, liberal arts education that is necessary to a robust democracy. It gives us an added incentive to mold our young citizens into well-prepared participants at all levels of the process, which can only be to the good of everyone.

All of this is contrary to the ethos of an authoritarian society. Journalists, encyclopedists, and teachers all bear a very heavy responsibility to fight against the authoritarian tendency—by being scrupulously neutral as they report the debate and not just the horse race.

14. The Argument from the Golden Rule

My second argument is much simpler: the Golden Rule holds that we should treat others as we want them to treat us. (For philosophers, I might just as well put this in terms of Kant's First Formulation of the Categorical Imperative, for example. Interestingly, perhaps, my first argument may be cast in terms of Kant's Second Formulation.)

Suppose you are writing an encyclopedia article about some topic on which you have a strong opinion, such as politics, religion, or sports, and you have to represent an opinion you think is completely wrong.

Well, the Golden Rule asks, how would you want to be treated in *this* situation? So let us imagine that someone else is doing the writing, and you are the reader. The issue is one you are fanatical about—but the writer takes the other side. Perhaps you would like them to ignore their own opinions and repeat yours. But that is not going to happen: they disagree with you. You would not want to put aside your own opinion and repeat theirs, either. At the very least, you would like your opinion represented in this encyclopedia article, not ignored. Indeed, you want it explained fully and fairly. In fact, you want the best arguments and the strongest evidence offered. But you will grudgingly admit that other opinions have to be given the same treatment, as long as yours is as well.

So the Golden Rule says that that is how you, too, should lay out opinions you disagree with. As a result, you will paint the whole dialectical landscape in its most vibrant colors, not just one part of it.

In short, when people set themselves up to be authorities, condescendingly telling you The Truth when you might want to disagree, you naturally find it irritating. You want to be treated like an adult, presented with all the best arguments, so you can make up your own mind. So, since that is how you want to be treated, the Golden Rule would have you treat your readers that way, when you sit down to write a traditionally neutral text.

15. The Argument from Cooperation

So far, I have given two main arguments for neutrality, which are conceptually related: first from autonomy and second from the Golden Rule. A third, from cooperation, and fourth, from reliability, remain.

Here is an argument from cooperation, which I can state briefly.

Wikipedia's predecessor, Nupedia, originally adopted a neutrality policy, which Wikipedia inherited, partly because neutrality provides a way to defuse potential problems when people collaborate. If people are working together on the same text, the text cannot take a controversial position without potentially alienating some co-writers. Of course, if the collaborators share the same views, this is not a problem. But if the collaboration is, as on Wikipedia, open-ended—if you do not know who, in the future, will be working on it—then the prudent way to avoid conflict is simply not to let the text take a position on controversial issues. Insisting that shared text in a collaborative project remain neutral provides the basic diplomatic framework that enables such projects to exist without permanent ideological warfare.

But since this argument is relevant only to open wikis and some other collaborative works, that is all I will say about that here.

16. The Argument from Reliability

Let us consider one last argument, from reliability. The basic claim is simple: neutral writing is truth-conducive. Neutrality makes it more probable that readers will arrive at true and nuanced beliefs.[8]

The conclusion here is that the exercise of rationality is truth-conducive: we are more likely to have true beliefs if we base those beliefs on cogent arguments and solid evidence. Neutral writing supports the exercise of rationality by presenting us with, ideally, a full battery of arguments, with all the relevant evidence on all sides. This better equips us to determine what is true than if we receive only one side *ex cathedra*.

We will be more likely to have true beliefs if, as a matter of policy, we are presented with neutral writing. The more points of view we consider, and the more fairly and sympathetically the arguments for the various competing views are represented (even if they are wrong), the more likely we will be to arrive at true beliefs as a result.

17. A Shotgun Has a Better Chance to Hit a Fuzzy Target

Some people might find this to be wrong or puzzling, in cases in which the truth is known. Ideally, they will say, of course the best way to ensure that a reader has the truth is to determine in advance what the truth is and then present it and only it in all its glorious detail. Generally, I find nothing wrong with that, as far as it goes. It does not go very far, however, as

---

[8] Compare the following argument to J.S. Mill, *On Liberty*, Ch. 2.

it assumes the truth to be known and—this being the sticking point—uncontroversial. What if there is significant disagreement about what the truth is, and undecided readers know this?

In such cases, undecided readers have no rational grounds on which to prefer one source over another, everything else being equal; if they wish to follow Kant's advice, *sapere aude*, they must make up their own minds. If they see different experts and credible resources saying different things, which are they to believe?

What if there are five different expert views on a question, each having adherence of 20% of the expert population? Suppose an article advocates only one of these, and it turns out to be the wrong one. Then the chance of the article's readers reaching a true belief, based on this biased account, is 0%. But if we canvass all five views, at least those readers who settle on the correct view will have a true belief.

More generally, if one side is ignored, or made to look very bad, and that side turns out to be correct, readers are discouraged from learning it. That is what my young friends would call a "fail." And even if the truth happens to be presented with a favorable bias, it will not be presented in its strongest, most rationally persuasive form if the reader cannot compare it to the other, wrong side.

Suppose instead that I have indeed made up my mind about something and, fortunately, I am correct; still, neutral sources inform me about other, incorrect views. That often helps me to understand and support my own position better.

In short, a neutral presentation at least exposes readers to the truth (if anybody has it) and, by comparing it with false views, enables them to understand it better.

18. A Complete Map of the Dialectical Landscape

It is more complicated than that, though, of course.

Frequently, there are not just competing, simple claims on some narrow question; instead, there are various competing systems, or webs of interdependent claims, which are best weighed at the same time. The claims, taken together, make up what I might call the "dialectical landscape" surrounding a position: all the arguments, facts, details, attacks on the other side, rebuttals to their attacks, history, and context of some core proposition. For example, the dialectical landscape of a typical Democratic Party approach to health care is very different from that of the Republican Party. Whatever you think of them, both are complex, both involve many subtopics and specialized claims, and they do not even always address the same questions.

Truly neutral text, then, fully maps out the dialectical landscape on both, or all, sides of an issue, in a way that the sides can recognize as fairly representing their views.

A map of the opposing camps provides an invaluable service to us undecided interlopers. This is not just because we have a better chance of deciding rationally whether the core claims are correct, but also because the quality of our understanding is greatly improved the more familiar we are with all parts of the landscape. Even if we finally embrace some false claims, our minds are improved by being exposed to the context of all the claims. After all, in the dialectical landscape surrounding all competing claims are typically many others that are uncontroversial and yet very important to evaluating both sides.

Biased writing, by contrast, tends to be comparatively simple, too often appealing to emotion and employing fallacies and simplistic versions of arguments. Even if a piece fully and fairly canvasses one side, a biased account that mentions the other side makes a caricature of it, often simply to make its own side look more reasonable. Such caricatures propagate falsehoods—they are false portrayals of what the best representatives of the other side actually believe. But the point is that such caricatures actually stand in the way of improving the sophistication of our acceptance of our own side.

Arguments Against Neutrality

19. Examples of "Good Enough" Neutrality Exist

Now that I have laid out the arguments for the policy of neutrality, next I want to deal with some objections. There are two big ones: (1) neutrality is impossible, and (2) in some cases, it is simply the wrong approach.

When defending neutrality as a policy, I often hear the following. We all have our views; nobody is unbiased. Those views are bound to come out, one way or another, in any exposition of a controversy. We can try to be unbiased, but we will always fail. It is inevitable.

Yet many of us have had the experience of taking a class from a teacher who presented both sides of controversial questions sympathetically, and at the end, the teacher asks, "So, what do you think my view is?" And nobody could tell. I taught a philosophy of religion course once and at the end of the course asked for a show of hands: "Who thinks I believe in God?" About a third of the class put their hands up. "Who thinks I believe God does not exist?" About the same number of hands went up. "Who thinks I am agnostic?" Again, about the same number of hands. That was a proud moment for me.

Similarly, many of us have—I certainly have—had the experience of reading a news or encyclopedia article covering some debate, and it occurs to us that we cannot tell what view the writer endorses. The article seems admirably even-handed.

Perhaps it is true that one can always, in any text above a certain length, find something to improve as regards neutrality. Neutrality is extremely difficult to achieve—a point I will elaborate toward the end of the paper. But "good enough" neutrality, neutrality robust enough to earn our praise, plainly exists. "Plainly," I say: we have seen many examples of it.

There is a different way into the latter objection. One of the main insights that motivate some people to say that neutrality is impossible is that *objectivity* is impossible. We all have a point of view, goes the objection, and this makes claims that certain propositions are "objectively true," or true independently of any observer, very problematic—perhaps indefensible.[9]

I doubt that this is a problem for claims about neutrality, however. As I said above, "objectivity" and "neutrality" are two quite distinct concepts. The first is a quality of beliefs or attitudes; the second is a method of or constraint on exposition. I can be as subjective and "biased" as you like, in my heart of hearts, even as I am crafting a supremely neutral text. Similarly, the claims made in such a text can be neutral, fair, balanced, or untendentious without being objectively or subjectively true or false. The point of neutrality is to be fair to what people actually believe. One can be fair despite personally taking a side.

20. Chomskyan Cynicism

Some people claim that neutrality is impossible basically because they have a cynical view of the world. To them, neutrality is always a front, a show—never sincere. Politics, like life, is nothing but a power struggle, they believe, and any claims to neutrality are instead just a cynical device for smuggling an ideology into a reader's thought-world under cover of such precious epithets as "fairness," "objectivity," or "neutrality."

Given the abundance of examples of apparently neutral writing, such a cynical stance seems unwarranted and merely puzzling. How can these people justify their cynical attitude in the face of such seemingly obvious examples to the contrary? What are they thinking of? They seem *too* cynical. Perhaps this is how they think; but it is most assuredly not how everyone thinks.

I find in conversation that the cynics frequently defend their views in terms of Noam Chomsky's influential book

---

[9] This issue is discussed in Thomas Nagel's well-known book *The View from Nowhere*, Revised edition (Oxford, 1989).

Manufacturing Consent. Chomsky and his followers state that the news media may be given a "propaganda model," i.e., the news serves merely propagandistic purposes for our corporate masters. They argue that the various "filters" that make up this model put the lie to pretensions of journalistic neutrality. Basically, the news is filtered: some legitimate stories are excluded, and others are distorted by mechanisms of "money and power," including such things as the size of mass-media firms, advertising, reliance on establishment sources, "flak," and "anti-communism."

The most common thing one hears, along these lines, is that the big news media organizations are owned by corporations and thus inevitably biased in favor of corporate interests—for example, ABC is owned by the Walt Disney Company, Comcast owns NBC, and National Amusements is majority shareholder of CBS. If corporate interests are in control of the news media, how could the news fail to be biased in favor of such interests and of capitalism generally?

21. Chomskyan Cynicism Does Not Support the Thesis

There is no brief way to address Chomsky's argument head-on, so I will not try. Instead, I will simply discuss this *type* of argument. The difficulty with it in this context is that it is a hypothesis formed more or less a priori—the news must be "filtered" because it is subject to the mechanisms of money and power—and while the hypothesis might be true, it can be confirmed only empirically.

What would go into confirming the claim? At a minimum, one would have to find some way to identify instances of bias and then confirm that that bias tends to be significantly associated with Chomsky's "filters" such as corporate interests. The question then devolves from the rarified, abstract air of "systemic bias" to the more humdrum, concrete instances of bias that can be detected in actual reporting. Even if Chomsky and his followers were able to marshal some convincing examples of bias in corporate-sponsored reporting, the fact remains that there are plenty of examples of unbiased reporting. At least, in my opinion, there have been lots of news articles that lack any significant amount of bias.

Even if it is completely correct—and falsifiable—Chomsky's cynical hypothesis appears to be that there is one *source* of thoroughgoing bias due to the influence of "filters." It does not follow that neutrality is in principle impossible. In other words, even if we can identify something like "systemic" bias, or the bias of the whole (unreconstructed capitalist) system, it does not follow that there is bias in every instance of every publication, every article, every paragraph, and every sentence.

Another response is simpler: Chomsky's criticisms concern only corporate news. What about private, independent media, individual and small bloggers, academic and independent encyclopedias, and various non-corporate textbooks? Even supposing that corporate news is hopelessly and systemically biased, that would not establish that neutrality *per se* is unachievable.

22. Is Neutrality Relative?

Next I will address a different sort of argument that neutrality is impossible. Its basic premise is that neutrality is relative.

This is hard to dispute: it seems to follow from the very definition of neutrality. If neutrality is a matter of fairly representing the various opinions on a question, one is right to ask *which* opinions should be included. We routinely exclude the extreme minority, idiosyncratic, and personal opinions from traditionally neutral texts, and we do not call them biased for this reason. But we also routinely exclude (or fail to weight) opinions from foreign cultures. And for this reason—I will have to agree—our texts are typically biased in favor of our own cultures.

A *New York Times* article about the American policy debate over gun rights and gun control, which is remarkably even-handed in its treatment of Republican and Democratic approaches, looks extremely biased to a Briton, for whom the very idea of "gun rights" seems ridiculous and horrible. And so it is. The *Times* article is indeed biased in that regard: it carries an American bias. One may also say that an encyclopedia article for the *Catholic Encyclopedia* might be unbiased with respect to liberal and conservative Catholics, while remaining biased, as one would expect, in favor of Catholicism generally. And the same may be said for textbooks and encyclopedias and so forth: even if they are neutral with respect to a particular community, they are biased in favor of the more distinctive aspects of the community's outlook.

This is interesting, but it is not very obviously a serious objection to a neutrality policy. It might cause us to review the arguments in favor of the policy. Indeed it seems we are indoctrinated, by our newspapers, encyclopedias, and textbooks, into our community's basic assumptions. Are we less free for that indoctrination? Cosmopolitan philosophers like Descartes[10] and Spinoza, again, certainly thought so—to say nothing of contemporary philosophers like Martha Nussbaum and Kwame Anthony Appiah. I think so too.

But it is surely too much to ask that writers somehow take account of the enormous range of views from across the whole globe when they write in traditionally neutral forms—or even always to care about those views. Arguably, it is human to be part of a culture, and, globalism notwithstanding, there is really no such thing as a "global monoculture" with respect to which writers should be expected to be neutral. Maybe that will exist someday, but it does not yet.

I suppose a committed multiculturalist or relativist might want to take me to task for this, saying that it would surely be a grand thing that we be exposed to the broadest range of views from across the globe and across all ideologies, religions, and philosophies. (But what about eras? Should we not canvass historical views as well? We are surely *present*-biased.) Such a perspective is what one hopes to gain from international travel and a broadening, liberal education. But with the possible

---

[10] Rene Descartes, *Discourse on Method*, Part I.

exception of remarkable polymaths, probably none of us has such a global perspective that we could write for, or even make sense of, a newspaper, encyclopedia, or textbook that is quite globally "neutral"—one that comprehensively takes account of an entirely global range of views.

Wikipedia itself might be thought to be committed to such a completely international neutrality, and in places, its policies and practices have seemed to hold it to that utopian ambition. But of course it cannot be and it is not. The English Wikipedia's articles about science most clearly betray its Western and especially Anglo-American provenance, and articles about, for example, philosophy are mostly about Western philosophy. I see nothing really wrong with that. There are many pages that report comparative information about conditions all over the world; but I have never seen a page that actually tries to synthesize and compare opinions from around the world, about controversial questions. It might, perhaps, be a worthy goal to create a new version of Wikipedia that is fully committed to being internationally neutral. If it succeeded, it would be the world's first and only encyclopedia (or traditionally neutral text of any sort) that is fully neutral.

I am not claiming that many people would find it to be very useful. Maybe it would. It would certainly be of interest to some scholars. Yet it is not clear that the general global public would find it all that interesting; to say so is to say something profound about the nature of human knowledge, surely. But what it says is a thing that a mere encyclopedia cannot change, it seems.

23. Unworthy Positions and "False Balance"

The last major objection to a neutrality policy that I will consider is perhaps the most potent for many journalists: sometimes, certain points of view simply do not deserve inclusion in a traditionally neutral text. Surely, some opinions are simply wrong—scientifically disproven, grossly offensive, or just plain idiotic.

Journalists sometimes make this objection. They react with exasperation at accusations of "liberal bias" from conservatives, arguing that sometimes, since one side of a dispute is clearly false, any balance on the dispute would be "false balance." The mission of journalism is to uncover the truth; its first commitment is to accuracy. Accuracy, these journalists say, forbids us to strike a spurious balance between two very unequal views.

I think some journalists can use this device as a cover for naked partisan bias: if there is a legitimate debate and an activist journalist refuses to find a "false balance," that is a fallacy. Whenever journalists choose a side, on grounds of avoiding "false balance," they owe us an argument that the disfavored side really does not deserve neutral treatment. What sort of argument would do the trick?

Consider some points of view that mainstream journalists often find unworthy of uncritical coverage: global warming skepticism; creationism, intelligent design, or creation science; the anti-vaccination movement. Those examples are from science, and similarly controversial examples might be drawn from recent events and history: Holocaust denial; the 9/11 conspiracy theory; the Bilderberger or Jewish banker conspiracy theory.

The popularity of such views, in certain unfashionable circles, combined with the relative silence about them in the media suggests that journalists would find neutral coverage of such topics to be "false balance." These also suggest at least two different variants of the argument to consider: a moral variant and an epistemological variant.

On the moral variant, the reason we should not fairly represent certain positions is that the positions are morally reprehensible, harmful, and/or dangerous. This is a common German attitude toward Holocaust denial. Moral concerns, therefore, outweigh society's interest in neutral reporting.

On the epistemological variant, the reason is that the positions are so unscientific or otherwise ill-supported that it simply insults readers' intelligence for a writer to treat them seriously. This is a common scientific attitude toward global warming skepticism and creationism. Here, epistemological concerns outweigh society's interest in neutral reporting.

In either case, the argument is simple: certain views are either morally or epistemologically bankrupt to an extreme degree. So, the claim goes, traditionally neutral texts are under no obligation to include them. Therefore, since there are exceptions, neutrality is not a universal, absolute principle. It has its place, journalists tell me, but it operates within ethical and epistemological constraints—which they determine, of course.

24. Morally Repugnant Views

This all seems reasonable to journalists. I shall proceed to disagree.

Let me begin by conceding that there do seem to be instances of positions that I would want to exclude from an encyclopedia, for example. Indeed, I might want to do so on grounds that they are thoroughly (morally) reprehensible or utterly (epistemologically) ridiculous. Is shoplifting to be represented as a legitimate hobby? Do the attitudes of child molesters or sociopathic killers toward their crimes merit serious discussion? Do we really need to spend any time on Holocaust denial? For some, these seem to be rhetorical questions; but I will not treat them that way.

In a list of hobbies covered by an encyclopedia, we would not include shoplifting, even though it has a function something like a hobby for some people. While a general encyclopedia might not include shoplifting among the hobbies, probably we can justify that exclusion not on grounds that it is immoral or criminal but because it simply is not ordinarily classified among the hobbies.[11]

---

[11] A thorough web search confirmed this for me, although one can find news stories referring to stealing as a hobby, and some kleptomaniacs admit that it serves a hobby for them.

Similarly, in news reports of crime statistics, crime's impact on communities, and police and legislative strategies to defeat it, discussion of the attitudes of child molesters and sociopathic killers is an unnecessary and unwelcome intrusion. That is because they are irrelevant to the concerns of most news readers. But criminal attitudes are certainly a focus of sociologists and criminal psychologists, who need to understand the motives of criminals; in criminology textbooks,[12] criminal attitudes are crucial to include in chapters about criminal psychology. And sometimes, criminal motives are newsworthy. For example, we wonder what impels some police offers to shoot inner-city blacks without obvious provocation—and vice-versa.

Even Holocaust denial is open to the same sort of context-based analysis. There is no need to include Holocaust denial as an "alternative theory" about German history in WWII, for the simple reason that it is an extreme minority position; textbooks are under no obligation to include extreme minority positions. Of course it is repugnant, but its repugnance is not why it is not covered in textbooks. After all, there are circumstances—e.g., the politics of modern Germany, or German sociology—in which the views of Holocaust deniers, and getting the facts about them correctly and even sympathetically stated, might be important.

This discussion should make it plausible that it is not the moral bankruptcy of certain views that would lead us to exclude them from traditionally neutral texts, after all, but just considerations of relevance. It depends on the purpose of the texts. In some sorts of texts, thoroughly reprehensible things are described in stunning detail. In others, they simply are not relevant.

But now, by contrast, let us consider much more common views held by political partisans and religious adherents in

---

[12] For example, Larry J. Siegel, *Criminology: The Core*, 5th ed. (Wadsworth, 2014).

modern American politics. Take, for example, the conservative religious position that gay marriage is impossible and homosexual behavior sinful. These positions are regarded as morally reprehensible by the modern left. But in marriage and social policy in American politics broadly, it would be *obviously* biased to take either side. It is not "false balance" to approach such issues, in journalism, neutrally, to analyze the two competing moral evaluations on two separate sides without favoring either side. As I said in the previous section, journalism aims to help an audience to understand competing sides in a lively, ongoing public debate in order to make up their own minds about it. Its function is not to participate as a partisan in the debate itself or to declare a winner.

25. Epistemologically Repugnant Views

So much for the moral argument. What about the epistemological version? Is such an analysis possible for those cases in which a position seems legitimate to exclude because (on the view of many scientists or scholars) it lacks any sound intellectual basis?

I cannot sidestep the issue when it comes to, for example, creation science or creationism in biology textbooks. I will not pretend to be able to adjudicate this politically charged issue in a short space, but I will make a few germane remarks and draw some limited, tentative conclusions.

On the one hand, the public and their representatives in Texas have the right to ensure that public school children are exposed to views about what Bible-touting Christians believe about the creation of the world and the origin of species. In the U.S., they do not have the legal right to teach *only* those views in public schools, because that would run afoul of First Amendment prohibitions of the state establishment of religion. But it seems perfectly unobjectionable that those views, if placed among others, are canvassed in public schools.

On the other hand, scientists have an excellent point when they maintain that creation science is an extreme minority view among scientists. Even scientists with a Christian point of view generally endorse evolutionary theory, as does the Catholic Church and many mainline Protestant denominations. If the purpose of teaching biology is to impart facts and theories that biologists stand behind, then biology classes should do so.

A policy of neutrality would have us determine what the relevant community is. In science class, that would seem to be the scientific community. But science class is taking place in the larger context of enculturation by the school system, and there the relevant community is the general public, not just scientists.

Bearing this in mind, I think adopting a policy of neutrality would entail the following recommendations.

Insofar as biology class is canvassing the views of actual biologists, creation science has no place there; for better or worse, the vast majority of scientists simply do not consider it to be a scientific theory at all, but a theological one. So it is simply incorrect to represent it as one view among many.

Insofar as biology class takes place in the context of a broader schooling context, however, the people of Texas (and other such places) have the right to insist, not that the science be taught a certain way, but that students be informed that a large number of citizens disagree with the science. Little time need be spent in informing them of this disagreement in science class, because the disagreement is not a topic in science but in the broader culture. But the dignity of students and their parents is best respected when their disagreement is officially and respectfully acknowledged.

In the interests of neutrality, in addition to evolution as taught in biology, students should be taught about (neutrally, of course) a variety of religious, philosophical, and scientific views about cosmology, creation stories, and other topics that religion, philosophy, and science all speak on. Such an interdisciplinary class or unit would be the place in which creationism would be canvassed. Needless to say, perhaps, students in that class whose parents do not want a neutral approach to this subject should not be forced to endure it.

This is a compromise solution, and I hope a neutral one as well.

I could give similar treatment to other issues. What I want to maintain is that for all the issues listed earlier, there exist sophisticated, often multi-part neutral solutions. In some cases I might seem to favor one part or another; but taken all together, the result will be fair. Journalists, or the state, will not unduly favor one position over another, affording readers and students the dignity and tools to decide important, controversial issues for themselves.

26. Neutrality and Global Climate Change

A few comments about how to write neutrally about climate change should clarify some more issues.

A majority of climate scientists believe in anthropogenic global warming (AGW); exactly which scientists to include as "experts," and exactly how to characterize their expert views, and thus which surveys to consider and what percentage endorse it, is a matter of debate. In any case, while some distinguished climate science experts are skeptics, probably a majority are not.

When explaining the science itself—so, in science textbooks and science research news—understanding the controversy is not the primary aim. Understanding the state of the science is. So, presumably, in that context, most of the issues and most of the evidence will appear to be on the AGW side, not because the writers are biased but because most of the actual science happens to be on that side. In other words, if the mission of the text is to canvass the science, the text will appear biased but it will not really be biased; any bias is to be found in the subject matter itself. Besides, there are many qualifications and objections that will be worth covering, which are dwelt upon by skeptics, even if they are dismissed by climate activists. One justification of covering them, apart from the requirements of neutrality, is that it helps the mastery of any very complex subject (like climate science) to consider objections and qualifications.

But matters are different in a political context—political journalism, or encyclopedia articles or textbook chapters about the politics of global warming. There, as important as understanding the science is, understanding the controversy is even more important. Coverage of such a controversy cannot be done without apportioning space at least roughly equally.

Climate change scientists and activists have dismissed the idea that journalists ought to report neutrally on climate change skepticism by arguing, "If you are going to give equal space to climate change skepticism, you should also give equal space to Holocaust denial—which is absurd." But I hope it is clear how I would respond to that argument: while among the American population, climate change skepticism appears to be a (large) minority position,[13] Holocaust denial is a tiny fringe phenomenon. In an American context, reporting neutrally about the climate change debate does not entail that reporters must so much as mention Holocaust denial. In certain other countries, however, things might be different.

I realize this section's discussion has a lot hand-waving on my part, and more needs to be said. Beyond this, the issues are to be taken up by the experts themselves (those who really care about neutrality). That, as we will see next, is the point: the specific requirements of neutrality in any particular case can be discovered only by careful study of the details of the case. The devil of bias and the angel of neutrality are in the details.

---

[13] A Pew survey said 39% of Americans regard "global climate change to be "minor threat" or "not a threat" to the United States. See Moira Fagan and Christine Huang, "A look at how people around the world view climate change," *pewresearch.org* by the Pew Research Center, April 18, 2019, https://pewrsr.ch/3g02GJM.

The Difficulty of Neutrality and Eliminating Bias

27. Neutrality Is Complex and Difficult

After this long discussion, I hope it will be abundantly clear that neutrality is not a simple concept. "Why cannot journalists just be more neutral?" readers ask, complaining about "media bias." But this assumes that bias is something simple and straightforward to fix, like a spelling mistake. It might appear simple, if you think of neutrality as no more than giving an equal amount of space to each position and avoiding certain loaded words.

Apportioning space evenly and avoiding words that imply judgment is a good place to begin, especially when you are reporting about a policy debate. But if your purpose is to construct a narrative about a multi-layered, developing situation, neutrality is instead a matter of relaying, while reporting the basic facts, that there are alternative views, mentioning them in the right places, providing different possible explanations, and so forth.

The failure to understand or acknowledge the complexity of neutrality is widespread, even among journalists. That failure in turn leads many writers, even of traditionally neutral texts, to underestimate the challenges and fail to take practical measures to meet them head-on. Writers often fail at this and end up writing biased stuff without realizing it, even when they sincerely believe and intend otherwise. The sheer difficulty of neutrality is at the root of this failure.

When we learn to spot instances of bias and look hard for it, we can see it everywhere. For some, this in turn causes cynicism about the very possibility of neutrality.

28. Eradicating Bias Deliberately

Cynicism is understandable. We should expect bias to be the norm, if it is not deliberately eradicated.

That bias is the natural state of affairs became obvious to me after I attempted to herd the many biased cats of Wikipedia and Citizendium, and later compared those experiences to what I learned about how the admirably even-handed ProCon.org operates.[14] ProCon's executive team told me they have detailed rules about neutrality as well as a thorough process in which people from a variety of ideological perspectives give brutally honest feedback on the fairness of drafts. The result is remarkably even-handed articles.

Well, if ProCon has to invest so much time and attention to make their pages neutral, what makes the rest of us think we can do it without spending a similar amount of time and attention?

29. How Publishers Can Improve Neutrality

Publishers, I propose, need to add two features to combat bias: first, detailed neutrality guidelines, and second, specific procedures for making writing more neutral, procedures to be carried out by specially assigned people.

Publishers need a complex set of neutrality guidelines to identify neutrality problems and adjudicate issues. I offer no such rules here. To a great extent, the rules will resemble a style guide. Wikipedia has an extensive guide, although I cannot recommend its current version.[15] Other publishing organizations that claim to be neutral or fair ought to be able to articulate exactly what guidelines they follow in identifying and resolving neutrality problems.

Beyond simply having rules, staff need to follow some procedure to ensure that the publication as a whole is neutral, as well as individual articles and their components. Some publishers invest money into copyediting and fact-checking,

---

[14] Disclosure: ProCon's publisher is an investor in a startup of mine; but we got to know each other some years before that due to our close alignment on the very issue of neutrality.

[15] See Chapter 3 in this volume. Wikipedia today has a few different pages about implementing neutrality according to its definition. I also helped to develop a guide for Ballotpedia in 2015.

presumably on grounds that it makes their publications more readable and accurate. Similarly, I propose that publishers of traditionally neutral texts ought to care much more than they apparently do about neutrality, and they might wish to assign editors and writers to handle the most difficult neutrality issues and otherwise implement their neutrality methodology.

Examples can be found in ProCon, which constantly worries about the issue and follows arduous procedures to achieve neutrality. Ballotpedia, too, hired people in 2015 to serve as "neutrality editors" to help with such issues.

30. The Discipline of Neutrality

Let me elaborate the latter point.

I am proposing that publishers add what would be for many a new layer of oversight: not just vague expressions of commitment to neutrality, but specially assigned neutrality editors, or some other way to more actively and aggressively edit for neutrality, in addition to the traditional disciplines of copyediting and fact-checking.

Ballotpedia recently hired its first writers specifically tasked to work on neutrality. The top candidates evaluated the neutrality of a report Ballotpedia had recently done. I immodestly prided myself on my ability to spot problems with neutrality, and the Ballotpedia piece struck me on a casual reading as having only a few problems—nothing too bad. But after the candidates got through with it, it was clear that the report had many more neutrality issues than I had noticed. The problems were mostly subtle and perhaps understandable, but the criticisms all made sense. And more to the point, they were all fixable. If the writer of that study had had feedback from a neutrality editor, the piece would have been substantially more neutral and better-written as a result.

Similar instances of surprising, hidden bias are rife in most reporting, textbooks, and encyclopedia articles. If we view neutrality as a discipline similar to spelling, then the bias of today will look clumsy and backward, like the spellings one finds in books published before spelling became standardized.

Professional publishing operations already take the time for the traditional disciplines of copyediting and fact-checking, because publishers and readers value readability and accuracy. For traditionally neutral forms, should they not also value neutrality just as much? As I showed earlier in this essay, the moral and political arguments in favor of a new discipline are strong. If you do not take the time to edit for neutrality very explicitly, you will simply fail to be neutral. How could you not? The same can be said of copyediting and fact-checking: if you do not take the time to edit explicitly for correct mechanics and accuracy, you will probably screw up. To err is human. If you try hard and are conscientious, you might do a decent job—maybe. If you want to be sure, hire some professionals and set up a neutrality editing process.

31. No Newspaper Has Ever Been Neutral

If I am right that bias is rife and yet we have good reason to value neutrality, there is a great latent demand for reporting that is neutral in the sense described here. We should take great interest (I would, anyway) in any publisher that credibly announced a claim to neutrality in the sense I have defined.

The emphasis here is on "credibly." Obviously, claims to being "unbiased" or "objective" have long been a cheap but meaningless selling point for various clearly biased publications. Idle claims to the effect of "we are already neutral, of course" are simply not credible.

After all, the reply is simple: *No, you are not. No newspaper has ever been neutral.* No newspaper has ever even tried, as a matter of policy.

Again, this is not a complaint about "liberal media bias." Fox News claims to be "fair and balanced" but of course very few people believe they are. Traditional news broadcasts project a tone of objectivity and generally claim not to be biased. But nobody really believes they are *neutral* in the sense defined in this paper. Again, I say this not because I am accusing them of liberal bias but because neutrality is difficult and simply will not be achieved except deliberately, recognizing the perhaps surprising complexity and difficulty of the job and devoting the effort needed to get it done.

A publisher's claim to neutrality could be substantiated by (a) publishing a statement of neutrality principles, (b) taking proactive measures to ensure that they are followed, (c) doing audits of reader opinion and of external neutrality editors, and finally (d) publishing the results of the audits.

32. The Unmet Latent Demand for Neutrality

There is a great latent demand for neutral content, and the demand is unmet.

There will always be a market for biased reporting and opinion. But publishing operations that can credibly state that they embrace neutrality would have an unusual advantage over others. So I speculate that startups in a new "neutrality niche" might do well. There could be newspapers, weeklies, wire services, and more.

I can also imagine startups in reference and textbook publishing that could *credibly* make similar claims. As an encyclopedia aficionado and former college teacher, I know I would be extremely interested.

Finally, I can imagine firms offering external audits of the neutrality of publications and research organizations.

Readers can help make this happen, too, simply by making their preference for neutral texts known. You simply need to promote the proposition that publishers should adopt both detailed neutrality guidelines and procedures for ensuring the guidelines are followed.[16]

---

[16] For discussion and other help with this essay, thanks to Kamy Akhavan, Courtney Collins, Angela Consani, Anthony DiPierro, Scott Duryea, Stephen Ewen, Mike Forsythe, Leslie Graves, Sara Key, Greg Lukianoff, Geoff Pallay, Terry Phillips, Jay Rakow, Gerry Sanger, Kristen Smith, Jason Swadley, Anton Sweeney, and Bryan White.

Five

Why Wikipedia Must Jettison
Its Anti-Elitism

In this essay, which appeared in December 2004, I made my first foray into Wikipedia criticism. Wikipedia made no special role for experts and empowered anonymous trolls. It was already full of problems. Was this really the best humanity could do? The current version is lightly edited for this volume; all footnotes are from 2020 and serve as either converted links or a running commentary.

WIKIPEDIA has started to hit the big time. Accordingly, several critical articles have come out, including a sniffy one by a former editor-in-chief of *Britannica*[1] and a skeptical AP piece titled, "When Information Access Is So Easy, Truth Can Be Elusive."[2]

---

[1] Robert McHenry, "The Faith-Based Encyclopedia," *Tech Central Station*, December 2004; article is no longer online.
[2] Anick Jesdanun, *The San Diego Union Tribune*, Dec. 10, 2004, https://bit.ly/2ZJ6nOr.

These articles were written by people who appeared not to appreciate the merits of Wikipedia fully. I did, however; I co-founded it.

Wikipedia does have two big problems, and attention to them is long overdue. These problems could be eliminated by eliminating a single root problem. If the project's managers are not willing to solve it, I fear a fork (a new edition under new management, for the non-techies reading this) will probably be necessary.[3]

Let me preface this by saying that I know Wikipedia is very cool. A lot of people do not think so, but of course they are wrong. So the following must be taken in the spirit of someone who knows and supports the mission and broad policy outlines of Wikipedia very well.[4]

First Problem: Lack of Credibility to the Public

The problem I would like to raise is not that Wikipedia is unreliable. The alleged unreliability of Wikipedia is something that the news articles mentioned above made much of, but that is not my concern, and I am not interested in discussing that point per se.

My concern is that, regardless of whether Wikipedia actually is more or less reliable than the average encyclopedia, it is not perceived as adequately reliable by many librarians, teachers, and academics. The reason for this is not far to seek: those librarians etc. note that anybody can contribute and that there are no traditional review processes. You might reply that it does work nonetheless, and I would agree with you to a large extent, but your assurances will not put this concern to rest.

---

[3] When I wrote this piece, I had not started any such fork myself.

[4] Again, one must bear in mind that I wrote this at the end of 2004, when Wikipedia still followed habits of neutral writing and sound dispute resolution that I could more or less respect. Despite growing in size, the project has gone downhill since then.

You might maintain that people are already using Wikipedia a lot, and that that implies a great deal of trust. This is true, as far as it goes; but people use many resources that they would admit are not quite reliable, via web searches, for example. (I do so all the time, though perhaps I should not.) Perhaps Wikipedia is better described as one of those sources regarded as unreliable which people read anyway. In this case, one might say there is no problem: Wikipedia is being read, and it is of minimally adequate and increasing reliability. What more could you ask? In other words, why does a perception of unreliability matter?

I am willing to grant much of this reply. I think merely that there are a great many benefits that accrue from robust credibility to the public. One benefit, but only one, is support and participation by academia. A great many of my colleagues in philosophy are not at all impressed with the project; but more about that in a bit.

Another benefit accruing from robust public credibility is even more widespread use and support by teachers, schools, libraries, and the general public—precisely the people who want to use what they believe to be a credible encyclopedia. To the extent that the project is not reaching, and being supported by, these people, it is not succeeding as well as it might.

Perhaps you might also maintain that, while Wikipedia does not now have a reputation for reliability, it will eventually, once enough studies proving its reliability are done, and once people are more familiar with the concept behind the project. This is hard to argue with. But it is also hard to support, because it involves predicting the future about public opinion—a risky business. It would be better to do something to help guarantee a reputation for reliability.[5]

---

[5] Interestingly, a few small, poorly-designed studies—nothing comprehensive yet—did come out later. They seemed to indicate that Wikipedia was indeed mostly reliable. In any case, it gained a broad

Wikipedia has another sort of credibility problem, mentioned in passing above, and I fear that time is not a solution to this problem, the way it might be to the foregoing one. Namely, one can make a good case that, when it comes to relatively specialized topics (outside of the interests of most of the contributors), the project's credibility is very uneven.[6] If the project was lucky enough to have a writer or two well-informed about some specialized subject, and if their work was not degraded in quality by the majority of people, whose knowledge of the subject is based on paragraphs in books and mere mentions in college classes, then there *might* be a good, credible article on that specialized subject. Otherwise, there will be no article at all, a very amateurish-sounding article, or an article that looks like it might once have been pretty good, but which has been hacked to bits by the rabble. One has only to compare the excellent *Stanford Encyclopedia of Philosophy* or *Internet Encyclopedia of Philosophy* to Wikipedia's philosophy section. From the point of view of a specialist, Wikipedia needs a lot of work.

Second Problem: Difficult People

I stopped participating in Wikipedia when funding for my position ran out. That does not mean that I am merely mercenary; I might have continued to participate, were it not for a certain poisonous social or political atmosphere in the project.

---

reputation for credibility among the public, although not so much among most professionals and educators.

So the points here still stand: (1) teachers still widely discourage the use of Wikipedia, and (2) it continues to lack a reputation for credibility among professionals and educators, such people continue to form a small minority of participants. Worse, especially in less technical fields, those students who do use it frequently rely on what happens to be substandard analysis.

[6] This remains the case, in my opinion, as of 2020.

There are many ways to explain this problem, and I will start with just one. Far too much credence and respect accorded to people who in other Internet contexts would be labeled "trolls." There is a certain mindset associated with unmoderated Usenet groups and mailing lists, one that infects the collectively-managed Wikipedia project: if you react strongly to trolling, that reflects poorly on you, not (necessarily) on the troll. If you attempt to take trolls to task or demand that something be done about constant disruption by trollish behavior, the other list-members will cry "censorship," attack you, and even come to the defense of the troll. This drama has played out countless times on unmoderated Internet groups, and since about the fall of 2001 on the unmoderated Wikipedia.[7]

Wikipedia has, to its credit, done something about the most serious trolling and other kinds of abuse: there is an Arbitration Committee that provides a process whereby the most disruptive users of Wikipedia can be ejected from the project.

But there are myriad abuses and problems that never make it to the mediation process, let alone the Arbitration Committee. A few of the project's participants can be, not to put a nice word on it, pretty nasty. And this is tolerated. So, for any person who can and wants to work politely with well-meaning, rational, reasonably well-informed people—which is to say, to be sure, most people working on Wikipedia—the constant fighting can be so off-putting as to drive them away from the project.[8] This explains why I am gone; it also explains why

---

[7] For most of us in 2020, difficult users are still a problem, but not quite the same one. This article was written just as the Internet was becoming flooded by new Internet users who completely rejected the tolerant attitude toward trolling expressed here.

[8] Everything stated in this paragraph is certainly still the case. In 2020, what sorts of behavior you will be confronted with all depends on who is dominant on a give page or WikiProject.

many others, including some extremely knowledgeable and helpful people, have left the project.

The Root Problem: Lack of Respect for Expertise

There is a deeper problem—I, at least, think so—which explains both of the above-elaborated problems. Namely, as a community, Wikipedia lacks the habit or tradition of respect for expertise. As a community, far from being elitist (which would, in this context, mean excluding the unwashed masses), it is anti-elitist (which, in this context, means that expertise is not accorded any special respect, and snubs and disrespect of expertise are tolerated). This is one of my failures: a policy that I attempted to institute in Wikipedia's first year, but for which I did not muster adequate support, was the policy of respecting and deferring politely to experts. (Those who were there will, I hope, remember that I tried.)

I need not recount the history of how this nascent policy eventually withered and died. Ultimately, it became clear that the most active and influential members of the project—beginning with Jimmy Wales, who hired me to start a free encyclopedia project and who now manages it—were decidedly anti-elitist in the above-described sense.

Consequently, nearly everyone with much expertise but little patience will avoid editing Wikipedia, because they will—at least if they are editing articles that are subject to any sort of controversy—be forced to defend their edits on discussion pages against attacks by non-experts. This is not perhaps so bad in itself. But if the expert should have the gall to complain to the community about the problem, he or she will be shouted down (at worst) or politely asked to "work with" persons who have proven themselves to be unreasonable (at best).[9]

---

[9] This cult of the amateur (in Andrew Keen's phrase: see his relevant *Cult of the Amateur*, Doubleday, 2008) remains a problem,

This lack of respect for expertise explains the first problem, because if they had it, project participants would have long ago invited a board of academics and researchers to manage a culled version of Wikipedia (one that, I think, would not directly affect the way the main project is run). But because project participants have such a horror of the traditional deference to expertise, this sort of proposal has never been taken very seriously by most Wikipedians leading the project now. So much the worse for Wikipedia and its reputation.[10]

This lack of respect for expertise and authority also explains the second problem, because again if the project participants had greater respect for expertise, there would necessarily be very little patience for those who deliberately disrupt the project. This is perhaps not obvious, so let me explain. To attract and retain the participation of experts, there would have to be little patience for those who do not understand or agree with Wikipedia's mission, or even for those who are not able to work with others constructively and recognize when there are holes in their knowledge (probably the most disruptive group of all). A less tolerant attitude toward disruption would make the project more polite, welcoming, and indeed open to the vast majority of intelligent, well-meaning people on the Internet. As it is, there are far fewer genuine experts involved in the project (though there are some, of course) than there could and should be.

It will probably be objected by some that, since I am not 100% committed to the most radical sort of openness, I do not

---

although Wikipedians have become much more fanatical about finding secondary sources, which does entail a kind of respect for expertise, as I argued it would in "The Fate of Expertise after Wikipedia," *Episteme* 6, no. 1 (2009): 52–73. But indeed, since Wikipedia's policies have made it rather snootily in favor of whatever is the Establishment view, this means only *some* experts are listened to.

[10] Again, Wikipedia has no such review project as of 2020.

understand why the project that I founded works: it works, I will be told, precisely *because* it is radically open—even anarchical.

I know, of course, that Wikipedia works because it is radically open. Indeed, that was part of the original plan I proposed. But I firmly disagree with the notion that that Wikipedia-fertilizing openness requires disrespect for expertise. The project can prize and praise its most knowledgeable contributors, while at the same time permitting contribution by persons with no credentials whatsoever. That, in fact, was my original conception of the project. It is sad that the project did not go in that direction.

One thing that Wikipedia could do now, although I doubt that it is possible in the current atmosphere and with the current management, is to adopt an official policy of respect of and deference to expertise.[11] Wikipedia's "key policies" have not changed since I was associated with the project; but if a policy of respect for and deference to expertise were adopted at that level, and if it were enforced somehow, perhaps the project would solve the problems described above.

But do not hold your breath. Unless there is the equivalent of a revolution in the ranks of Wikipedia, the project will not adopt this proposal and make it a "key policy"; or if it does, the policy will probably be not be enforced. I certainly do not expect Jimmy Wales to change his mind. I have known him since 1994 and he is a smart and thoughtful guy; I am sure he has thought through his support of radical openness and his (what I call) anti-elitism. I doubt he will change his mind about these things. Unless he does change his mind, the project itself will probably not change.

Nevertheless, everyone familiar with Wikipedia can now see the power of the basic Wikipedia idea and the crying need to get more experts on board and a publicly credible review

---

[11] This is precisely what another wiki project I founded, Citizendium, did about two years after I wrote this.

process in place (so that there is a subset of "approved" articles—not a heavy-handed, complicated process, of course). The only way Wikipedia can achieve these things is to jettison its anti-elitism and to moderate its openness to trolls and fools; but it will almost certainly not do these things. Consequently, as Wikipedia increases in popularity and strength, I do not see how there can fail to be a more academic fork of the project in the future.[12]

I hope that a university, academic consortium, or think tank can be found to pursue a project to release vetted versions of Wikipedia articles, and I hope that the new project's managers will understand very well what has made Wikipedia work as well as it has, before they adopt any policies.[13]

---

[12] With Citizendium, I made one myself.

[13] I still think this is an excellent idea, and it is both more needed and more viable than it was in 2004.

Part II

THE POLITICS OF
INTERNET KNOWLEDGE

Six

How the Internet Is Changing
What (We Think) We Know

This is a speech I gave in 2008, updated here for 2020, and it serves as a good introduction to and foundation for the topics of the second part of the book: knowledge, how it should be distinguished from mere information, and how we should evaluate the contributions of anonymous amateurs and experts in an age when "info lite" reigns.

Information Is Easy, Knowledge Is Difficult

THERE is a mind-boggling amount of information online. And this is a wonderful thing. I am serious about that. A good search engine is like an oracle: you can ask it any question you like and be sure to get an answer. The answer might be exactly what you are looking for, or it might be, well, oracular—difficult to interpret and possibly incorrect. I draw the usual distinction between knowledge and information. You can find information online very easily. Knowledge is another matter altogether.

Now, this is not something new, something that emerged with the Internet. It is a basic feature of human life that while information is easy, knowledge is difficult. There has never been a shortage of mere data and opinion in human life. It is a very old observation that the most ignorant people are usually full of opinions, while many of the most knowledgeable people are full of doubt. Other people are certainly sources of knowledge, but they are also sources of half-truths, confusion, misinformation, and lies. If we simply want information from others, it is easy to get; if we want knowledge in any strong sense of the word, it is very difficult. Besides that, long before the Internet, there was far more to read, far more television shows and movies to watch, than anyone could ever absorb in many lifetimes. Before the Internet, we were already awash in information. Wading through all that information in search of some hard knowledge was already difficult.

The Internet is making this old problem even worse. If we had an abundance of information in, say, the 1970s, the Internet has created a superabundance of information today. Out of curiosity, I looked up some numbers. According to one estimate, as of 2020, there are now over 4.6 billion people online[1]; Internet Live Stats estimated that there are over 1.5 billion active websites.[2]

With that many people, and that many active websites, clearly there is, as I say, a superabundance of information. Google is stingy with its data, but one tech blog estimated they had over five billion searches performed per day; that is about

---

[1] InternetWorldStats.com, May 31, 2020, https://bit.ly/3eKOwL0. "Internet usage information comes from data published by Nielsen Online, by the International Telecommunications Union, by GfK, by local ICT Regulators and other reliable sources."

[2] InternetLiveStats.com, 2018 estimate, https://bit.ly/2WyQb02. "Source: NetCraft and Internet Live Sites (elaboration of data by Matthew Gray of MIT and Hobbes' Internet Timeline and Pingdom)".

two trillion in a year, an unimaginably vast number.[3] Google, by the way, was responsible for over 90% of web searches. Now, you might have heard such numbers before; I do not mean to be telling you news. But I want to worry out loud about a consequence of this situation.

My worry is that the superabundance of information is devaluing knowledge. The more that *information* piles up on Internet servers around the world, and the easier it is to be found, the less that *knowledge* will appear distinctive and attractive by comparison. I fear that the Internet has already greatly weakened our sense of what is distinctive about knowledge, and why it is worth seeking. I know this might seem rather abstract, and not something worth getting worked up about. Why, really, should you care?

It used to be that in order to learn some specific fact, like the population of France, you had to crack open a big thick paper encyclopedia or other reference book. One of the great things about the Internet is that that sort of searching—for very specific, commonly-sought-after facts—has become dead simple. Even more, there are many facts one can now find online that, in the past, would have taken a trip to the local library to find. The point is that the superabundance of information has actually made it remarkably easy to get information. Today, it is easy not just to get some information about something or other, it is easy to get boatloads of information about very specific questions and topics we are interested in.

For all that, knowledge is not getting much easier, I am afraid. To be quite sure of an answer still requires comparing multiple sources, critical thinking, sometimes a grasp of statistics and mathematics, and a careful attention to detail when it comes to understanding texts. In short, knowledge still requires hard thought. Sure, technology is a great time-saver in various ways; it has certainly made research easier, and

[3] seotribunal.com, accessed July 2020, https://bit.ly/2WyRyMe.

it will become only more so. But the actual mental work that results in knowledge of a topic cannot be made much easier, simply because no one else can do your thinking for you. So while information becomes nearly instantaneous and dead simple, knowledge is looking like a doddering old uncle.

I do not mean to be glib. I have a serious point. Not only is information easy to find, it is easy to digest. Just think of the different types of pages that a typical web search turns up: news articles, which summarize events for the average person; blogs, which are usually very brief; web forums, which only rarely go into depth; and encyclopedia articles and other mere summaries of topics. Of course, there are also more substantive websites, as well as resources buried in the "deep web" (that is, things harder to find with a search engine), which contains books and journal articles and white papers. But most people do not use those other resources. The point is that most of the stuff that you typically and easily find on the Internet is pretty lightweight. It is Info Lite.

"Right," you say, "what is wrong with that? Great taste, less filling!" Sure, I like easy, entertaining information as much as the next guy. But the problem is that it makes the hard work of knowledge much less appealing by comparison. For example, if you are coming to grips with what we should do about illegal immigration, or some other very complex issue, you must escape the allure of all the dramatic and entertaining news articles and blog posts on these subjects. Instead, you must be motivated to wade through a lot of far drier material. The sources that are more likely to help you in your quest for knowledge look very boring by comparison. My point here is that the superabundance of information devalues knowledge, because the means of solid knowledge are decidedly more difficult and less sexy than the Info Lite that it is so easy to find online.

There is another way that the superabundance of information makes knowledge more difficult. It is that, for all the terabytes upon terabytes of information on the Internet, society does not employ many more (and possibly fewer) editors than it had before the advent of the Internet. When you go to post something on a blog or a web forum, there is no one called an editor who decides to "publish" your comment. The Internet is less a publishing operation than a giant conversation. But most of us still take in most of what we read fairly passively. Now, there is no doubt that what has been called the "read-write web" encourages active engagement with others online, and helps us overcome our passivity. This is one of the decidedly positive things about the Internet, I think: it gets people to understand that they can actively engage with what they read. We understand now more than ever that we can and should read critically. The problem, however, is that, without the services of editors, we need our critical faculties to be engaged and very fine-tuned. While the Internet conversation has made it necessary for us to read critically, still, without the services of editors, there is far more garbage out there than our critical faculties can handle. We end up absorbing a lot of nonsense passively: we cannot help it.

In short, we are reading reams of content written by amateurs, without the benefit of editors, which means we must as it were be our own editors. But many of us, I am afraid, do not seem to be prepared for the job. In my own long experience interacting with Internet users, I find heaps of skepticism and little respect for what others write, regardless of whether it is edited or not. Now, skepticism is all well and good. But at the same time, I find hardly anything in the way of real critical thinking. The very opinionated people I encounter online rarely demonstrate that they have thought things through as they should, given the strength of their convictions. I have even encountered college professors who cite easy-to-find news articles in the commission of the most elementary of logical fallacies. It is not necessarily just a lack of education that accounts for the problem I am describing. Having "information at our fingertips," clearly, sometimes makes us skip the hard thinking that knowledge requires. Even those of us who ought to know better are too often content to be impressed by the sheer quantity and instant availability of information, and let it substitute for their own difficult thought.

The Nature and Value of Knowledge

Easy information devalues hard knowledge, I say. But so far I have merely been appealing to your understanding of the nature and value of knowledge. Someone might ask me: well, what do you mean by knowledge, anyway, that it is so different from mere information? And why does that matter?

Philosophers since Plato have been saying that knowledge is actually a special kind of belief. This does not mean that we hedge everything we say we know, as if we were not quite sure. It means only that, if we say we know something, that means, at a minimum, that we accept or buy into some truth. Second, it must indeed be true, and finally, it must also be justified, or have good reasons or evidence to support it.

For example, let us suppose I read something for the first time in some social media post, without any further source: some celebrity died, say. Suppose I just uncritically believe this. Well, even if that is true, I do not know that it is true, because social media is full of all sorts of made-up garbage. One random post saying something really is not a good enough reason to believe it. But if I then read the news in a few other, more credible sources, then my belief becomes much better justified, and then I can be said to *know*.

Now, I do not want to go into a lot of unnecessary details and qualifications, which I could at this juncture. So let me get right to my point. I say knowledge is, roughly speaking, justified, true belief. Well then, I want to add that knowledge is difficult not because getting truth is difficult, but because justifying our beliefs is. In other words, it is really easy to get truth. Google is a veritable oracle of truth. The problem is recognizing truth, and distinguishing it from falsehood. The ocean of information online contains vast seas of truth. The difficulty comes in knowing when you have got it.

That is what justification is for. We use reasons, or evidence, to determine that, indeed, if we accept a piece of information, we will have knowledge, not error. But producing a good justification for our beliefs is extremely difficult. It requires, as I said before, good sources, critical thinking, sometimes a knowledge of statistics and mathematics, and a careful attention to detail when it comes to understanding texts. This all takes time and energy, and while others can help, it is something that one must do for oneself.

Here you might wonder: if justification, and therefore knowledge, is really so difficult, then why go to all the trouble? Besides, justification is not an all-or-nothing matter. How much evidence is needed before we can be said to know something? After all, if that social media post says the celebrity is dead, that is at least some weak evidence. Do I really need stronger evidence? Why?

These are difficult questions. The best brief answer is, "It depends." Sometimes, if someone is just telling an entertaining story, it does not matter at all whether it is true or not. So it does not matter that you know the details of the story; if the story entertains, it has done its job. I am sure that celebrity trivia is similar: it does not matter very much whether the latest gossip in TMZ about the royals is true, it is just entertaining to read.

But there are many other subjects that matter. I certainly cannot presume to tell you how much evidence you need for your positions on such issues, before you can claim to have knowledge. Being a skeptic, I would actually say that we cannot have knowledge about such complex issues, or at least, not very certain knowledge. But I would say that it is still important to get as much evidence as possible about these issues. Why? Quite simply because a lot is riding on our getting the correct answers, and the more that we study the issues and justify our beliefs, the more likely our beliefs are to be correct.

To passively absorb information from the Internet, without caring about whether we have good reasons for what we believe, is really to roll the dice. Like all gambling, this is pleasant and self-indulgent. But if the luck does not go your way, it can come back to bite you.

Knowledge matters, and as wonderful as the Internet can be for getting knowledge, it can also devalue knowledge. It does so, I have said, by making passive absorption of information seem more pleasant than the hard work of justifying beliefs, and also by presenting us with so much unedited, low-quality information that we cannot absorb it as carefully as we would like. But there is another way that the Internet devalues knowledge: by encouraging anonymity.

Knowledge and Anonymity

We get much of our knowledge from other people. Of course, we pick some things up directly from conversation or chatting online. We also read books, news, and opinion; we watch videos and films. In short, we get knowledge either directly from other people, or indirectly, through various media.

Now, the Internet is very different, importantly different, from both face-to-face conversation and from traditional, pre-Internet media. Let us talk about that.

The Internet has been called, again, a giant conversation. But it is a very unusual conversation, if so. For one thing, it is not a face-to-face conversation. We have comparatively few video conferences, probably fewer than old science fiction stories described. In fact, in many of our interactions online, we have no names, pictures, or any information at all about the people that we converse with online. Like the dog said in the famous *New Yorker* cartoon, "On the Internet, nobody knows you are a dog."

In modern MMPORGs, there are sometimes elaborate systems in which you can choose the precise physical characteristics for the person you are online—your "avatar." Not surprisingly, in such games, there are a lot more beautiful and striking-looking people than there are in real life. This practice of make-believe is very self-conscious, and many academic papers have been written about how "identity" is "constructed" online in general.

When I went to make an avatar for myself in Second Life, long ago, I was pretty uncomfortable representing myself as anything other than what I am. Of course, I know that is supposed to be half the fun. Clearly, it is no fun for me. So I actually made an avatar that looks like me, more or less; it was hard to get right. I have always been personally uncomfortable representing myself online in any other way than how I really am. But I realize that I am unusual in this regard. Obviously, privacy matters.

Now, think of this. People who care very much about getting their facts right generally consult authoritative sources; they do not usually get their knowledge from casual conversation with friends and relatives. But at least, when we do get knowledge from a friend or relative, we have some idea of how reliable they are. Maybe you have an uncritical acquaintance who beliefs all sorts of crazy stuff. He spends little time considering the merits of his sources, or the plausibility of their claims. Your acquaintance may have many fascinating factoids and interesting stories, but probably, you are not going to take what he says very seriously.

But imagine if you were chatting online about conspiracy theories or UFOs, or other weird stuff, with someone you did not know was actually this acquaintance. You might actually take him more seriously in that case. You might take his bizarre claims somewhat more seriously. I do not mean that you would simply believe them—if you are like most of us, you would not—but you would not have any specific reasons to discount them, as you would if you knew you were talking to your acquaintance. Your only positive reason to discount the claims would be: I do not know this person, this person is anonymous. But you know that among anonymous people online, there can be smart, very reliable people, as well as crazies.

I think many of us would actually trust an anonymous person more than we would trust people we know are crazy. Now do not get me wrong, I do not mean to accuse anyone of being a dupe. Of course, we are able to spot really daft stuff no matter who it comes from. But without knowing who a person is, we are operating without a basic bit of information that we are used to having, in evaluating what people tell us face-to-face. If we lack any information at all about how reliable a source is, we will not simply conclude that the source is completely unreliable; we will often give the person the benefit of the doubt. That is sometimes more respect than we would give the person if we knew a few damning facts about him or her.

There is an attitude online—a common but not universal attitude—that it is not supposed to matter, in fact, who you are. We are supposed to be more or less equal in many online communities, except for what we say or do in those communities. Who we are offline is our private business so it does not really matter for many purposes online. But as it turns out, facts about us do matter when it comes to evaluating what people say about offline topics, like science and politics. The more time we spend in the Internet's egalitarian communities, the more contempt we might ultimately have for information about a person's real-world credibility. The very notion of personal credibility, or reliability, is ultimately undermined by online anonymity, I think. On a certain utopian view, no one should be held up as an expert, and no one should be dismissed as a crackpot. All views, from all people, about all subjects, should be considered with equal respect.

If that is what you think, be careful. Personal credibility is a universal notion; it can be found in all societies and throughout recorded history. There is a good reason that it is universal, as well: knowledge of a person's credibility, or lack thereof, is a great time-saver. If you know that someone knows a lot about a subject, then that person is, in fact, more likely to be correct than some random person opining about that subject. Now, the expert's opinion cannot take the place of thought on your part; usually, you probably should not simply adopt the expert's opinion. It is rarely that simple. But that does not mean the information about personal credibility is irrelevant or useless.

Two Ideas for a Solution

So far, I have mainly been criticizing the Internet, which you might find it odd for me to do. After all, I work online. I build and advise websites.

I do not think that the Internet is an unmitigated bad influence. I will not bore you by listing all the great things there are about the Internet, like being able to locate the source of a quote in a book quickly. Besides, I have only focused on a small number of problems, and I do not think they are necessarily Earth-shatteringly huge problems, either. But they are problems, and I think we can do a little bit to help solve them, or at least mitigate them.

First, we can make a role for experts in Internet knowledge communities. Of course, make the role so that does not conflict with what makes the community work. Do not simply put all the reins of authority in the hands of your experts; doing that would ensure that the project remains a project by and for experts, and of relatively little broader impact. But give them the authority to approve content, for example, or to post reviews, or other modest but useful tasks.

My hope is that, when the general public work under the "bottom up" guidance of experts, this will have some good effects. I think the content such a community might produce would be more reliable than the run of the mill on the Internet. I would also hope that the content itself will be more conducive to seeking knowledge instead of mere information, simply by modeling good reasoning and research.

I do worry, though, that if expert-reviewed information online were to become the norm, then people might be more likely to turn off their critical faculties.

Second, we can create new communities, in which real names and identities are expected, and we can reward people in old communities for using their real names and identities. This is something that Amazon.com has done, for example, with its "real name" feature on product reviews, and that Twitter used to do with its blue check system. If contributors are identified, we could use the same sort of methods to evaluate what they say online, that we would use if we were to run into them on the street.

I began by laying out a general problem: superabundance of information online is devaluing knowledge. I do not know if we can really solve this problem, but the two suggestions I just made might go a little way to making it a little better. First, if we identify the sources of our information, we will be in a better position to evaluate whether it actually justifies any belief. Second, if we include a modest role for experts in more of our Internet communities, we will have better information to begin with and better role models.

In any event, getting the nuggets of knowledge out of the mountains of information online begins with us—individually. We never really know anything if we are not willing to do the hard work of critically evaluating evidence. That is work we must do for ourselves. The Internet can only help.

Seven

Who Says We Know: On the
New Politics of Knowledge

This was an invited essay for Edge.org in 2007, as I was starting work on another wiki encyclopedia project, Citizendium. The piece goes into more detail about the balance I urged between amateur and expert contributions in online knowledge communities. Again, I have edited the essay for this volume while relegating linked citations and updates in my thinking to footnotes.

I

There are a lot of things that "everybody knows." Everybody knows that Everest is the tallest mountain on Earth, that 2+2=4, that most people have two eyes—and a lot of other things. If I were to go on, it would get tedious very fast, because, after all, these *are* things that everybody knows.

But there are also a lot of other things that we—some of us—say "everybody knows" except that not everybody agrees that everybody knows them. I am afraid this is very woolly so let me give an example. Everybody knows that there has been significant global warming recently, and also that human beings caused this by burning fossil fuels. We know that evolution is as solidly proven as most of the rest of science, and that intelligent design is not science at all; and that the U.S. government had nothing to do with the destruction of the World Trade Center. Except that, for each of these things "we all know," significant minorities insist that they are false.

Those dissenters, however, do not seem to matter much when it comes to most journalism, reference, and education. Society forges ahead, reporting and teaching things without usually mentioning the dissenters, or only in a disparaging light. As a result, certain claims that some of us do not accept end up being background knowledge, as I will call it.[1] If you question such background knowledge, or even express some doubt about it, you will look stupid, crazy, or immoral. Maybe all three.

To be able to determine society's background knowledge—to establish what "we all know"—is an awesome sort of power. This power can shape legislative agendas, steer the passions of crowds, educate whole generations, direct reading habits, and tar as radical or nutty whole groups of people who otherwise might seem perfectly normal. Exactly how this power is wielded and who wields it constitutes what we might call "the politics of knowledge." The politics of knowledge has changed tremendously over the years. In the Middle Ages, Europeans were told what they knew by the Church; after the printing press and the Reformation, by state censors and the licensers of publishers; with the rise of liberalism in the 19th

---

[1] This is not my own phrase. It is used especially by educationists, who treat such knowledge as that which it is important for students to know in order to, for example, be able to read a certain book. This is much discussed by E.D. Hirsch, e.g., in his *Why Knowledge Matters* (Harvard Education Press, 2016). Philosophers also deal with a similar concept, especially in social epistemology, in discussing the framework of beliefs in which a proposition is justified, or not.

and 20th centuries, by publishers themselves, and later by broadcast media and academics—in any case, by a small, elite group of professionals.

But we are now confronting a new politics of knowledge, with the rise of the Internet and particularly of the collaborative web—YouTube, Wikipedia, the Blogosphere, Reddit, and in short every website and type of aggregation that invites all comers to offer their knowledge and their opinions, and to rate content, products, places, and people. It is particularly the aggregation of public opinion that instituted this new politics of knowledge. In the 1990s, lots of people posted essays on their personal home pages, put up fan websites, and otherwise "broadcasted themselves." But what might have seemed merely vain and silly at the beginning of the World Wide Web is now, thanks to aggregation of various sorts, a contribution to an online mass movement. The collected content and ratings resulting from our individual efforts allow us to tap into a sort of collective authority that we did not have in the 20th century.

So today, it practically goes without saying that, if you want to find out what "everybody knows," you are not limited to looking at what *The New York Times* and *Encyclopedia Britannica* are taking for granted. You can turn to online sources that reflect a far broader spectrum of opinion than that of the aforementioned "small, elite group of professionals." Professionals are no longer needed for the bare purpose of the mass distribution of information and the shaping of opinion. The hegemony of the professional in determining our background knowledge is disappearing—a deeply profound truth that not everyone has fully absorbed.

The votaries of Web 2.0, and especially the devout defenders of Wikipedia, know this truth very well indeed. In their view, Wikipedia represents the democratization of knowledge itself, on a global scale, something possible for the first time in human history. Wikipedia allows everyone equal authority in stating what is known about any given topic. Their new politics of knowledge is deeply, passionately egalitarian.

Today's Establishment is nervous about Web 2.0 and Establishment-bashers love it, and for the same reason: its egalitarianism about knowledge means that, with the chorus (or cacophony) of voices out there, there is so much dissent, about *everything*, that there is a lot less of what "we all know." Insofar as the unity of our culture depends on a large body of background knowledge, handing a megaphone to everyone has the effect of fracturing our culture.[2]

I, at least, think it is wonderful that the power to declare what we all know is no longer exclusively in the hands of a professional elite. A giant, open, global conversation has just begun—one that will live on for the rest of human history—and its potential for good is tremendous. Perhaps our culture is fracturing, but we may choose to interpret that as the sign of a healthy liberal society, precisely because knowledge egalitarianism gives a voice to those minorities who think that what "we all know" is actually false.[3] And—as one of the fathers of modern liberalism, John Stuart Mill, argued—an unfettered, vigorous exchange of opinion ought to improve our grasp of the truth.

This makes a nice story; but it is not the whole story.

As it turns out, our many Web 2.0 revolutionaries have been so thoroughly seized with the successes of strong collaboration that they are resistant to recognizing some hard truths. As wonderful as it might be that the hegemony of professionals over knowledge is lessening, there is a downside: our grasp of and respect for reliable information suffers. With the rejection of professionalism has come a widespread rejection of expertise—of the proper role in society of people who make it

---

[2] It is all the more stunning, then, that in 2020 the social media successors of "Web 2.0" have fallen in line with the Establishment. More on this theme in this volume's final essay.

[3] Much of this once-heralded democratization of knowledge is now, in 2020, called "fake news": again, a theme in this volume's final essay.

their life's work to know stuff. This, I maintain, is not a positive development; but it is also not a necessary one. We can imagine a Web 2.0 with experts. We can imagine an Internet that is still egalitarian, but which is more open and welcoming to specialists. The new politics of knowledge that I advocate would place experts at the head of the table, but—unlike the old order—gives the general public a place at the table as well.

II

We want our encyclopedias to be as reliable as possible. There is a good reason for this. Ideally, we would like to be able to read an encyclopedia, believe what it says, and arrive at knowledge, not error. Now, according to one leading account of knowledge called "reliabilism," associated with philosophers like Alvin Goldman and Marshall Swain, knowledge is true belief that has been arrived at by a "reliable process" (say, getting a good look at something in good light) or through a "reliable indicator of truth" (say, proper use of a calculator).

Reliability is a comparative quality; something does not have to be perfectly reliable in order to be reliable. So, to say that an encyclopedia is reliable is to say that it contains an unusually high proportion of truth versus error, compared to various other publications. But it can still contain some error, and perhaps a high enough proportion of error that—as many have said recently—you should never use just one reference work if you want to be sure of something. Perhaps, if one could know that an encyclopedia were perfectly reliable, one could get knowledge just by reading, understanding, and believing it. What a wonderful world that would be. But I doubt both that there is a way of knowing that about an encyclopedia, and also that humanity will ever be blessed with such a reference work. Call such a thing a *perfect encyclopedia*. Well, there is no such thing as a perfect encyclopedia, and if there were, we would never know if we were holding one.

Why not? Well, when we say that encyclopedias should state the truth, do we mean the truth itself, or what the best-informed people take to be the truth—or perhaps even what the general public takes to be the truth? I would like to say "the truth itself," but we cannot simply point to the truth in the way we can point to the North Star. Some philosophers, called pragmatists, have said there is no such thing as "the truth itself," and that we should just consider the truth to be whatever the experts opine in "the ideal limit of inquiry" (in the phrase of C. S. Peirce). While I am not a pragmatist in this philosophical sense, I do think that it is misleading to say simply that encyclopedias aim at the truth. We cannot just leave it at that. Unfortunately, statements do not wear little labels reading "True!" and "False!" We need a criterion of encyclopedic truth—a method whereby we can determine whether a statement in an encyclopedia *is* true.

Let us suppose our criterion of encyclopedic truth is encoded in how encyclopedists decide whether to publish a statement. The method no doubt used by *Encyclopedia Britannica* and many other reference works goes something like this. If an expert article-writer states that *p* is true, and the editors find *p* plausible, and *p* gets past the fact-checkers (who consult other experts and expert-compiled resources), then *p* is true, at least as far as this encyclopedia is concerned.

The problem is that this is a highly fallible process. Sometimes, we discover that *p* is false. Sometimes, it is false because somebody made a typo or misinterpreted expert opinion; but sometimes it is false because, though faithful to expert opinion, expert opinion itself turned out to be false. Even if there were a beautifully reliable method of capturing expert opinion, that would not be an infallible criterion of encyclopedic truth, because expert opinion is frequently wrong. Unfortunately, as a society, we usually cannot do any better: if we learn that expert opinion is wrong, the corrected view becomes the new expert opinion. Besides, experts disagree about a lot of things. It is presumptuous, and a great disservice to readers, for editors to choose one expert to believe over another.

So we should not say that encyclopedias aim to capture either the truth itself or any perfectly reliable indicator of truth. That is too much to hope for from an encyclopedia. Instead, consider: what do we most *want*, as responsible, independent-minded researchers, out of an encyclopedia? Primarily, I think most of us want mainstream expert opinion stated clearly and accurately; but we do not want to ignore minority and popular views, either, precisely because we know that experts are sometimes wrong, even systematically wrong. We want well-agreed facts to be stated as such, but beyond that, we want to be able to consider the whole dialectical enchilada, so that we can make up our own minds for ourselves.

Notice that the word "expert" is used in various ways. For instance, journalists, interviewers, and conference organizers—people trying to gather an audience, in other words—use "expert" to mean "a person we can pass off as someone who can speak with some authority on a subject." Also, we say the "local expert" on a subject is the person who knows most, among those in a group, about the subject. Neither of these are the very interesting senses of "expert."

We also speak of experts in the *credentials* sense, that is, any person who meets a (vague) standard of credentials, or evidence of having studied (or practiced) some matter, to whatever extent is thought needed for expertise—for example, as defined by professional organizations. And finally, surely we also speak of experts in a more *objective* sense: someone who really does have expert knowledge of a subject, whatever that amounts to. On my view, objective expertise amounts to something like this: if we rely on the expert's opinion in matters of his or her expertise, that really does increase the probability that we have the truth. The higher the probability, the greater the expertise.

The hope is that expertise in the credentials sense is a good but imperfect sign of expertise in the objective sense.

Personally, I am not so cynical as to deny this. So, I believe that if someone meets a certain standard of credentials about some topic, then that person is probably more reliable on that topic than someone picked at random. Bear in mind, however, that "credentials" should be construed very broadly, and can mean much more than simply degrees and certifications; it can mean any sort of evidence of knowledge.

I say that encyclopedias should represent expert opinion first and foremost, but also minority and popular views. Here, surely we are stuck with the credentials sense of "expert opinion." Just as statements do not bear labels announcing their truth values, people do not bear labels announcing their objective expertise. When decision makers have to decide whether a person really is, objectively, an expert, they have to use evidence that they can agree upon. But any such evidence can count as a "credential" in a broad sense. No doubt some wholly uncredentialed people have expertise in the objective sense—some autodidacts must fit the bill. Moreover, it is surely possible for other people to come to recognize such hidden expertise. But when groups must make decisions about who is an expert, they must have evidence; if evidence of expertise, or credentials, is lacking, the decision makers cannot be expected to acquaint themselves deeply with each person individually. What if someone who is unquestionably an expert does interview, and declare to be an expert, an autodidact who is wholly uncredentialed? Then that opinion is the autodidact's first credential.

Even given this goal, why not simply grant the authority to articulate what we know to experts, as *Britannica* does? Can experts not do a good job of representing mainstream and minority expert views as well as popular views? Or, on the other hand, why not give this authority to the general public, as Wikipedia does? Can the general public in time get expert opinion right? Surely.

First, why open up encyclopedia projects to the general public? While the whole body of people called "experts" (in any very restrictive sense) are probably capable of writing about and representing the interests and views of the larger public, the trouble is that they will not actually want to do so, or they lack the time to do so, in as much detail as the public itself is capable of. It is difficult and tedious enough for experts to cover their own areas. While there are people with expertise about popular culture—from celebrity journalists, to video game designers, to master craft workers—there are far more people who can do a good job summarizing information about "popular" topics than there are experts about them. Similarly, there are usually a number of experts about theories that are far out of the mainstream—one thinks of people who have expert knowledge of astrology, or some kinds of alternative medicine—but again, the quantity of non-expert people able to write reasonably well about such theories is much greater.

I will have no truck with the view that simply because something is out of the mainstream—unscientific, irrational, speculative, or politically incorrect—it therefore does not belong in an encyclopedia. Non-mainstream views need a full airing in an encyclopedia, despite the fact that "the best expert opinion" often holds them in contempt. Such views need an airing if for no other reason than that we will then have better grounds on which to reject them. Moreover, as we are responsible for our own beliefs, and as the freedom to believe as we wish is essential to our dignity as human beings, encyclopedias do not have any business making decisions for us that we, who wish to remain as intellectually free as possible, would prefer to make ourselves.[4]

There is another reason to engage the public: due to its sheer size, the public can also contribute enormous breadth and extra eyeballs for all sorts of the more usually "expert" topics, too. The general public may add a far greater assortment of topics and perspectives than one would get if one assigned only experts to write about only their areas of expertise. Moreover, the sheer quantity of eyeballs gazing at obvious mistakes

---

[4] For elaboration of this argument, see Chapter 3 in this volume.

means that such mistakes will be fixed more quickly and reliably than if one engages only experts working only on their areas of expertise. Finally, and perhaps most importantly, the inclusion of the general public in an encyclopedia project, and ensuring that all subjects are treated at once, will tend to reduce the insularity common to many specialized fields: the result is that the encyclopedia's readers will be subjected less to dogmatic presentations of wrongheaded intellectual fads.[5]

Therefore, the assistance of the general public is needed in encyclopedia projects. Now let us turn to the other group: why are experts needed? Or perhaps a better question is: why it is important to ensure that experts are involved?

Experts, or specialists, possess unusual amounts of knowledge about particular topics. Because of their knowledge, they can often sum up what is known on a topic much more efficiently than a non-specialist can. Also, they often know things that virtually no non-specialist knows. Due to their personal connections and their knowledge of the literature, they often can lay their hands on resources that extend their knowledge even further.

Another thing that experts can do, that few non-experts can, is write about their specializations in a style that is credible and professional-sounding. Frequently, students and dabblers possess an adequate understanding of the basics of a topic, but they are wholly incapable of saying much about it without revealing their inexpert knowledge, in one way or another—even if they are superb writers and even if what they say is correct, strictly speaking. This is a common problem on Wikipedia. Furthermore, while a great many specialists are terrible writers, some of the very best writers on any given topic are specialists about that topic. Many experts take great

---

[5] This has turned out to be false. I was assuming that a public project would not artificially limit itself, say, to expert opinion as articulated by secondary Establishment sources—as the Wikipedia of 2020 generally does.

pride in their ability to write about their own fields for non-experts.

Finally, experts are—albeit fallibly—the best-suited to articulate what expert opinion is. It is for the most part experts who create the resources that fact-checkers use to check facts. This makes their direct input in an encyclopedia invaluable.

For these reasons, I believe experts should share the main responsibility of articulating what "we know" in encyclopedia projects; but they should share this responsibility with the general public. Involving both groups in a content production system has the best chance of faithfully representing the full spectrum of expression. To exclude the public is to put readers at the mercy of wrongheaded intellectual fads and propaganda masquerading as scholarship; and to exclude experts, or to fail to give them a special role in an encyclopedia project, is to risk getting expert opinion wrong.

III

The most massive encyclopedia in history—well, the most massive thing often called an encyclopedia—is Wikipedia. But Wikipedia has no special role for experts in its content production system. So, can it be relied upon to get mainstream expert opinion right?

Wikipedia's defenders are capable of arguing at great length that expert involvement is not necessary. They are entirely committed to what I call *dabblerism*, by which I mean the view that no one should have any special role or authority in a content creation system simply on account of their expertise. I apologize for the neologism, but there is no word meaning precisely this view. I did not want to use "amateurism," since that word is opposed to "professionalism," and the view I want to discuss attacks not the privileges of professionals, per se, but of experts. The issue here is not whether people should make money from their work, but whether their special knowledge should give them some special authority. To the latter, dabblerism says no.

Wikipedia's defenders have a great many arguments for dabblerism: non-experts can create great things; the "wisdom of crowds" makes deference to experts unnecessary; studies appear to confirm this in the case of Wikipedia; there is no *prima facie* reason to give experts any special role; it is only fair to judge people by what they do, and not by their credentials; and making a role for experts will actually ruin the collaborative process.

Not one of these arguments is any good.

First, it is absolutely true that dabbleristic (if you will), expert-spurning content creation systems can create amazing things. That is what Web 2.0 is all about. While many might sneer at these productions generally, Web 2.0 has created some quite useful and interesting websites. Wikipedia and YouTube are not popular for nothing, and for many people they are endlessly fascinating.

This does not go the slightest way toward showing, however, that some sort of expert guidance is neither needed, nor would be a positive addition to, content creation systems, and particularly to encyclopedia projects. Many people have looked at Wikipedia's articles and concluded that they sure could use work by experts and real editors. It is one thing to say that Wikipedia is amazing and useful; it is quite another to say that we could not do better by adding a role for experts.[6]

At this point, my opponent might pull out a very interesting and popular book called *The Wisdom of Crowds* by James Surowiecki,[7] and say that it shows that Wikipedia has no need of expert reviewers. Surowiecki explains some fascinating phenomena, but nowhere does he say that Wikipedia does not need experts. And no surprise: by Surowiecki's own criteria,

---

[6] This is still evident to me today, in 2020, when I look at articles on topics I know a great deal about. Looking at articles on topics one is ignorant about is no test of anything.

[7] Anchor Books, 2005.

there is no reason to think that Wikipedia displays "the wisdom of crowds." Let me explain.

In the introduction of the book, Surowiecki describes an agricultural fair in England in 1906, at which all manner of people competed to guess the weight of an ox. There were many non-experts in the crowd, so the average of the guesses should have been ridiculously far off; but in fact, while the ox actually weighed in at 1,198 pounds, the average of the guesses was 1,197 pounds. This, Surowiecki says, illustrates a widely-recurring phenomenon, in which ordinary folks in great numbers acting independently can display behavior that, in aggregate, is more "wise," or accurate, than the greatest expert among them.

Of course, Surowiecki is no fool. His claim is not that whatever "crowds" produce is reliable, regardless of circumstances. Among other things, each member of a "crowd" needs make decisions independently of each other. But this is precisely how Wikipedia does not work. As he writes:

Diversity and independence are important because the best collective decisions are the product of disagreement and contest, not consensus or compromise. An intelligent group, especially when confronted with cognition problems, does not ask its members to modify their positions in order to let the group reach a decision everyone can be happy with.[8]

But that is exactly what happens on wikis, and on Wikipedia. To be able to work together at all, consensus and compromise are the name of the game. As a result, the Wikipedian "crowd" can often agree upon some pretty ridiculous claims, which are very far from both expert opinion and from anything like an "average" of public opinion on a subject. I do not mean to say that the Wikipedia process is not robust and does not produce a lot of correct answers. It is and

---

[8] *Ibid*, p. xix.

it does: that is why Wikipedia is useful, a point I have never denied. But the process does not closely resemble the "wise crowd" phenomena that Surowiecki is explaining.

Besides, the standard examples demonstrating the strength of group guessing—say, that a classroom's average guess of the number of jelly beans in a jar is better than all individual guesses, or that experts cannot outperform financial markets—do not lend the slightest bit of support to the notion that experts and editors are not needed for publishing or content creation. There are objective facts about the number of jelly beans, or about market prices, that experts can be right or wrong about. But what facts are Wikipedians attempting to describe? Objective facts that you can point to like a stock price in a newspaper? Only rarely. The facts they want to amass are facts contained in the books and articles that, it so happens, they are so keen on citing. Who writes those books and articles? Experts, mostly. To say that expert guidance is not really needed in encyclopedia construction is like saying the opinion of the person who counted out the jelly beans before putting them in the jar is not really useful.

It is easy to be impressed with the apparent quality of Wikipedia's articles. One must admit that some of the articles look very impressive, replete with multiple sections, surprising length, pictures, tables, a dry, authoritative-sounding style, and so forth. These are all good things (except for the style). But these same impressive-looking articles are all too frequently full of errors or half-truths, and—just as bad—poor writing and incoherent organization.[9] In short, Wikipedia's dabblerism often unsurprisingly leads to amateurish results.

Some might point to *Nature*'s December 2005 investigative report—often billed as a scientific study, though it was not peer-reviewed—that purported to show, of a set of 42 articles, that whereas the *Britannica* articles averaged around three

---

[9] Jaron Lanier was eloquent on the latter points in his essay "Digital Maoism," *Edge.org*, May 29, 2006, https://bit.ly/3f914fE.

errors or omissions, Wikipedia averaged around four. Wikipedia did remarkably well. But the article proved very little, as *Britannica* staff pointed out a few months later. There were many problems: the tiny sample size, the poor way the comparison articles were chosen and constructed, and the failure to quantify the degree of errors or the quality of writing. But the most significant problem, as I see it, was that the comparison articles were all chosen from scientific topics. Wikipedia can be expected to excel in scientific and technical topics, simply because there is relatively little disagreement about the facts in these disciplines. (Also because contributors to wikis tend to be technically-minded, but this probably matters less than that it is hard to get scientific facts wrong when you are simply copying them out of a book.) Other studies have appeared, but they provide nothing remotely resembling statistical confirmation that Wikipedia has anything like *Britannica*-levels of quality. One has to wonder what the results would have been if *Nature* had chosen 1,000 *Britannica* articles randomly, and then matched Wikipedia articles up with those, and finally invited raters to participate in a controlled, double-blind study removing all evidence of where articles came from.[10]

Let us set aside the question whether Wikipedia's quality does, at present, rival *Britannica*'s. One might argue that, even if it does not, there is still no *prima facie* reason to give experts any special role in the project. To give authority to people simply on the basis of their expertise is simply "credentialism"—as Wikipedians often say—and no more rational than rejecting an application from a stellar programmer simply because he lacks a B.S. in Computer

---

[10] To my knowledge, no one has yet constructed a comprehensive, comparative study of this sort, as of 2020. Wikipedia itself maintains a review of the literature, in its "Reliability of Wikipedia" article (accessed July 2020), https://bit.ly/2EpmiZT.

Science. People should be judged based on their demonstrated abilities, not degrees.

But I can agree with that. There is no reason whatsoever to insist on any simpleminded approach to identifying experts. Some of the finest programmers in the world lack any computer science degrees, and it would be silly to fail to recognize that fact. But there is no reason why a content creation system could not recognize as a "credential," or as proof of expertise, all manner of evidence, not just degrees.

Similarly, Wikipedians have a sort of moral argument for their dabblerism: they say, sometimes, that it is only fair to judge people based on what they do, not who they are. Meritocracy is the only fair way to justify differing levels of editorial authority in open projects; and a genuine meritocracy would assign authority not based on "credentials," but only based on what people have demonstrated they can do for the project. It is wrong and unfair to hand out authority based on credentials.

But, interestingly, Wikipedians cannot help themselves to this argument. If they are fully committed to dabblerism, then they cannot justify different levels of editorial authority on *any* grounds. Dabblerism, as I said, is the view that no one should have any special role or authority in a content creation system simply on account of their expertise. But we can easily identify, as a kind of expertise, the proven ability to do excellent work. So dabblerism, as I defined it, is incompatible with meritocracy itself. There is another way to make this point. Define "credential" as "evidence of expertise." If we reject the use of credentials, we reject all evidence of expertise; ergo, lacking any means of establishing who is an expert, we reject expertise itself. Meritocrats are necessarily expert-lovers.

I find the moral argument annoying for another reason, however. It implies that degrees, certificates, licenses, association memberships, papers, books, presentations, awards, and all other possible evidence of expertise—the whole gamut of "credentials"—just do not matter. They do not constitute good evidence of anything. But if they do not count as good evidence of expertise, why should the ability to do something on behalf of a mere Internet project count as good evidence? In fact, there is a bizarre reversal in the insular world of Wikipedia: mere *quantity* of wiki-writing is a credential there, while it is useless for academic tenure and advancement committees; meanwhile, degrees and peer-reviewed papers are credentials for tenure and advancement committees, but not for Wikipedia and its ilk. Wikipedians will protest that quantity of work does not really matter. But, of course, it very much does.

The last hope for rescuing dabblerism might come in the form of an argument that the use of experts will render the project less collaborative; it will "kill the goose that lays the golden eggs." Wiki-style collaboration requires that there be no differences in authority. According to this argument, we are committed to dabblerism if we want to enjoy the fruits of bottom-up collaboration.

But this is little better than an untested prejudice. The notion that experts cannot play a gentle guiding role in a genuinely bottom-up collaborative project seems to be plain old bigotry. No doubt this prejudice stems from a fear that experts will twist what should be an efficient process into the sort of slow, top-down, bureaucratic drudgery that they are used to. But this need not be the case.[11] Surely it is not impossible for professors to exit the cathedral—to borrow Eric Raymond's metaphor in his essay "The Cathedral and the

---

[11] Citizendium, which was launching as I wrote this essay in spring of 2007, can be regarded as an experiment testing this hypothesis. I will not explore the results here, except to say the following. Citizendium showed quite definitively that experts and the general public can work together side-by-side without slowing the process in any way at all. If Citizendium failed to take off, it was probably because it was attempting to launch a project too similar to Wikipedia at precisely the time when Wikipedia was enjoying its own greatest rate of growth. It was hard to beat a young 800-pound gorilla on its own turf.

Bazaar"[12]—and wander the bazaar, offering guidance and highlighting what is excellent. Will that necessarily make the bazaar less of a bazaar?

None of these arguments for dismissing special roles for experts in encyclopedia projects is any good. The support for dabblerism—as I have defined the term—would appear irrational. Is it really?

IV

Here is a little dilemma. Wikipedia pooh-poohs the need for expert guidance; but how, then, does it propose to establish its own reliability? It can do so either by reference to something external to itself or else something internal, such as a poll of its own contributors. If it chooses something external to itself— such as the oft-cited *Nature* report—then it is conceding the authority of experts. In that case, who is it who says "we know"? Experts, at least partially: their view is still treated as the touchstone of Wikipedia's reliability. And if it concedes the authority of experts that far, why not bring those experts on board in an official capacity, and do a better job?

If, on the other hand, Wikipedia proposes to establish its own reliability "internally," for example through polls of its contributors, or through sheer quantity of edits, they have a ridiculously untenable position. The position entails that the word of an enormous, undifferentiated, and largely anonymous crowd of people is to be trusted, or held reliable, for no other reason than that it is such a crowd. It is one thing to argue for "the wisdom of crowds" by reference to an objective benchmark, or a reasonable proxy thereof. It is quite another thing to maintain that crowds are wise simply because they are crowds. That is a philosophical view, a variety of relativism,

---

[12] Free online, and also in Eric S. Raymond, *The Cathedral and the Bazaar: Musings on Linux and Open Source by an Accidental Revolutionary*, Revised & Expanded edition (O'Reilly, 2001).

according to which the only truth there is, the only facts there are, are literally "socially constructed" by crowds like the contributors to Wikipedia.

It is this view that Stephen Colbert was able to mock so effectively as "wikiality": reality is what the wiki says it is.[13] Colbert has in effect added to what "we all know." By skewering the notion that facts are whatever Wikipedians want them to be, Colbert has added to our culture's modest stock of background knowledge—about philosophy. Thanks to Colbert, we all know now that reality is not created by a wiki. That is no mean feat for a humorist.

But nobody really believes that reality is constructed by Wikipedia. Instead, Wikipedians attempt to take my dilemma by the horns, supporting the credibility of Wikipedia's content through a combination of both external and internal means. On the one hand, they insist that citations suffice support claim; after all, what else would? If a fact has been supported by a footnote, then, apparently, it is credible. This, we might say, is an external means of fact-checking; but it is up to rank-and-file Wikipedians, not any fancy experts, to add and edit the footnotes, and so it is also an internal means of fact-checking. So, where is the dilemma?

The dilemma is easy to apply here, too. If Wikipedians actually believe that the credibility of articles is improved by citing things written by experts, or articles summarizing the work of experts,[14] will it not improve them even more if people like the experts cited are given a modest role in the project? And, on the other hand, if (somehow) it is not the fact that the cited references were created by experts, one has to wonder what the references are for. They have a mysterious, talismanic value, apparently. It seems that we all know that

---

[13] The segment aired on the Colbert Report, July 31, 2006; see https://on.cc.com/2P5SN1r.

[14] I say this because Wikipedia officially avoids primary sources in favor of secondary sources.

footnotes makes articles much more credible—but why? Whatever the reason, Wikipedians would not want to say that it is because the people cited are credible authorities on their subjects.

The dilemma Wikipedia finds itself in, then, is that if it wants to establish its credibility literally by reference to expert opinion, then it has no reason not to invite experts to join in some advisory capacity. But this is completely intolerable for Wikipedians. Now, why is that?

Wikipedia is deeply egalitarian. We might describe one of its guiding principles as *epistemic* (knowledge) *egalitarianism.* According to epistemic egalitarianism, we are all fundamentally equal in our authority or rights to articulate what should pass for knowledge; the only grounds on which a claim can compete against other claims are to be found in the content of the claim itself, never in who makes it.

Notice that (on my account) this is a doctrine about rights or authority, not about ability; it would be simply absurd to say that we are equal in ability *to* declare what should pass for knowledge. Someone who has never had a course in physics is unlikely to be equal to a Nobel laureate in physics in his ability to declare what is known about physics. But epistemic egalitarianism would hold them equal in rights—for example, in the right to change a wiki page about a topic in physics—nonetheless.

Note also that epistemic egalitarianism does not declare we have the right to say what really is known—that too would be absurd—but only what passes for knowledge, or what is presented as known, for example through Wikipedia's mechanisms, or through those kinds of social media, like Reddit and Quora, that operate like a democratic popularity contest. In fact, Wikipedia would be the perfect vehicle for epistemic egalitarianism, or it would be if it actually did allow virtually everyone to edit virtually any page. In fact, Wikipedia's "administrators" have rights that others do not have, and some participants do tend to dominate and shut down others, as often happens in egalitarian communities.

Epistemic egalitarianism is fashionable.[15] It is precisely the fact that this doctrine speaks about our rights to declare what passes for knowledge that makes epistemic egalitarianism a doctrine about the politics of knowledge. So, who says "we know"? We all do.

Put that way, perhaps the appeal of the doctrine should be plain. I find it rather compelling myself. I began this essay by saying that the power to declare society's background knowledge is awesome, and that many consequential decisions, including political decisions, are deeply influenced by that background knowledge. If the Internet now makes it possible for society's background knowledge to be shaped by a far broader, more open and inclusive group of people, that would seem to be a good thing. Indeed, perhaps it is only an accident of history, not any good reason, that placed the epistemic leadership of society almost exclusively in the hands of a fairly small class of professionals. But now, through another accident of history—the rise of the Internet—the general public may partake in the conversations that determine what "everybody knows." I think this is mostly a positive development.

No doubt the main philosophical reason for epistemic egalitarianism is, like the reason for egalitarianism generally, the now-common and overarching desire for fairness. The desire for fairness creates hostility toward any authority—and not just when authority uses its power to gain an unfair advantage, but toward authority as such. That is, the most radical egalitarians advocate that our situations be made as equal as possible, including in terms of authority. But, in our specialist-friendly modern society, expertise can confer much authority not available to non-experts. Perhaps the most

---

[15] Insofar as Wikipedia circa 2020 has become yet another mouthpiece of the Establishment, however, I do not think that in the end it really did end up as a good representative of epistemic egalitarianism, even if it was one in 2007. See Chapter 12 of this volume.

important and fundamental authority experts have is the authority to declare what is known. This authority, then, should be placed in the hands of everyone equally, according to a thoroughgoing egalitarianism.

I support meritocracy: I think experts deserve a prominent voice in declaring what is known, because knowledge is their life. As fallible as they are, experts, as society has traditionally identified them, are more likely to be correct than non-experts, particularly when a large majority of independent experts about an issue are in broad agreement about it. In saying this, I am merely giving voice to an assumption that underlies many of our institutions and practices. Experts know particular topics particularly well. By paying closer attention to experts, we improve our chances of getting the truth; by ignoring them, we throw our chances to the wind. Thus, if we reduce experts to the level of the rest of us, even when they speak about their areas of knowledge, we reduce society's collective grasp of the truth.

That said, the public deserves a seat at the table it did not have throughout most of history. Wikipedia's tremendous usefulness shows the wisdom of that policy.

Still, it is no exaggeration to say that epistemic egalitarianism, as illustrated especially by Wikipedia, places Truth in the service of Equality. Ultimately, at the bottom of the debate, the deep modern commitment to specialization is in an epic struggle with an equally deep modern commitment to egalitarianism. It is Truth versus Equality, and as much as I love Equality, if it comes down to choosing, I am on the side of Truth.[16]

---

[16] I stand by the conclusions of this essay. The fight that turned out to matter fifteen years later was not the one between amateurs and experts, but about *de facto* control of Wikipedia. Control has been wrested from a broad cross-section of the public and placed in the hands of operatives of all sorts. Given how powerful knowledge is, this was inevitable in retrospect. More about this in Chapter 12.

Eight

Individual Knowledge
in the Internet Age

Published April 2010, this paper seeks to restrain the irrational exuberance many had for education technology tools applied outside of their proper sphere, failing to appreciate the enduring importance of individual knowledge and its perennial requirements. Lightly edited for this volume.

IN the last several years, many observers of education and learning have been stunned by the abundance of information online, the ever-faster findability of answers, and the productivity of online "crowds," which have created information resources like Wikipedia and YouTube. The enormous scope of these developments has surprised me too, despite the fact that they are more or less what many of us had hoped for and deliberately tried to bring into being. These sudden, revolutionary developments demand analysis: How is this latest information explosion changing the way we live? Is the relationship between society and individual changing?

More to the point for this article, how is the Internet revolution changing learning and knowledge?

I will analyze three common strands of current thought about learning, knowledge, and the Internet. First is the idea that the instant availability of information online makes the memorization of facts unnecessary or less necessary. Second is the celebration of the virtues of collaborative learning as superior to outmoded individual learning. And third is the insistence that lengthy, complex books, which constitute a single, static, one-way conversation with an individual, are inferior to knowledge co-constructed by members of a group.

Though seemingly disparate, these three strands of thought are interrelated. Each tends to substitute the Internet—both a resource and an innovative way to organize people—for individual learning and knowledge. I have devoted my Internet career to creating educational tools, so I am sympathetic to the use of the Internet for education. But I believe that it is a profound mistake to think that digital tools can replace the effortful, careful development of the individual mind—the sort of development that is fostered by a solid liberal arts education.

Unnecessary Memorization

Whenever I encounter yet another instance of educationists' arguments against "memorizing," the following rather abstract yet simple thought springs to mind: Surely the only way to know something is to have memorized it. How can I be said to know something that I do not remember? So being opposed to memorizing has always sounded to me like being opposed to knowledge. I realize this argument likely seems glib. The thing educationists object to, of course, is not remembering or even memorizing but rather memorizing *by rote*—that is, by dull repetition and often without experience or understanding.

In a December 2008 interview, Don Tapscott, a popular author on the subject of the Internet and society, argued that the Internet is now "the fountain of knowledge" and that students need not memorize particular facts such as historical dates. "It is enough that they know about the Battle of Hastings," he said, "without having to memorize that it was in 1066. They can look that up and position it in history with a click on Google."[1] Or, I would add, on Wikipedia. This attitude is so common among student users of Wikipedia that some teachers bemoan its very existence. They sometimes declare that since the free online encyclopedia is so huge and easy to use, they feel less pressure to commit "trivia" to memory. In 2010, the website *Edge* asked 172 prominent scientists and thinkers: "How is the Internet changing the way you think?"[2] One of the main themes of the responses was that, metaphorically put, we will soon be "uploading our brains" to the Internet—or more literally, we will be relying increasingly on the Internet as an extension or prosthesis of our memory.[3] As then-18-year-old David Dalrymple (to take just one example) noted:

Before the Internet, most professional occupations required a large body of knowledge, accumulated over years or even decades of experience. But now, anyone with good critical thinking skills and the ability to focus on the important information can retrieve it on demand from the Internet, rather than her own memory. On the other hand, those with wandering minds, who might once have been able to focus by isolating themselves with their work, now often cannot work without the Internet, which simultaneously furnishes a

---

[1] Tapscott quoted in Alexandra Frean, "Google Generation Has No Need for Rote Learning," *Times* (London), December 2, 2008, https://bit.ly/3hjpJzI.

[2] "How is the Internet changing the way you think?" The *Edge* Annual Question of 2010, https://bit.ly/32EIZ6C.

[3] This curious description of the Internet as a mental "prosthesis" is not my own. See, for example, Stephen M. Kosslyn, "A Small Price to Pay," *Edge*, https://bit.ly/2OGZHdm, and Clifford Pickover, "The Rise of Internet Prosthetic Brains and Soliton Personhood," *Edge*, https://bit.ly/2ZFyf5Y. I myself addressed the issue in "The Un-Focusing, De-Liberating Effects of Joining the Hive Mind," *Edge*, https://bit.ly/3hmeQNz.

panoply of unrelated information—whether about their friends' doings, celebrity news, limericks, or millions of other sources of distraction. The bottom line is that how well an employee can focus might now be more important than how knowledgeable he is. Knowledge was once an internal property of a person, and focus on the task at hand could be imposed externally, but with the Internet, knowledge can be supplied externally, but focus must be forced internally.[4]

Dalrymple explicitly draws the conclusion—that the Internet has made acquiring "a large body of knowledge" unnecessary, since it can be "supplied externally"—that Tapscott implicitly conveyed in his interview. Of course, nobody is saying that knowledge is unimportant. Tapscott, for example, says simply that knowing the exact date of the Battle of Hastings is not important. Dalrymple says only that acquiring a "large" body of knowledge is not necessary. So is this merely a practical problem of detail, the problem of distinguishing the essential, important-to-remember items from the trivial, just-look-it-up-on-Google items?

No. In fact, this is a deeply theoretical and crucial issue. What counts as trivial? How much knowledge is enough, so that more than that would be a large body of (presumably unnecessary) individual knowledge? And what makes acquiring knowledge valuable in the first place? I suspect that these questions are ultimately beside the point for those who suppose the Internet makes knowledge less important. Their point is merely that we can now learn less than we have learned in the past, again because the Internet is such a ready mental prosthesis.

But to claim that the Internet allows us to learn less, or that it makes memorizing less important, is to belie any profound grasp of the nature of knowledge. Finding a fact about a topic with a search in Wolfram Alpha, for example, is very different

---

[4] David Dalrymple, "Knowledge Is Out, Focus Is In, and People Are Everywhere," *Edge* (as of 2020, no longer online).

indeed from grasping and integrating some piece of knowledge. Having well-understood knowledge ready to recall is far different from merely getting an unfamiliar answer to a question. Reading a few sentences in Wikipedia about some theories on the causes of the Great Depression does not mean that one thereby knows or understands this topic. Being able to read (or view) something quickly on a topic can provide one with information, but actually having a knowledge of or understanding about the topic will always require critical study. The Internet will never change that.

Moreover, if you read an answer to a question, you usually need fairly substantial background knowledge to interpret the answer. For example, if you have never memorized any dates, then when you discover from Wikipedia that the Battle of Hastings took place in 1066, this fact will mean absolutely nothing to you. (Anyone who has tried to teach a little history to young children, as I have to my three-year-old, knows this.) Indeed, you need knowledge in order to know what questions to ask. Defenders of liberal arts education often remind us that the point of a good education is not merely to amass a lot of facts.[5] The point is to develop judgment or understanding of questions that require a nuanced grasp of the various facts and to thereby develop the ability to think about and use them. If you do not have copious essential facts at the ready, then you will not be able to make wise judgments that depend on your understanding of those facts, regardless of how fast you can look them up.

If public intellectuals can say, without being laughed at and roundly condemned, that the Internet makes learning ("memorizing") facts unnecessary because facts can always be looked up, then I fear that we have come to a very low point in our intellectual culture. I fear we have completely devalued or, perhaps worse, forgotten about the deep importance of the sort

---

[5] John Henry Newman, in *The Idea of a University* (1873), is my favorite example.

of nuanced, rational, and relatively unprejudiced understanding of issues that a liberal education provides.

That I make this point may seem ironic. After all, in place of rote memorizing of trivia, practically everybody agrees that we should "learn how to learn"—and this is one of the hallmarks of a liberal education. Tapscott argued that the ability to learn new things is more important than ever "in a world where you have to process new information at lightning speed." He added: "Children are going to have to reinvent their knowledge base multiple times. So for them memorizing facts and figures is a waste of time."[6] This is an old argument of many educationists: the ever-changing nature of science and technology in the information age makes it unnecessary to amass a lot of soon-to-be-out-of-date knowledge. Since an ever-expanding amount of information and research is frequently updating our understanding of disciplines, there is no reason to insist on memorizing facts and figures—and no reason to insist on a core of basic knowledge and books that should be mastered.

But this argument seems fallacious. It implies that the new information has either replaced or made trivial the old information. This is obviously not so in most subjects. Think of all the things typically taught in primary schools: reading, writing, mathematics, basic science. How much of this has changed in the last one hundred years? Even granting that some of our understanding, especially at more advanced levels, has been replaced (as in nuclear physics and geography) or refined (as in biology and history), the vast body of essential facts that undergird any sophisticated understanding of the way the world works does not change rapidly.[7] This is as true

---

[6] Quoted in Frean, "Google Generation."

[7] In an article footnote, John Seely Brown and Richard P. Adler approvingly quote someone as saying that the "half life" of much technical information is "now less than four years." Perhaps. Some, not much, information changes fast, as long as we are talking about

in biology and medicine, fields with stunning recent advances, as it is in mathematics and philosophy.[8] To return to my point, unless one learns the basics in those fields, Googling a question will merely allow one to parrot an answer—not to understand it.

It also will not do to make the facile reply that there is no such thing as "the basics." The basics can be understood as what is commonly taught in introductory courses or what commonly appears in introductory textbooks. Granted, there are some new and specialized fields in which there are relatively few basics that everyone is taught—I am thinking of computer programming, design, social media, and knowledge management. But in most fields, there is certainly a body of core knowledge.

To possess a substantial understanding of a field requires not just memorizing the facts and figures that are used by everyone in the field but also practicing, using, and internalizing those basics. To return to my "glib" argument, surely the only way to begin to know something is to have memorized it.

Outmoded Individual Learning

Belittling substantial knowledge as unnecessary rote memorization, in the new age of Internet searching, is only one way in which the Internet is being made to substitute for

---

technology—but that is the nature of technology. It is not the nature of the basic arts and sciences. Formulating educational policy about all of knowledge based on the nature of technical knowledge seems like a very bad idea. John Seely Brown and Richard P. Adler, "Minds on Fire: Open Education, the Long Tail, and Learning 2.0," *EDUCAUSE Review*, vol. 43, no. 1 (January/February 2008), p. 32 (note #21), https://bit.ly/2ZIsIeU.

[8] Would you like to be treated by a doctor who believed that he or she did not need to memorize the basic facts and figures of the field because the field is changing quickly, and facts can looked up in a medical database?

the difficult work of developing individual minds. Another way is to suggest that collaborative work via the Internet makes more traditional modes of study old-fashioned and also unnecessary. The first attack is on the content of learning; the second is on the method.

I have some acquaintance with the use of online collaboration in learning. My appreciation for it began in the mid-1990s when I was a philosophy graduate student. I started several mailing lists and organized careful readings of some philosophy books. I also started an online philosophical society, which hosted fascinating discussions of many topics. I learned quite a bit from these extracurricular activities. Later, in the first years of Wikipedia, I saw collaboration being used in course assignments. Then a few years later, I had students in my philosophy of law course post their writings and discussions on a wiki. Another wiki encyclopedia project I started, Citizendium, officially invited college teachers to assign group-written encyclopedia articles via our Eduzendium program. These various experiences have given me some practical idea of the merits and drawbacks of collaborative learning online.

My own view of online collaborative learning is that it *can* be an excellent method of (1) exchanging written ideas, especially when those involved are interested and motivated, via student forums, and (2) obtaining free public reviews of students' work, on wikis. There are drawbacks with each of these, however. First, as to online student forums, attempting to spark a lively online, real-time, always-on conversation among reluctant students is apt to be about as easy as sparking a more traditional lively conversation among similarly reluctant students. To be sure, things can go brilliantly, if you are lucky; but the remarks can be disappointingly perfunctory and not apt to teach much to anyone except, maybe, the student making them. I think some teachers who are early adopters of online student forums probably became enthusiastic about the prospects because of their own experiences, in which conversing online with colleagues and fellow hobbyists can be a fantastic way of learning about one's interests. But there is no reason to think that adopting the tool—online conversation—will necessarily reproduce, in students, either the motivation to pursue interests or the resulting increase in knowledge.

Regarding the second method—getting reviews of students' work via online discussion, and wikis in particular—I and my colleagues have discovered that can be a handy way for teachers to avoid having to read and give feedback on early drafts of student work. Having students post their work on Citizendium,[9] which has many important topics still wide open, can result in their getting feedback from "the regulars," and that can be very valuable. One problem, however, is that a significant level of useful feedback cannot be guaranteed. Some students might get a huge amount of feedback, and others might get none, and that hardly seems fair.

Another way of using wikis (and similar online collaborative tools) is to require students to work together online on co-written papers. But collaboration alone will not reliably create the same magic and excitement among students as was created in the days of Wikipedia's growth. For one thing, many Wikipedians have been motivated by vanity—by a desire see their own words prevail as representing "what is known" on a subject. In contrast, students who are required by a teacher to write articles together do not suddenly acquire such a motivation from the use of the tool, especially when using a private collaboration tool such as Google Docs.

So it goes, I suspect, with all social media. There is no reason to think that repurposing social media for education will magically make students more inspired and engaged.

---

[9] When this essay first appeared, it was still plausible to suggest that Wikipedia be used for this purpose. As of 2020, this is no longer the case. Wikipedia has become so closed and discouraging in its typical operation that it can no longer be recommended as a place to develop student work. Citizendium is still in operation, however, and continues to be recommendable.

What inspires and engages some people about social media is the passion for their individual, personal interests, as well as the desire to stay in touch with friends. Remove those crucial elements, and you merely have some neat new software tools that make communication faster.

Some of the claims made on behalf of online collaborative learning are quite dramatic. It seems that some educationists are conceiving of a whole new pedagogy centered on group work done online. In a recent *EDUCAUSE Review* article, for example, John Seely Brown and Richard P. Adler position "social learning" online as the cornerstone of "Learning 2.0."[10] And in another *EDUCAUSE Review* article, Don Tapscott and Anthony D. Williams argued that we should "adopt collaborative learning as the core model of pedagogy," with "the Internet and the new digital platforms for learning" being "critical to all of this."[11]

Brown and Adler do not view the Internet as merely a fancy new set of tools, as I am inclined to.[12] They regard it as potentially revolutionary for educational methods:

The most profound impact of the Internet, an impact that has yet to be fully realized, is its ability to support and expand the various aspects of social learning. What do we mean by "social learning"? Perhaps the simplest way to explain this concept is to note that social learning is based on the premise that our *understanding* of content is socially constructed through conversations about that content and through grounded interactions, especially with others, around

---

[10] Brown and Adler, "Minds on Fire."

[11] Don Tapscott and Anthony D. Williams, "Innovating the 21st-Century University: It's Time!" *EDUCAUSE Review*, vol. 45, no. 1 (January/February 2010), p. 26, https://bit.ly/3fLT3yd.

[12] One thing I am not mentioning here is using the Internet as a way to organize education, as opposed to a way to *deliver* education. I wrote a speculative "2.0" article on just that topic: "Education 2.0," *The Focus* (German-based English-language magazine), Spring 2007.

problems or actions. The focus is not so much on *what* we are learning but on *how* we are learning.

They draw a distinction between social learning and what they call "Cartesian" learning:

The emphasis on social learning stands in sharp contrast to the traditional Cartesian view of knowledge and learning—a view that has largely dominated the way education has been structured for over one hundred years. The Cartesian perspective assumes that knowledge is a kind of substance and that pedagogy concerns the best way to transfer this substance from teachers to students. By contrast, instead of starting from the Cartesian premise of "*I think, therefore I am,*" and from the assumption that knowledge is something that is transferred to the student via various pedagogical strategies, the social view of learning says, "*We participate, therefore we are.*"[13]

One might quibble with their incorrect description of Descartes' epistemology,[14] but my focus here is specifically on the notion that the opportunities afforded by the Internet ought to fundamentally change the way that we teach.

First, they draw a distinction between the Cartesian view of learning and the social view of learning. In Cartesian learning, knowledge is "transferred" from a teacher to a student, whereas social learning involves students "constructing" knowledge collaboratively. Brown and Adler apparently think that since knowledge is transferred, according to this supposedly Cartesian view, there must be something that is transferred, like a baton that is passed. But why saddle Cartesian learning with the notion of a transferred substance?

---

[13] Brown and Adler, "Minds on Fire," p. 18 (italics in original).

[14] Brown and Adler opine that "The Cartesian perspective assumes that knowledge is a kind of substance," which is not really true. Descartes thought that each person's mind, not "knowledge" itself somehow, was a mental substance (a thinking thing, *res cogitans*). The notion that knowledge itself is a "substance" would have been incoherent to him.

That seems like a straw man. One can simply say instead that Cartesian learning involves the teacher *causing* the student to believe something that is true, by communicating a true thought.

In Cartesian learning, a person learns by himself or herself with the help of a teacher—hence the article drawing of the lone "I think, therefore I am" student. On the other hand, in social learning, students learn together in a group—hence the article drawing of the two "We participate, therefore we are" students.

The distinction here, as best as I can make out, does not need this confusing philosophical scaffolding, because it is simply the common-sense distinction between learning with and without the help of peers.[15] Examples of Cartesian learning would involve reading a book, doing homework alone, or writing a paper by oneself. Examples of social learning would involve discussions, doing homework together, co-writing papers, and working or doing practica together. As Brown and Adler explain, the social view of learning

shifts the focus of our attention from the content of a subject to the learning activities and human interactions around which that content is situated. This perspective also helps to explain the effectiveness of study groups. Students in these groups can ask questions to clarify areas of uncertainty or confusion, can improve their grasp of the material by hearing the answers to questions from fellow students, and perhaps most powerfully, can take on the role of teacher to help

---

[15] The authors do go on to posit "a second, perhaps even more significant, aspect of social learning"—namely, becoming a practitioner in a field. I think this means that according to Brown and Adler's view, one cannot really have learned something "socially" without becoming part of the social community of practice that "does" whatever is learned about. This raises even further issues, which would require much more space for me to address them.

other group members benefit from their understanding (one of the best ways to learn something is, after all, to teach it to others).[16]

The conclusion here is that social learning is superior to Cartesian learning because students who use study groups score better than those who study alone (says one group of researchers cited by our authors), students in groups can ask questions and hear answers more readily, and students in groups can teach each other. This reasoning hardly clinches the matter. But then, I doubt this is meant as a rigorous argument. It is simply an articulation of a view for those educationists who are already inclined to agree with both the premises and the conclusion, so that they can nod their head as they move on to the meat of the paper.

The meat of Brown and Adler's paper comes when they present some Internet tools for "extending education." These tools provide examples of how social learning flourishes online. The examples include the Terra Incognita project and a Harvard Law School course, which were developed in virtual classrooms within Second Life; Digital StudyHall, an online help center for students in India; the Faulkes Telescope Project, which allows students to access high-powered telescopes via the Internet, and a couple of other astronomy tools; the Decameron Web, a site for study of and scholarship about the classic work by Giovanni Boccaccio; and public blogging by David Wiley's students in a course called "Understanding Online Interaction."

I am sure that such educational tools are exciting, fascinating, and no doubt excellent learning resources. The Internet in general is the greatest educational tool that has been devised since, perhaps, the invention of the printing press. But the question under examination is whether the mere existence of such learning resources somehow establishes the conclusion that social learning is superior to "Cartesian"

---

[16] Brown and Adler, "Minds on Fire," p. 18.

learning—that the Internet makes it possible for social learning to replace or displace more traditional individual learning.

To see just how difficult it would be to establish this conclusion, consider all the many aspects of a quality liberal arts education—not a technical education but a more foundational, liberal one—that involve necessarily individual acts:

- You can find the *Decameron* online, you can even listen to another person reading it to you, but you must mentally process it yourself. No one else, certainly no group, can do your reading comprehension for you, no matter how helpful they may be in discussing it or summarizing it. Either you read/process it or you do not.

- Similarly, you may post your essays online in public blogs and benefit from comments others offer, but you will not become well educated unless you engage in the essentially solitary act of writing,[17] no matter how much others may assist you with drafts and no matter how much you may help others with collaboratively written papers.

- It is one thing to engage in a discussion—whether online, in a traditional classroom, or in a study session—and thereby be inspired to think fascinating thoughts, but it is quite another to think creatively and critically for oneself. A person who has no experience or inclination for the latter may work well in groups but would seem to be missing something essential to the ordinary notion of scholarship. *My* notion of a good scholar—perhaps standards are changing—is someone who is capable of thinking independently.

- Similarly, you may get tremendous help solving problems in your math and science classes by working in groups, online or off, but ultimately the knowledge and skills

---

[17] Most original acts of writing, even on wikis, are solitary. You, an individual, are the producer of the sentences that others may edit.

developed are your own. After you have engaged in a study session with others, you had better make sure you can do the problems by yourself. If you cannot, you probably do not understand the material.

These four activities—reading, writing, critical thinking, and calculation—should make up the vast bulk of a liberal education. Social learning could not replace these individual, "Cartesian" activities without jettisoning liberal education itself.

Boring Old Books

But perhaps the point is that liberal education is outmoded. Perhaps the advantage found in collaborative learning lies in a new mode of life, an online social life perhaps sought for its own sake, even as knowledge itself is said to be sought for its own sake. Online communities that are open to students and that promote collaboration count as practical training in that social life. But is fostering a deeply networked online social life among the proper tasks of education independent of (or in addition to or instead of) the more traditional tasks of a liberal education? Is participating in online communities via social media a replacement for reading boring old books?

Until recent years, the question would have been very puzzling, but now the suggestion will sound familiar to many readers. Books, we hear, are old-fashioned: they are not interactive, and they constitute a single, static, one-way conversation with an individual. The Internet theorist Clay Shirky has noted that we are undergoing another, inevitable "transformation of the media landscape"—as happened previously with Gutenberg's printing press—in which an older "monolithic, historic, and elite culture" is sacrificed in favor of "a diverse, contemporary, and vulgar one." An "upstart literature" is destined to become "the new high culture."

Taking on this "challenge" will mean "altering our historic models for the *summa bonum* of educated life."[18]

Shirky was writing in response to Nicholas Carr's essay "Is Google Making Us Stupid?"[19] Carr explained that the fracturing of our attention may be making us less capable of processing broad, complex information and, more simply, less capable of reading books. For example, Carr noted that an acquaintance of his, a medical professor, admitted to not being able to read *War and Peace* anymore. On the *Britannica Blog*, Shirky wrote: "It is not just Carr's friend, and it is not just because of the web—no one reads *War and Peace*. It's too long, and not so interesting." He underscored his seriousness by saying: "This observation is no less sacrilegious for being true." Shirky proceeded to argue that "the literary world is now losing its normative hold on culture." Both Shirky and Carr quote the playwright Richard Foreman, who observed that the "complex, dense and 'cathedral-like' structure of the highly educated and articulate personality" is at risk.[20]

Shirky's argument implies that the now supposedly dying medium of paper publishing encouraged "wordy, abstract, and dense" writing and that such writing is now falling away with the demise of the medium. Works like *War and Peace*—and no doubt most other classics—are outmoded. They are outmoded because the highly networked nature of communication and publishing presents us with a different "media landscape," one with different requirements. The requirements of the new medium make not just books but also personalities that are "complex, dense and 'cathedral-like'" positively anachronistic. But it seems to me that to say so is to declare the irrelevance of

---

[18] Clay Shirky, "Why Abundance Is Good: A Reply to Nick Carr," *Encyclopaedia Britannica Blog*, July 17, 2008, https://bit.ly/3eD1Y3K.

[19] Nicholas Carr, "Is Google Making Us Stupid?" *The Atlantic*, July/August 2008, https://bit.ly/2Bjt1DG.

[20] Richard Foreman, "The Pancake People; or, 'The Gods Are Pounding My Head'," *Edge*, March 8, 2005, https://bit.ly/2WyAJAY.

most of the thinkers throughout history—as Shirky notes, "the literary world is now losing its normative hold" on our culture. What does this mean if not that we as a society hold all traditional authors in contempt? In other words, it *seems* that Shirky is saying that blog and Twitter posts, and Wikipedia and YouTube contributions, which arguably weaken our attentional capabilities, are becoming dominant in our culture and that more challenging, pre-Internet modes of expression, like books, are going by the wayside.

But is knowledge, even the knowledge contained in great books, now something that can be *adequately* replaced by the collaborative creations of the students themselves? Perhaps the answer is yes; perhaps that is the point. Perhaps the notion is that knowledge-as-co-created by students is superior to knowledge-as-passed-along-by-teachers-and-books, regardless of quality. Perhaps the accuracy of the information co-created by students does not matter, because as shared information it enjoys a social validity that dusty old volumes and teachers speaking from authority cannot. Perhaps the subtlety and depth of thinking that comes from critical reading and evaluation of great writers does not matter, because information is now ultimately best understood as belonging to and produced by large groups of people. Perhaps being acquainted with the original sources of great ideas does not matter, because reproducing those ideas, even if in stunted ways, enjoys an authenticity that convoluted old texts do not. Perhaps the perennial nature of the classics, the fact that they have been loved and learned from for generations, does not matter, because in the new publishing and societal paradigm, they are being replaced by an "upstart literature"—literature that is more realistic about the capabilities of attention-challenged students.

It might now sound as if I am attacking a straw man, with no one really talking about wholesale replacement. I hope that is true. To be well educated, to be able to pass along the liberal and rational values that undergird a civilization worth keeping, we must as a culture retain our ability to comprehend long, difficult texts written by individuals. Indeed, the single best method of getting a basic education is to read increasingly difficult and important books. To be sure, other tasks are essential, especially for training in scientific and applied fields; there are some people who are very well trained for various trades without reading many books. But when it comes to getting a solid intellectual grounding—a foundational, liberal education—nothing is less dispensable than getting acquainted with many books created by the "complex, dense" minds of deep-thinking individuals.

Conclusion

Considering the amount of play that collaborative learning and Web 2.0 educational methods have received, I suspect that the above discussion may sound pedestrian and even backward. My attitude is probably not what one would expect from a co-founder of Wikipedia. But I am not alone in my perspective.

The inherent merits of online communities have not at all been universally agreed-upon. Wikipedia, YouTube, Facebook, and Twitter all have harsh critics. More to the point, some of the digerati have contempt specifically for the more collectivist aspects of Internet communities. In this genre, Andrew Keen's *The Cult of the Amateur*[21] is well known. Other examples include Maggie Jackson's *Distracted*,[22] which argues that the sheer amount of information and activity in our always-on culture is fracturing our attention and hence our ability to process information. Mark Bauerlein's *The Dumbest Generation*,[23] far from celebrating social networks for

---

[21] Andrew Keen, *The Cult of the Amateur: How Today's Internet Is Killing Our Culture* (New York: Doubleday/Currency, 2007).

[22] Maggie Jackson, *Distracted: The Erosion of Attention and the Coming Dark Age* (Amherst, N.Y.: Prometheus Books, 2008).

[23] Mark Bauerlein, *The Dumbest Generation: How the Digital Age Stupefies Young Americans and Jeopardizes Our Future* (or, *Don't Trust Anyone under 30*) (New York: Jeremy P. Tarcher/Penguin, 2008).

enhancing education, instead blames them for turning the "digital natives" into the "dumbest generation." Perhaps the criticism most relevant to the current discussion is Jaron Lanier's essay "Digital Maoism."[24] Lanier maintains that online collaboration in what he (along with Kevin Kelly and others) calls "hive minds" (e.g., Wikipedia) unsurprisingly tends to depersonalize and alienate us, cheapening our individuality and sapping the interest and idiosyncrasy from our writing and thinking.

While I tip my hat to such thinkers, my main interest in this article was to analyze the recent boosterism of the educational merits of using Internet tools to replace the effortful, careful development of the individual mind. The three strands of current thought explored above—about how the Internet might change the educational role of memorization, about individual versus collaborative learning, and about the future of books and book-reading—are really just an extension of the older debate over the value of Western civilization, liberal arts, and "the canon." The key assumption underlying my view is that liberal education and the Western enlightenment ideals that it inculcates not only are valuable but are essential to our future.

This is worth emphasizing. Some Internet boosters argue that Google searching serves as a replacement for our memory and that students need not memorize—need not learn—as much as they did before the Internet. Educationists inspire us with the suggestion that collaborative learning online can serve as "the core model of pedagogy." Knowledge is primarily to be developed and delivered by students working in online groups. And finally, the co-creation of knowledge can and should take the place of reading long, dense, and complex books. Such claims run roughshod over the core of a liberal education. They devalue an acquaintance with (involving much

---

[24] Jaron Lanier, "Digital Maoism: The Hazards of the New Online Collectivism," *Edge*, May 30, 2006, https://bit.ly/3jjFTuz.

memorization of) many facts about history, literature, science, mathematics, the arts, and philosophy. Such claims also ignore the individual nature of much of liberal education. Reading, writing, critical thinking, and calculation, however much they can be assisted by groups, are ultimately individual skills that must, in the main, be practiced by individual minds capable of working independently. And such claims dismiss the depth of thinking that results from a critical reading and evaluation of many long and complex books.

The educational proposals and predictions of the Internet boosters described above point to a profoundly illiberal future. I fear that if we take their advice, in the place of a creative society with a reasonably deep well of liberally educated critical thinkers, we will have a society of drones, enculturated by hive minds, who are able to work together online but who are largely innocent of the texts and habits of study that encourage deep and independent thought. We will be bound by the prejudices of our "digital tribe," ripe for manipulation by whoever has the firmest grip on our dialogue. I see all too much evidence that we are moving headlong in that direction. Indeed, I fear this is already happening. I honestly hope that I prove to be an alarmist, but I am a realist reporting on my observations. I wish the news were better.[25]

---

[25] Thanks to Teddy Diggs, Founding Editor of *EDUCAUSE Review*, for extensive editorial assistance with this essay.

Nine

Is There a New Geek

Anti-Intellectualism?

Here is a LarrySanger.org blog post from 2011. It was very controversial; it turns out "geeks" do not like being called "anti-intellectual." It is a fitting conclusion for this part of the book. The collectivization of knowledge meant the decline of our respect for "the life of the mind," even among geeks. The trend is even more evident today. Updated for this volume, with comments in footnotes.

IS there a new anti-intellectualism? I mean one that is advocated by Internet geeks and some of the digerati. I think so: more and more mavens of the Internet[1] are coming out firmly against academic knowledge in all its forms. This might sound outrageous to say, but it is sadly true.

---

[1] I more specifically mean technologists—not necessarily programmers—who comment about all matters Internet. But indeed a good many computer programmers too, as we will see, but they are not what I mean exclusively by "geeks" here.

Let us review the evidence.

1. The Evidence

Programmers have been saying for years that it is unnecessary to get a college degree in order to be a great coder—and this has always been easy to concede. I never would have accused them of being anti-intellectual, or even of being opposed to education, just for saying that. It is just an interesting feature of programming as a profession—not evidence of anti-intellectualism.

In 2001, along came Wikipedia, which at least for a time gave everyone equal rights to record knowledge. This was only half of the project's original vision, as I explained in a memoir.[2] Originally, we seriously discussed adding some method of letting experts approve articles. But the Slashdot geeks who came to dominate Wikipedia's early years, supported by Jimmy Wales, nixed this notion repeatedly. The digerati cheered and said, implausibly,[3] that experts were no longer needed, and that "crowds" were wiser than people who had devoted their lives to knowledge. This ultimately led to a debate, now a bit passé, about experts versus amateurs in the mid-2000s.[4] There were certainly notes of anti-intellectualism in that debate.

Around the same time, some people began to criticize books as such, as an outmoded medium, and not merely because they are traditionally paper and not digital. The Institute for the Future of the Book has been one locus of this criticism.[5]

---

[2] This volume's Chapter 1. Cf. also Chapter 7.

[3] That this is implausible is the thesis of my "The Fate of Expertise after Wikipedia," *Episteme* 6, no. 1 (2009): 52–73.

[4] In the age of the first amateur politician for president, it is not surprising that amateurs would dominate social media, while experts have mostly retreated to the strongholds of publishing and academia.

[5] They still exist, in 2020, but seem to be more or less inactive. Perhaps we now know what the future of the book is going to be.

But nascent geek anti-intellectualism really began to come into focus around with the rise of Facebook and Twitter, when Nicholas Carr asked, "Is Google making us stupid?" in *The Atlantic.*[6] More than by Carr's essay itself, I was struck by the reaction to it. Altogether too many geeks seemed to be assume that if information glut is sapping our ability to focus, this is largely out of our control and not necessarily a bad thing. But of course it is a bad thing, and it is in our control, as I pointed out.[7] Moreover, focus is absolutely necessary if we are to gain knowledge. We will be ignoramuses indeed, if we merely flow along with the digital current and do not take the time to read extended, difficult texts.[8]

Worse still was Clay Shirky's reaction[9] in the *Britannica Blog*, where he opined, "no one reads *War and Peace*. It's too long, and not so interesting," and borrows a phrase from Richard Foreman, claiming, "the 'complex, dense and "cathedral-like" structure of the highly educated and articulate personality' is at risk." As I observed at the time,[10] Shirky's views entailed that Twitter-sized discourse was our historically determined fate, and that, if he were right, the Great Books and civilization itself[11] would be at risk. But he was not right—I hope.

At the end of 2008, Don Tapscott got into the act,[12] claiming that Google makes memorization passé. "It is enough that they

---

[6] July/August 2008, https://bit.ly/2BjtlDG.

[7] Reply to Carr, *Edge*, July 11, 2008, https://bit.ly/39g9n8c.

[8] And frankly, that seems to be where are today, in 2020.

[9] Clay Shirky, "Why Abundance Is Good: A Reply to Nick Carr," *Encyclopaedia Britannica Blog*, July 17, 2008, https://bit.ly/3eD1Y3K.

[10] "A Defense of Tolstoy & the Individual Thinker: A Reply to Clay Shirky," *Encyclopedia Britannica Blog*, July 18, 2008, https://bit.ly/2ZMiVVm.

[11] "The Internet and the Future of Civilization," *Encyclopedia Britannica Blog*, July 30, 2008, https://bit.ly/3eSSVvO.

[12] Tapscott quoted in Alexandra Frean, "Google Generation Has No Need for Rote Learning," *Times* (London), December 2, 2008, https://bit.ly/3hjpJzI.

know about the Battle of Hastings," Tapscott boldly claimed, "without having to memorize that it was in 1066. [Students] can look that up and position it in history with a click on Google."

In 2010, *Edge* took up the question, "Is the Internet changing the way you think?"[13] and the answers were very sobering. Here were some prominent scientists, thinkers, and writers, and all too many of them were saying—once more, with feeling—that the Internet was making it hard to read long pieces of writing, that books were passé, and that the Internet was essentially becoming a mental prosthesis. We were, as one writer put it, uploading our brains to the Internet.

Again, I did not buy the boosterism, the implicit techno-determinism, and the notion that the Internet makes learning unnecessary.[14] Anyone who claims that we do not need to read and memorize some facts is saying that we do not need to *learn* those facts. Reading and indeed memorizing are the first, necessary steps in learning anything.

That brought us to 2011. Sir Ken Robinson has got a lot of attention by speaking out—inspiringly to some, outrageously to others—saying that K-12 education needs a sea change away from "boring" academics and toward collaborative methods that foster "creativity."[15] At the same time, PayPal co-founder Peter Thiel sparked much discussion by claiming that there is a "higher education bubble," that is, the cost of higher education greatly exceeds its value.[16] This claim by itself is

---

[13] "How is the Internet changing the way you think?" The *Edge* Annual Question of 2010, https://bit.ly/32EIZ6C.

[14] See the previous chapter in this volume, as well as "The Un-Focusing, De-Liberating Effects of Joining the Hive Mind," *Edge*, 2010, https://bit.ly/3jsd1Ay.

[15] "On Robinson on Education," *LarrySanger.org* (blog), May 27, 2011, https://bit.ly/3eMDftQ.

[16] Sarah Lacy, "Peter Thiel: We're in a Bubble and It's Not the Internet. It's Higher Education," *TechCrunch*, April 11, 2011, https://tcrn.ch/3fPz5m8.

somewhat plausible. But Thiel much less plausibly implies that college *per se* is now not recommendable for many, because it is "elitist." With his Thiel Fellowship program he hopes to demonstrate that a college degree is not necessary for success in the field of technology. Leave it to a 19-year-old recipient of one of these fellowships to shout boldly that "College is a waste of time."[17] Unsurprisingly—even if I do detest how much higher education now resembles indoctrination—I disagree.[18]

2. Geek Anti-Intellectualism

In the above, I have barely scratched the surface. I have not mentioned many other commentators, blogs, and books that have written on such subjects. But this is enough to clarify what I mean by "geek anti-intellectualism." Let me step back and sum up the views mentioned above:

- Experts do not deserve any special role in declaring what is known. Knowledge is now democratically determined, as it should be.

- Books are an outmoded medium because they involve a single person speaking from authority. In the future, information will be developed and propagated collaboratively, something like what we already do with the combination of Twitter, Facebook, blogs, Wikipedia, and various other websites.

- The classics, being books, are also outmoded. They are outmoded because they are often long and hard to read, so those of us raised around the distractions of technology cannot be bothered to follow them. Besides, they concern foreign worlds, dominated by dead white guys with

---

[17] Dale Stephens, "College is a waste of time," *CNN.com*, June 3, 2011, https://cnn.it/2WFLBx9.

[18] "Is college a waste of time?" *LarrySanger.org* (blog), June 5, 2011, https://bit.ly/30ubnWi.

totally antiquated ideas and attitudes. In short, they are boring and irrelevant.

- The digitization of information means that we do not have to memorize nearly as much. We can upload our memories to our devices and to Internet communities. We can answer most general questions with a quick search.

- The paragon of success is a popular website or well-used software, and for that, you just have to be a bright, creative geek. You do not have to go to college, which is overpriced and so reserved to the elite anyway.

If you are the sort of geek who loves all things Internet uncritically, then you are probably nodding your head. If so, I submit this as a new epistemological manifesto that might well sum up your views:

You do not really care about knowledge; it is not a priority. For you, the books containing knowledge, the classics and old-fashioned scholarship summing up the best of our knowledge, the people and institutions whose purpose is to pass on knowledge—all are hopelessly antiquated. Even your own knowledge, the contents of your mind, can be outsourced to databases built by collaborative digital communities, and the more the better. After all, academics are boring.

A new world is coming, and you are in the vanguard. In this world, the people who have and who value individual knowledge, especially theoretical and factual knowledge, are objects of your derision. You have contempt for the sort of people who read books and talk about them—especially classics, the long and difficult works that were created alone by people who, once upon a time, were hailed as brilliant. You have no special respect for anyone who is supposed to be "brilliant" or even "knowledgeable." What you respect are those who have created stuff that many people find useful today. Nobody cares about some Luddite scholar's ability to write a book or get an article past review by one of his peers. This is why no decent school requires reading many classics, or books generally, anymore— books are all tl;dr for today's students.

In our new world, insofar as we individually need to know anything at all, our knowledge is *practical*, and best gained through projects and experience. Practical knowledge does not come from books or hard study or any traditional school or college. People who spend years of their lives filling up their individual minds with theoretical or factual knowledge are chumps who will probably end up working for those who skipped college to focus on more important things.

Do you find your views misrepresented? I am being a bit provocative, sure, but have I not merely repeated some remarks and made a few simple extrapolations? Of course, most geeks, even most Internet boosters, will not admit to believing all of this manifesto. But I submit that geekdom is on a slippery slope to the anti-intellectualism it represents.[19]

So there is no mistake, let me describe the bottom of this slippery slope even more forthrightly.

You are opposed to knowledge as such. You contemptuously dismiss experts who have it; you claim that books are outmoded, including classics, which contain the most significant knowledge generated by humankind thus far; you want to memorize as little as possible, and you want to upload what you have memorized to the net as soon as possible; you do not want schools to make students memorize anything; and you discourage most people from going to college.

In short, at the bottom of this slippery slope, you seem to be opposed to knowledge wherever it occurs, in books, in experts, in institutions, even in your own mind.

But, you might say, what about Internet communities? Is that not a significant exception? You might think so. After all, how can people who love Wikipedia so much be "opposed to knowledge as such"? Well, there is an answer to that.

It is because there is a very big difference between a statement occurring in a database and someone having, or learning, a piece of knowledge. If all human beings died out, there would be no knowledge left even if all libraries and the

---

[19] In 2020, I submit that this manifesto is even more plausible as a fair representation of "geek anti-intellectualism" than it was in 2011.

whole Internet survived. Knowledge exists only inside people's heads. It is created not by being accessed in a database search, but by being learned and mastered. A collection of Wikipedia articles about physics contains text; the mind of a physicist contains knowledge.

3. How Big of a Problem Is This?

How serious am I in the above analysis? And is this really a problem, or merely a quirk of geek life in the 21st century?

It is important to bear in mind what I do and do not mean when I say that some Internet geeks are anti-intellectuals. I do not mean that they would admit that they hate knowledge or are somehow opposed to knowledge. Almost no one can admit such a thing to himself, let alone to others. Also, of course, I doubt I could find many geeks who would say that students should not graduate from high school without learning a significant amount of math, science, and some other subjects as well. Most geeks have significant respect for the knowledge of people like Stephen Hawking or Richard Dawkins, of course. Many geeks, too, are planning on college, are in college, or have been to college. And so forth—for the various claims (1)-(5), while many geeks would endorse them, they could also be found contradicting them regularly as well. So is there really anything to worry about here?

Well, yes, there is. Attitudes are rarely all or nothing. The more that people have these various attitudes, the more bad stuff is going to result, I think. The more that a person really takes seriously that there is no point in reading the classics, the less likely he will actually take a class in Greek history or early modern philosophy. Repeat that on a mass scale, and the world becomes—no doubt already has become—a significantly poorer place, as a result of the widespread lack of analytical tools and conceptual understanding. We can imagine a world in which the humanities are studied by only a small handful of people, because we already live in that world[20]; just imagine the number of people all but vanishing.

But is this not just a problem for geekdom? Does it really matter that much if *geeks* are anti-intellectuals? The question is whether the trend will move on to the population at large. One does not speak of "geek chic" these days for nothing. The digital world is the vanguard, and attitudes and behaviors that were once found mostly among the geeks of yesteryear are now mainstream. Geek anti-intellectualism is another example. Most of the people I have mentioned in this essay are not geeks per se, but the digerati, who are frequently non-geeks or ex-geeks who have their finger on the pulse of social movements online. Via these digerati, we can find evidence of geek attitudes making their way into mainstream culture. One now regularly encounters geek-inspired sentiments from business writers like Don Tapscott and education theorists like Ken Robinson—and even from the likes of Barack Obama.

Let us just put it this way. If, in the next five years, some prominent person comes out with a book or high-profile essay openly attacking education or expertise or individual knowledge as such, because the Internet makes such things outmoded, and if it receives a positive reception not just from writers at CNET and Wired and the usual suspects in the Blogosphere, but also serious, thoughtful consideration from Establishment sources like *The New York Review of Books* or *Time*, I will say that geek anti-intellectualism is in full flower and has entered the mainstream.[21]

---

[20] The National Center for Education Statistics' "Digest of Education Statistics," Table 322.10 (https://bit.ly/3ghQkgm), says English bachelor's degrees earned declined by an *absolute* value of 22% in the period from 2005-6 to 2015-16 (3.62% of all bachelor's degrees to 2.23%). Philosophy and religious studies declined by 15%.

[21] Bryan Caplan, *The Case Against Education: Why the Education System Is a Waste of Time and Money* (Princeton, 2018). Glowing Establishment reviews. Caplan, an acquaintance of mine, qualifies as a geek.

Part III

FREER KNOWLEDGE

Ten

Introducing the Encyclosphere

First a speech delivered at a TheNextWeb conference in Amsterdam in October 2019, this short manifesto argues for a new, decentralized network of encyclopedias rather than a new encyclopedia. Big Tech has become increasingly powerful and centralized in the last decade. We can maintain our freedom only by organizing ourselves in ways that respect that freedom and do not depend on giant corporations. The text is very slightly updated for this book.

WE are fed up.

After ten years of domination by big social media—which might finally be in decline—we are tired of giant Silicon Valley corporations using us contemptuously. We still remember an Internet in which we charted our own destiny and owned our own data.

It is not just social media. It is Wikipedia, too. If you want to participate in the world's largest encyclopedia, you must collaborate with a shadowy group of anonymous amateurs and paid shills on exactly one article per topic. If you are new, you will not be treated very nicely. If you do not play their strange game, you will be summarily dismissed. Like the social media giants, Wikipedia has become an arrogant and controlling oligarchy.

Like Facebook, Wikipedia is also controlling its readers. It feeds them biased articles, exactly one per topic, does not let users give effective, independent feedback on articles (you are forced to become a participant if you just want to give feedback) or to rate articles. They have, in a very real way, centralized epistemic authority in the hands of an anonymous mob. This is worse than Facebook. At least with Facebook, Congress can call Mark Zuckerberg to testify. There is not anyone who is responsible for Wikipedia's content—certainly not Jimmy Wales. The situation is, in some ways, more dire than with Facebook, because you cannot effectively talk back to Wikipedia.

The old proverb tells us that knowledge is powerful. More specifically, authoritative statements of what is known on various subjects are powerful. How? Such statements can be used to influence elections, justify policies, and articulate controversial points of view—in effect to gain, wield, and build and consolidate power. The power to declare what is known is nearly the power to rule the world. No small group—no person, corporation, oligarchy, or cadre of insiders—should wield such power.

We believe in democracy, or we should: we believe that political power is best spread out, not concentrated in the hands of a few, where it is apt to be abused. We should also believe, therefore, in epistemic democracy: the power to declare what is known should also be very widely distributed.[1]

So it should not be concentrated in the hands of Wikipedia, Facebook, Twitter, *The New York Times*, or any such exclusive group. The history of publishing, including Internet publishing, makes all too clear that the authority to declare what is known is wielded by selfish, powerful interests to

---

[1] This is the theme of this volume's Chapter 7.

advance their own agendas, which always unsurprisingly have the effect of consolidating their own power.

We do not have to tolerate this. We do not have to be at the mercy of these people.

A few thousand people work regularly on Wikipedia. But what if millions more—orders of magnitude more—wrote encyclopedia articles and rated them, as part of a completely decentralized knowledge network, with no individual, group, corporation, or government in charge of the whole? That is surely possible. There are surely that many people who, if given the freedom to do so, would be highly motivated to volunteer their time to add to the world's largest collection of knowledge.

We could create a knowledge commons, defined by neutral, open, technical standards and protocols: a network that decentralizes encyclopedias, exactly as the Blogosphere has done for blogs.

The Encyclosphere

Blogs give everyone an independent voice. All blogs taken together are called the "Blogosphere," but there is no single, central blog repository and no blogging authority. It is a good thing, too. Can you imagine what it might be like if all our blogs were ultimately controlled by a giant, powerful organization like Facebook, Twitter, or Wikipedia?

What made the Blogosphere possible were technical standards for formatting, sharing, and interlinking blog posts: the RSS[2] and Atom specifications. The nontechnical basics about these standards are easy and important to understand. They are simply a way to format information about blog posts in a consistent, machine-readable way and to let bloggers alert

---

[2] "RSS," short for "Really Simple Syndication," is the most common technical specification for publishing blogs and blog-like feeds of articles.

the world when their blog has changed. In general, they allow for an organized type of interconnected, networked activity—blogging—without a central, controlling body.

Plenty of websites, like WordPress.com, Tumblr, Medium, and Blogger.com, have tried to become the home of blogging online.[3] But none has been able to gain exclusive dominance, because it is just too easy to move your blog elsewhere. The existence of common blogging standards makes that possible.

We need to do for encyclopedias what blogging standards did for blogs: there needs to be an "Encyclosphere." We should build a totally decentralized network, like the Blogosphere—or like email, IRC, blockchains, and the World Wide Web itself. The Encyclosphere would give everyone an equal voice in expressing knowledge (or claims to knowledge), and in rating those expressions of knowledge. There would be no single, central knowledge repository or authority.

So, considering that RSS and Atom enabled the development of the decentralized Blogosphere, we clearly need to develop technical standards for encyclopedias. That is the mission of a new organization I want to introduce: the Knowledge Standards Foundation (KSF).

Writers and publishers would be able to post feeds of encyclopedia articles (or metadata about articles, and ratings of articles). App developers would be able to collect the data from all of those feeds and use the data to construct massive search engines, and other neat features, for all the encyclopedia articles in the world. No one app would be privileged, but all would tap into—and help build—a "knowledge commons." Ultimately there would be a massive knowledge competition to best express human knowledge on every topic and from every point of view.

There has never been anything like this. But if we get together, we can build it. Nobody's stopping us. We need only the desire to get it done. We will never run out of runway

---

[3] WordPress.com is leader according to Alexa.com as of July 2020.

because it is not a startup. It is a distributed, collective project, an open source movement that is bigger than any of us—and certainly much bigger than the KSF, which will serve only as the catalyst, not the owner. The Encyclosphere will have no owner just as the Blogosphere has no owner.

Epistemic power should be spread out among the public. But how? I call it the "Encyclosphere," but how would a more democratic Encyclosphere work?

- Writers should be able to publish their own articles wherever and whenever they want, without asking anyone.

- Raters—the general public, including people identified as experts—should be able to rate those articles.

- The data for both articles and ratings are published according to standards, or a single common format, in a feed, similar to an RSS feed.

- Users should be able to sort and re-sort articles according to all ratings, or selected ratings.

- The control over whose ratings to pay attention to should always be in the hands of the user.

- The data is copied and aggregated into different databases, including distributed databases such as Torrent, IPFS, and open APIs.

- Many competing apps, all around the world, use the aggregated data to build encyclopedia readers according to their own editorial standards. The Foundation's technical standards will be completely neutral with regard to such editorial standards.

This is not a completely new concept, but I am sure it will sound somewhat confusing. So I want to try to clarify by listing a few things that the Encyclosphere is not, or will not be:

- The Encyclosphere is not an encyclopedia. It is a network of encyclopedic content. It is no more an encyclopedia than the Blogosphere is a blog.

- The Encyclosphere is not a platform or network for building encyclopedias. It will be basically just a series of feeds. It is not a piece of software or a library or API you can build on. It is an old-fashioned Internet network.
- The Encyclosphere is not a blockchain. You could deliver it over a blockchain, to be sure, but it will be built directly on more basic Internet protocols.

By building the Encyclosphere, we, all of us little people, can, in a decentralized and democratic system, do an end run around giants like Google and Wikipedia.

The Knowledge Standards Foundation

This is the vision I have had for encyclopedias since around 2014. That was when I first started talking about something I called "GreaterWiki"; I even started learning to code more seriously partly in order to execute the vision. I went to work for Everipedia, the blockchain encyclopedia, in late 2017 with the promise that I would be able to work on this project. When I joined the startup (three years after the co-founders began work on it), one thing we discussed was the necessity of creating a nonprofit organization holding technical standards for encyclopedias. I thought that heading up such a foundation was a job I would like to have.

For almost two years, I developed and promoted this vision[4] (and related ideas, like decentralizing social media) as CIO of Everipedia. It is time to start executing the plan. For that, I have made a start on the KSF, for which reason I left my position as CIO of Everipedia. To demonstrate that the Foundation and Everipedia are independent entities, I have given back my equity to Everipedia—without compensation,

---

[4] Larry Sanger, "Wikipedia co-founder's 8,000-word essay on how to build a better Wikipedia," *The Next Web*, April 21, 2018, https://bit.ly/2OGMukF.

i.e., they did not pay me for my returned equity and I did not receive any cash or tokens when I left.

The Foundation's purpose will be to publish technical standards for the Encyclosphere. We will host open source tools and other software mainly for the developer community. We will serve as a neutral public forum for discussion of such standards. We will be mostly a volunteer organization. Hundreds of people have stepped forward to help. I expect many more volunteers in the coming months.

There are also a few things that the Foundation is not, or will not be doing:

- It is misleading to call the Encyclosphere "a project" of the KSF, insofar as that implies a centralized development project. We just want to be the organization to get the ball rolling and to articulate the content publishing and aggregation specifications.

- The KSF is not itself developing an encyclopedia. There will be no "official" Encyclosphere reader. We want there to be lots of competing reader software, just as there are competing blog readers.

- The KSF is not an industry consortium; it is not a project paid for and controlled by reference publishers. I will have an announcement about how we will raise money for our modest operations next month.

I and future Foundation staff and volunteers will confer with the leadership and technical teams of a number of different app developers, standards experts, online reference publishers, and other potential stakeholders—including, of course, anyone from the interested general public. We will develop draft standards together, while vetting them in a very public, open, civil, and moderated process. As we develop software, we will host it in a Git repository controlled by the Foundation.

I hope a better kind of knowledge repository will result from our efforts.

Eleven

Declaration of Digital
Independence

This widely-publicized petition, posted on LarrySanger.org in June 2019, is in reaction to the encroachments on privacy and free speech, and to centralized control tactics generally, found throughout the corporate Internet. Wikipedia is now a part of that world, considering that its hegemony (its de facto power to declare what "we all know," in the language of Chapter 7) now closely matches that of the Establishment and deliberately eliminates minority views. Version 1.3 of the petition is reproduced here with no changes. You can still sign copies of it online as of this writing.

HUMANITY has been contemptuously used by vast digital empires. Thus it is now necessary to replace these empires with decentralized networks of independent individuals, as in the first decades of the Internet. As our participation has been voluntary, no one doubts our right to take this step. But if we are to persuade as many people as possible to join together and make reformed networks possible, we should declare our reasons for wanting to replace the old.

Declaration of Digital Independence

We declare that we have unalienable digital rights, rights that define how information that we individually own may or may not be treated by others, and that among these rights are free speech, privacy, and security. Since the proprietary, centralized architecture of the Internet at present has induced most of us to abandon these rights, however reluctantly or cynically, we ought to demand a new system that respects them properly. The difficulty and divisiveness of wholesale reform means that this task is not to be undertaken lightly. For years we have approved of and even celebrated enterprise as it has profited from our communication and labor without compensation to us. But it has become abundantly clear more recently that a callous, secretive, controlling, and exploitative animus guides the centralized networks of the Internet and the corporations behind them.

The long train of abuses we have suffered makes it our right, even our duty, to replace the old networks. To show what train of abuses we have suffered at the hands of these giant corporations, let these facts be submitted to a candid world.

They have practiced in-house moderation in keeping with their executives' notions of what will maximize profit, rather than allowing moderation to be performed more democratically and by random members of the community.

They have banned, shadow-banned, throttled, and demonetized both users and content based on political considerations, exercising their enormous corporate power to influence elections globally.

They have adopted algorithms for user feeds that highlight the most controversial content, making civic discussion more emotional and irrational and making it possible for foreign powers to exercise an unmerited influence on elections globally.

They have required agreement to terms of service that are impossible for ordinary users to understand, and which are objectionably vague in ways that permit them to legally defend their exploitative practices.

They have marketed private data to advertisers in ways that no one would specifically assent to.

They have failed to provide clear ways to opt out of such marketing schemes.

They have subjected users to such terms and surveillance even when users pay them for products and services.

They have data-mined user content and behavior in sophisticated and disturbing ways, learning sometimes more about their users than their users know about themselves; they have profited from this hidden but personal information.

They have avoided using strong, end-to-end encryption when users have a right to expect total privacy, in order to retain access to user data.

They have amassed stunning quantities of user data while failing to follow sound information security practices, such as encryption; they have inadvertently or deliberately opened that data to both illegal attacks and government surveillance.

They have unfairly blocked accounts, posts, and means of funding on political or religious grounds, preferring the loyalty of some users over others.

They have sometimes been too ready to cooperate with despotic governments that both control information and surveil their people.

They have failed to provide adequate and desirable options that users may use to guide their own experience of their services, preferring to manipulate users for profit.

They have failed to provide users adequate tools for searching their own content, forcing users rather to employ interfaces insultingly inadequate for the purpose.

They have exploited users and volunteers who freely contribute data to their sites, by making such data available to others only via paid application program interfaces and privacy-violating terms of service, failing to make such freely-contributed data free and open source, and disallowing users to anonymize their data and opt out easily.

They have failed to provide adequate tools, and sometimes any tools, to export user data in a common data standard.

They have created artificial silos for their own profit; they have failed to provide means to incorporate similar content, served from elsewhere, as part of their interface, forcing users to stay within their networks and cutting them off from family, friends, and associates who use other networks.

They have profited from the content and activity of users, often without sharing any of these profits with the users.

They have treated users arrogantly as a fungible resource to be exploited and controlled rather than being treated respectfully, as free, independent, and diverse partners.

We have begged and pleaded, complained, and resorted to the law. The executives of the corporations must be familiar with these common complaints; but they acknowledge them publicly only rarely and grudgingly. The ill treatment continues, showing that most of such executives are not fit stewards of the public trust.

The most reliable guarantee of our privacy, security, and free speech is not in the form of any enterprise, organization, or government, but instead in the free agreement among free individuals to use common standards and protocols. The vast power wielded by social networks of the early 21st century, putting our digital rights in serious jeopardy, demonstrates that we must engineer new—but old-fashioned—decentralized networks that make such clearly dangerous concentrations of power impossible.

Therefore, we declare our support of the following principles.

Principles of Decentralized Social Networks

1. We free individuals should be able to publish our data freely, without having to answer to any corporation.
2. We declare that we legally own our own data; we possess both legal and moral rights to control our own data.
3. Posts that appear on social networks should be able to be served, like email and blogs, from many independent services

that we individually control, rather than from databases that corporations exclusively control or from any central repository.

4. Just as no one has the right to eavesdrop on private conversations in homes without extraordinarily good reasons, so also the privacy rights of users must be preserved against criminal, corporate, and governmental monitoring; therefore, for private content, the protocols must support strong, end-to-end encryption and other good privacy practices.

5. As is the case with the Internet domain name system, lists of available user feeds should be restricted by technical standards and protocols only, never according to user identity or content.

6. Social media applications should make available data input by the user, at the user's sole discretion, to be distributed by all other publishers according to common, global standards and protocols, just as are email and blogs, with no publisher being privileged by the network above another. Applications with idiosyncratic standards violate their users' digital rights.

7. Accordingly, social media applications should aggregate posts from multiple, independent data sources as determined by the user, and in an order determined by the user's preferences.

8. No corporation, or small group of corporations, should control the standards and protocols of decentralized networks, nor should there be a single brand, owner, proprietary software, or Internet location associated with them, as that would constitute centralization.

9. Users should expect to be able to participate in the new networks, and to enjoy the rights above enumerated, without special technical skills. They should have very easy-to-use control over privacy, both fine- and coarse-grained, with the most private messages encrypted automatically, and using tools for controlling feeds and search results that are easy for non-technical people to use.

Declaration of Digital Independence

We hold that to embrace these principles is to return to the sounder and better practices of the earlier Internet and which were, after all, the foundation for the brilliant rise of the Internet. Anyone who opposes these principles opposes the Internet itself. Thus we pledge to code, design, and participate in newer and better networks that follow these principles, and to eschew the older, controlling, and soon to be outmoded networks.

We, therefore, the undersigned people of the Internet, do solemnly publish and declare that we will do all we can to create decentralized social networks; that as many of us as possible should distribute, discuss, and sign their names to this document; that we endorse the preceding statement of principles of decentralization; that we will judge social media companies by these principles; that we will demonstrate our solidarity to the cause by abandoning abusive networks if necessary; and that we, both users and developers, will advance the cause of a more decentralized Internet.[1]

---

[1] Please sign the Declaration on *LarrySanger.org*, where it will be available indefinitely (https://bit.ly/3jXwlFL).

Twelve

The Future of the Free Internet

I wrote this essay as a conclusion to this volume. How can we save free information and knowledge on the Internet?

I AM—I flatter myself—a truth-seeker. That is part of the reason I have spent so much of my life studying the standards of truth. So, when given the opportunity to start a free encyclopedia, I began to philosophize about free encyclopedias; I developed a vision. The task is fascinating since an encyclopedia is, after all, a compendium of truths.

You might well think my vision came to fruition. After all, Wikipedia now stands triumphant, seemingly, as the largest, most popular, most global encyclopedia in history. But, like a reflection in a funhouse mirror, my vision appears to me in a twisted, monstrous form, which I disown. Wikipedia is of no great help to truth-seekers. I would prefer to be known as the project's ex-founder.

Wikipedia now defends Establishment views, and the Establishment loves it for that reason. But it began as an idealistic, democratic project, one that would bring the world together to represent all of human knowledge, in all its messy, fascinating glory, on a neutral playing field. No more. It has been transformed into a thuggish defender of the epistemic prerogatives of the powerful. It began as an outgrowth of the open source software movement and its deeply decentralizing and democratic tendencies. In time, its operations became a black box, an enigma thriving on anonymity and the dark arts of dishonest social games and back-room deals. It is a mockery of an "encyclopedia anybody can edit."

Wikipedia's moral decline—for its decline is as much moral as epistemological—reflects that of the larger Internet. The short text and visual nature of social media is a poor replacement for the relatively long-form intellectual discussions we used to have on blogs, Usenet, and mailing lists. This is not necessarily what all users wanted, but it is what Big Tech corporate executives pushed on us with their careful experiments in gamification and user experience. It is a machine, of which so many of us are cogs, brilliantly and dangerously addictive and attention-hogging, dumbing us down, radicalizing us,[1] and amplifying voices in our ideologically separate silos. This state of affairs is similar to that of Wikipedia, which promotes a single silo, that of the Establishment. It absolutely refuses to consult the opinions and needs of readers, and in so doing, radicalizes its true believers and would simplify our grasp of complex, many-sided truths, if we let it.[2]

Even more fundamentally, what the decline of Wikipedia and social media have in common is the concentration—the centralization—of authority on the Internet. This centralization of Internet authority has many and terrible consequences. It turns out that placing so much power in the hands of Internet executives undermines us, our relationships,

---

[1] See my "Social Media Stupidifies and Radicalizes Us," *Free Press* (Tampa Bay, tampafp.com), June 19, 2020, https://bit.ly/3kdrjVQ.

[2] See my "Wikipedia Is Badly Biased," *LarrySanger.org* (blog), May 14, 2020, https://bit.ly/3icnuhZ.

our minds, even our sanity, and ultimately our politics. Who knew this would happen, even ten years ago? Some open source software stalwarts foresaw some of it. But as to the general public, they had little notion, perhaps beyond a vague inkling. It is all too plain now.

My vision for free encyclopedias was naïve, but then, Internet geeks at the turn of the millennium mostly shared a naïve vision of the permanence of the freedom of the Internet. In this essay I propose to revisit that vision, diagnose some flaws in it, and trace how the flaws allowed once free social structures to be closed and controlled, representing a distortion of the original vision. Finally, I will glean some lessons for restoring the vision in a more mature and strengthened form. We need, in short, systems for the free exchange of information that are provably decentralized. If we reliably regain control of our own data and take back our own identities, we will throw off the shackles of our arrogant digital masters.

I. The Naïve Vision of Wikipedia

Netscape Navigator—the first browser that supported something that looked roughly like the World Wide Web today—was released in 1994, the same year I started spending a lot of time on the Internet. That was when I met Jimmy Wales online for the first time. We became friendly acquaintances. Six years later, the World Wide Web was no longer virgin territory, but instead resembled, as we said, the "Wild West." Regardless, it was still easy to be naïve and idealistic. In 2000, Wales hired me to develop, as project lead, editor, and co-founder, the project of a free, public-built encyclopedia, which we called Nupedia. While developing it, I had the idea for and started Wikipedia.

Together, Nupedia and Wikipedia were the first serious online encyclopedia project.[3] We were fired up by new possibilities: (1) essentially free publishing and (2) collaborative work at a distance, as and when users wanted to—it was a golden opportunity to do the sort of distributed work that built Diderot's *Encyclopédie*[4] and the *Oxford English Dictionary*.[5]

In developing this vision, we took our cues from another new activity: the messy, open, and free culture of the early open source software (OSS) movement, as well as the Open Directory Project, which was itself inspired by OSS. Just consider Linux, for example. A bunch of programmers led by Linus Torvalds, and earlier and separately, Richard Stallman, were building an open source operating system—a project for the public good, without a single owner, free in cost, with source code open to view and available to everyone to contribute to. We wanted to do the same, but for an encyclopedia. The notion that we might catalog "the sum total of human knowledge," as we put it, struck many as charming but daft. Others thought it was somewhat dangerous-

---

[3] See Chapter 1, especially, as well as Chapters 2 and 3 in this volume. There were other early encyclopedia projects, but they were unserious either in terms of purpose (as in the case of Everything2 and the BBC's H2G2 project) or in terms of organization and execution (as in the case of Richard Stallman's early GNUpedia project). There was also earlier "vaporware," i.e., ideas that never came to fruition.

[4] On this, I can recommend Philipp Blom's *Enlightening the World: Encyclopédie, the Book that Changed the Course of History* (Palgrave Macmillan, 2004).

[5] I read Simon Winchester's fascinating account of the construction of the OED, *The Professor and the Madman: A Tale of Murder, Insanity, and the Making of the Oxford English Dictionary* (Harper Perennial, 2005), soon after it appeared. It sounded a great deal like the story of Nupedia and Wikipedia to me—even down to the interactions with madmen.

sounding. All of these descriptions were eventually proven correct.

Jimmy Wales and I were both, at least at the time, individualists and libertarians, like many people at work on the early Internet. It is not surprising that the Internet at first had such a culture. It was built by geeks who sat by themselves looking at computer screens all day long, fascinated by code, not people. The Internet was still mostly a thing for geeks, a few academics, and a few entrepreneurs. "Everybody and his grandma" had not arrived yet.

A certain vision of human nature and motivation inspired both Wales and, for a while at least, me too. We had the notion that most people really did simply want to share their knowledge, and those were the people who mattered. There was a certain amount of ego or narcissism involved, sure, but ultimately, people just wanted to do the right thing and build a great encyclopedia. That is surely true of many people, maybe even most people who were involved. So it was possible for me in 2001 to declare, "The grandest days of free content have not yet begun."[6] Even in 2005, I could write, "Wikipedia as it stands is a fantastic project."[7] It was all possible, ultimately, because of all public-spirited volunteers. Criticism seemed just churlish and mean toward those volunteers.

Many early criticisms concerned the amateurism: how could anyone trust the "encyclopedia anybody can edit"? My response to this[8] was to maintain that Wikipedia would work in tandem with the expert community of Nupedia, which would vet the amateurs' work. It did not work out that way, however, when Jimmy Wales let Nupedia wither without leadership or support. Wikipedia went it alone.

---

[6] Chapter 2 above.

[7] Chapter 1 above.

[8] As can be seen in Chapter 2 in this volume.

In the contempt for experts that it was easy to detect in Wikipedia,[9] there was a crusading and radical egalitarianism at work, an attitude it was easy to see in operation in the geekdom of the early Internet. I later called it *epistemic egalitarianism*,[10] the notion that any random person online is as good as another for purposes of declaring what is known; what matters is evidence, not credentials.

There were two kinds of naïveté battling here. On my side was the naïve notion that, in the early 21st century Internet, a big, popular project *could* feature cooperation between academics and amateurs. I did try, though, with Citizendium. Looking back, I do not think that was ever going to happen, but it was a worthy experiment and something like it still might work today, with changes.[11] On the other side, which I rejected from the beginning, was the probably more naïve notion that a bunch of amateurs could run an encyclopedia project, with the result ultimately being anything other than amateur and grossly biased.

In fact, strict amateurism could not and did not last long. Criticisms from me and others clearly galled Wikipedians. So they went, as it were, to another extreme. They began to strictly enforce the rule that all claims must be "verifiable," or given some specific citation, and that sources themselves must be "reliable," or taken from a dwindling list of approved, credentialed, expert-informed publications, and mostly secondary, not primary, sources.[12] In this way, a locked-down version of Wikipedia began developing in wake of my criticisms and of books like Andrew Keen's *The Cult of the*

---

[9] See Chapter 5.

[10] See Chapter 7. The phrase has other meanings, too.

[11] I understand that, as of summer 2020, the Citizendium project's new managers were busy making some changes leading to a relaunch.

[12] Primary sources apparently require too much interpretation, which looks like "original research."

Amateur.[13] Increasingly limited to Establishment sources, Wikipedia began to exhibit a decided Establishment orientation. The once-populist encyclopedia turned 180 degrees and today snootily rebuffs the "democratization of knowledge." It has less of a neutral point of view and more of an Establishment point of view today, as it fetishizes "official" expertise. Verifiability policies now operate as a control mechanism. Long gone and forgotten are any concerns that Wikipedia empowers amateurs. It is not "the encyclopedia anybody can edit" anymore. It empowers those who can win at the arcane Wikipedia game of representing some claim as "verifiable" by "reliable sources"; the deck seems stacked in favor of those who can afford to pay off the right people.

That brings me to another kind of criticism I ignored at first, which should not have done. As I said, a sunny view of human nature informed our thinking early on: people just want to share their knowledge; some people do. As it turns out, the fantasy that the other sorts of people did not matter—the bad actors and the cranks, to say nothing of the frauds, spies, PR flacks and political hacks—that really was naïve, and their involvement proved to be the project's Achilles' heel. The original optimism I had about participants disappeared as Wikipedians were rather ridiculously enjoined to "assume good faith"[14] (over my protests when the misbegotten idea was first bruited), when there was abundant evidence that some people were almost constantly acting in bad faith. Moreover, using Wikipedia to make biased edits to articles was within the first year something that the usual suspects were already pressuring the community to accept as being "good faith" editing.

----

[13] *The Cult of the Amateur: How Today's Internet Is Killing Our Culture* (New York: Doubleday/Currency, 2007).

[14] "Assume good faith," Wikipedia.org guideline page, accessed August 2020, https://bit.ly/3fyLB8F.

Here is another example of our naïveté. Wikipedia began when anonymity was still a normal and expected way of interacting. Indeed, it was all right when we were just having academic debates online. With the advent of free encyclopedias, that changed.[15] When Wikipedia gained clout and credibility as a source of information, taking responsibility for what you write—and more importantly, how you edit and how you make decisions for a powerful Internet resource—became much more important. Wikipedia is still, even today, ruled by anonymous administrators. There is no easy way to learn who officially calls the shots. They give free rein to certain powerful anonymous editors, who constantly break rules; at the same time, they punish anyone who does not fall in line with the more favored cadres, those with the most *de facto* authority in the system.

Decisions in Wikipedia-land are supposed to be made first according to rules that apply equally to all, and then in accordance with another poorly-executed fantasy, that of "consensus." This is a problem for several reasons. First, there is supposed to be one person, one vote. But it is all too easy for clever users to make multiple accounts (with extra accounts called "sock puppets") and stack the deck. Second, maybe more importantly, there can be nothing even remotely resembling a "consensus" text, not when it concerns important issues and there is an open, global community of potential participants.[16]

---

[15] See my "A Defense of Modest Real Name Requirements," speech at the *Harvard Journal of Law & Technology* 13th Annual Symposium, March 13, 2008, https://bit.ly/3ha3rjZ.

[16] This is not a claim about the possibility of neutrality, but about the possibility of getting a large, diverse, self-selecting group of humans to agree on a text. It hardly matters that are they instructed to work toward neutrality. Too many people simply will not play nicely. Wikipedia's official position seems to be to deny that this is possible and to bless the results of a "vote" among sock puppets, or

The notion of the possibility of anything deserving the name "consensus" as a decision-making stratagem for a collaborative project makes sense only in the context of a small community with a strong neutrality policy. This became obvious to me even while I was still working on Wikipedia. But consensus was seized upon by unscrupulous (usually anonymous) people who were all too eager to declare themselves to be the voice of the community consensus. That requires jaw-dropping levels of hubris, but the Wikipedia's sociopathic leaders have enough. The same people are routinely willing to simply declare their own controversial views "neutral."

The adoption of neutrality itself as a policy[17] was naïve as well, but not because of anything inherently invalid about the concept (there is not) or even because neutrality is practically impossible for groups (it is not).[18] The problem is this. It is ridiculous to suppose that, in an open, collaborative community, the language of neutrality and the procedures for maintaining it would not be taken over for ideological ends. The only way to avoid that inevitable outcome, I imagine, would have been to adopt a charter, i.e., firm constitutional safeguards,[19] and intelligent, independent methods of enforcement.[20] Of course, that did not happen. Naturally, the neutrality policy was indeed distorted, so that as of 2020, there

---

an arbitrary decision of some administrator, as "community consensus."

[17] The last iteration that I worked on is reproduced in Chapter 2.

[18] See Chapter 4.

[19] See Chapter 1, the "The Governance Challenge" and "Conclusions" sections.

[20] No one has yet solved this problem for collaborative communities. Although Citizendium has done a better job than Wikipedia, we have yet to see whether Citizendium's system can work at a large scale when confronted by motivated partisans. I doubt it, frankly. I suspect that what all such dispute resolution problems require is a jury of uninvolved, independent, and uniquely identified peers.

was a section of the "Neutral point of view" page that declares, "Giving 'equal validity' can create a false balance," "false balance" being the canard used by activist journalists to justify their failure to give fair treatment to competing views.[21] True neutrality is now a distant memory.[22] Wikipedia now takes the Establishment point of view.

We never did adopt anything like a charter. Indeed, that we could get by in project governance via consensus and neutrality without clear rules and especially without a way to arrive at a properly adjudicated, legitimate corporate decisions was one of the most damaging and ridiculous of our early, naïve errors. *Some* rules were eventually clarified, but anything resembling fair decision-making procedures never were. An Arbitration Committee, sort of the Wikipedia Supreme Court, did arise, but it did not officially have the authority to settle content disputes or to bless new projects or change rules and procedures. It is more like a court, not an editorial board or a legislature. After the Wikimedia Foundation got its start, then there was a Board of Trustees and Foundation staff members, but again, they rejected most official responsibility for the content of the wiki, rules, and procedures, which naturally leads to questions about what they do to earn their money. Editorial issues are even today supposed to be primarily the province of an imaginary "consensus" of editors.

---

[21] For one of many examples of the utter failure of journalists to appreciate the importance of neutrality, see Ned Resnikoff, "'Neutral' journalism can't die fast enough," *Salon.com*, June 29, 2010, https://bit.ly/2CjasQi. You might be interested to know that Resnikoff was a "researcher" for Media Matters for America, which is itself possibly the organization more responsible than any other for the rapid descent of journalism into partisanship and smears. Their work is ably laid bare by Sharyl Attkisson in *The Smear: How Shady Political Operatives and Fake News Control What You See, What You Think, and How You Vote* (Harper, 2017). Wikipedia appears to be abused in a similar way.

[22] See "Wikipedia Is Badly Biased," *ibid.*

There has been, in short, something like a power vacuum, and the culture of anonymity made it possible for unscrupulous people of all sorts to strike back-room deals and to wield real power in the project that way. There are many, many stories of how perfectly reasonable edits are summarily deleted, and the accounts of those who made them blocked merely for having the temerity to try to change the wiki. This was relatively rare and outrageous in Wikipedia's first five or ten years, but in the last decade it has become the system, crusty and pungent.

To motivate the powerful to exert control over Wikipedia, it needs only to be popular and widely trusted—and it became that within a few years of its founding. Thus it seems likely that powerful people, organizations, and regimes hire flacks and make necessary payments to ensure that the text reads as they wish it to. Even if we did not have direct testimony to this effect, which we do, the whitewashing of some subjects and slandering of others would be reasonable evidence that this is taking place. In short, while I will not attempt to prove it here, I believe Wikipedia is thoroughly corrupt—the information in it is carefully massaged through behind-the-scenes control and payoffs.[23]

---

[23] In public discussion of Wikipedia corruption, among the topics that come up are the CIA and other government agencies editing; the "Philip Cross" account which cannot be that of a single person; the "Wiki-PR" company which edited Wikipedia for pay on behalf of many famous and powerful people and companies; and certain of Jimmy Wales' associates, including Tony Blair and officials in Kazakhstan. I make no specific accusations here. Moreover, I have heard a lot over the years, including credible reports from a couple different people who made a good living from what is officially detested as "paid editing," but which is in fact better described as corruption. While I have casually paid attention to such things, I leave the investigation of such things up to others. To be honest, the whole subject turns my stomach.

I might engage in further hand-wringing about more instances of naïveté, but I hope I have made my point clear. The Wikipedia vision was based on a number of well-meaning fantasies, themselves charmingly rooted in the Wild West experience and the free and open values of the early Internet. It was all too easy for dishonest schemers and manipulators to twist those fantasies into the fun-house distortion I now disown. Power-mongers celebrate whenever they see open systems they can dominate by such dishonest tactics. Wikipedia certainly gave them much to celebrate.

I do confess that at Wikipedia's founding I had some naïve ebullience, but I hope you can see from the examples I have given, I also tried to rein it in—but failed to do so. So, especially in hindsight, I refuse to take too much responsibility for this easily-twistable idealism. I am still idealistic about some of it (as I will explain below), but policies like decision-making through "consensus" and anonymity even for administrators were fostered not by me but by other forces, both by (or certainly with the acquiescence of) Jimmy Wales and by certain participants and groups of participants. And now, as I said, I wash my hands of it entirely and urge us to start over.

II. The Social Media Disaster

For a long time I thought Wikipedia was doomed to a slow decline while the big social sites thrived. Aside from a bit of bias, I did not see many problems in common between Wikipedia and social media. But then social media, between approximately 2012 and the present, got a lot worse, first in terms of the amount of autonomy permitted to users, then in terms of privacy, and finally in blatant political restrictions on free speech. Now, on reflection, I see the issues with these websites as being all of a piece, with the same root. Like Wikipedia, the social media sites began life in the naïve, idealistic culture of the earlier Internet—which naïveté social media executives twisted, exploited, and abused.

Have a look. Let us begin with a brief history lesson.

Interactive sites for social presence and interaction in the early- to mid-2000s included Friendster, Myspace, Second Life, and Digg. The great innovation was that they were fun places for people to promote what would later be called their "personal brand" as well as to interact with each other in real time online. Dynamic, AJAX-driven pages, which did not require users to refresh the browser to update, made such interaction easy. Due to its own interactivity and rapid updating, the early Wikipedia tended to be lumped in with such sites. The new websites were dubbed "Web 2.0" at first. But then another descriptor, which excluded Wikipedia, emerged: "social media." That was about when the biggest social media giants of today—Facebook (2004), YouTube (2005), Reddit (2005), Twitter (2006), and Instagram (2010)—also emerged.

The original, failed early contenders had social features, to which the new social media giants added speed, brevity, ease of use, and slick, modular, modern design.

Alongside social media we should discuss blogging, which really came into its own in the early 2000s. Blogging differed from all of these in that you could own your own blog and move it around, without depending on any giant Silicon Valley company to manage the software and for all intents and purposes control your data and presence. The heyday and boom of blogging was the mid-2000s, but it continues to be more popular than you might think.

Blogging was really a direct, organic outgrowth of the original World Wide Web and the "personal home pages" (my first website was one) that proliferated in the 1990s. The longer messages that you might put in an email message to a mailing list or a Usenet newsgroup could also be placed on your blog. Blogging, as quick and easy as later blogging software made it, was still primarily a "long-form" medium, suitable for essays and arguments that could go on for months.

Social media was something different. Social media was way briefer and speedier than blogging, and made traditional mailing list and Usenet posts seem laughably outdated. The most extreme example of brevity, I guess, was Twitter, which limited its "microposts"—tweets—to 140 characters. (The 280-character limit arrived in 2017.) Contributions to Reddit tended to be links and terse comments about them, Facebook posts were typically short, and the basic post of social image sharing like Instagram is a picture and a brief comment. It was fun but insipid, kind of like the television of the Internet. It was the "killer app" of the Internet itself, just the sort of thing to attract everybody and his grandma.

As social media took off, some of the Internet commentariat—dubbed the "digerati"—oohed and aahed. But others, like me,[24] Nicholas Carr,[25] and Jaron Lanier,[26] found this to be a worrisome trend. The tendency to push users more and more toward brief, superficial interaction was terrible for users but excellent for the profits of soon-to-be giant social media companies.

The original geek skepticism about the merits of higher education for purposes of advancing Internet careers—something I bemoaned as "geek anti-intellectualism"—was itself a kind of naïveté. I suspect that our collectively dumbed-down civic discourse led many, more and more, to suppose that education and objective, difficult, hard-won knowledge was just not worth the effort. One professor wrote a 2018 book subtitled, "Why the Education System Is a Waste of Time and Money."[27] Meanwhile, the title of my 2008 speech that

---

[24] See Chapters 6-9 in this volume, especially Chapter 9.

[25] Nicholas Carr, "Is Google Making Us Stupid?" *The Atlantic*, July/August 2008, https://bit.ly/2BjtlDG; also *The Shallows: What the Internet Is Doing to Our Brains* (W.W. Norton, 2011).

[26] Jaron Lanier, *You Are Not a Gadget* (Vintage, 2011).

[27] Bryan Caplan, *The Case Against Education: Why the Education System Is a Waste of Time and Money* (Princeton, 2018). I said, presciently, at the end of Chapter 9 in this volume that I would know if some professor wrote a well-received book arguing that education

explained "How the Internet Is Changing What (We Think) We Know" now seems prophetic, but only because then-current trends continued and got worse. Our expectations for K-12 education and even for universities seem to have declined in recent years. I am not laying this problem solely at the step of social media and Wikipedia, but the ways in which messages tend to be simplified by the brief, instant, amateur medium means that our "reality" is "socially constructed" in ways that require little wisdom. It only makes sense that our education would become more foolish as well.

My present point is that these companies dumbed down the once-rich interaction of the early Internet. The early Internet was dominated by smart folks: computer scientists, programmers, and academics. It would have been silly to suppose the Internet would always be that way, and I am not saying anybody did think so. But we did not listen to the Cassandras who, quite correctly, warned us that, if we let them, these shiny new social media toys would steal our attention, our civility, and even our intelligence.

But they stole something else: our autonomy.

Like Wikipedia, early social media thrived on libertarian-flavored freedom. YouTube pushed the envelope by allowing people to upload all sorts of copyrighted material: music, movies, and more. There were not many advertisements in the early years, either—being ad-free was a feature of various social media platforms noticed by many at the time, and forgotten today. It was almost as if YouTube was promoting itself as a free speech locus of rebellion against copyright and commercialism. That was, of course, cynical pretense from the beginning, but it won YouTube a lot of good will.

Video was the stock example of the creative "mashup." That is, the new amateur videos featured components drawn from many different sources—images found at random online,

---

is a waste of time, then that would establish that geek anti-intellectualism had reached full flower. So it has.

music sampled or stolen, new or old videos altered for fun—creating something brand new and greater than the component parts. It would not be possible without the fantastic free culture of abundance and sharing. Larry Lessig, the originator of Creative Commons, was the prophet of this culture.[28] Wikipedia, too, was a good example of how free information brought together by free agents from many different sources could be combined to create something new, free—better. How great.

Even then, a lot of us thought it could not last, and we were right. Hollywood was going to find some way to monetize YouTube; it was only a matter of time. But it was nice that, for a while still, the individualistic, amateur, creative, "Wild West" spirit of the Internet was still respected and encouraged.

By 2008, YouTube was making a lot of money from ads. That signaled that corporate control was around the corner, and so it was. Soon it was locking down the use of music—videos that used proprietary music could be "monetized" by the music owner (or rather, by their industry representative) and made a source of ad revenue. By the 2010s, YouTube was carefully editing feeds in a way that was in line with their corporate policies and marketing strategies; no longer were recommendations and related videos merely a function of your interests.

Particularly in search, YouTube showed you what they wanted you to see. They were ignoring individual choice and autonomy—something absolutely paramount in the culture of the early Internet. Policy decisions governing the operation of the community were made by corporate executives with no meaningful input from users (you could not call them "participants" or "volunteers" anymore; they were "users," as if they were on the drugs the executives hooked them on). By 2019, *The Verge* was reporting that "The Golden Age of

---

[28] *Free Culture: The Nature and Future of Creativity* (Penguin, 2004).

YouTube Is Over," in part because referral traffic was being driven away from small user-made videos and funneled toward videos made by big companies.[29]

My disillusionment with social media began early, but the bloom really left the rose around 2018,[30] the year YouTube started obtrusively placing links to Wikipedia—now the mouthpiece of the Establishment—underneath videos deemed offensively controversial. Then it became clear that Big Tech websites like YouTube, once devoted to empowering the little guy, had become tools of social control.

The discovery that Wikipedia and social media would combine forces to shore up the epistemic privileges of the Establishment would have been surprising once, perhaps. In "Who Says We Know" in 2007,[31] I wrote, "Insofar as the unity of our culture depends on a large body of background knowledge, handing a megaphone to everyone has the effect of fracturing our culture." It is all the more stunning, then, that in 2020 Wikipedia and the social media successors of "Web 2.0" have fallen in line with the Establishment, trying (and so far failing) to create a global monoculture. They have become quite aggressive about defining "what we all know."

Matters were similar with Facebook and Twitter, which became more and more controlled. Facebook added its "News Feed" in 2006, but by 2011 it was editing this feed to display news it thought users would find most "relevant."[32] After that, the editing of information shown to you—and bear in mind, this is personal information from your "friends"—became quite openly political, as when Facebook tried to "stop fake

---

[29] Julia Alexander, "The Golden Age of YouTube Is Over," *The Verge*, April 5, 2019, https://bit.ly/33Wgulx.

[30] Brandon Weber, "YouTube now displays facts below conspiracy theory videos," *BigThink.com*, August 8, 2018, https://bit.ly/3aoEyhO.

[31] Chapter 7 in this volume.

[32] Samantha Murphy, "The Evolution of Facebook News Feed," *Mashable.com*, March 12, 2013, https://bit.ly/3ap2Zvy.

news."[33] Twitter exhibited a similar pattern. Moderation on discussion platforms such as Quora and Medium became more and more blatant in its political bias, which drove me away permanently in 2018-19. As I put it then:

Clearly, they aren't serving you; you're serving them.

We've been in an experiment. Many of us were willing to let Internet communities be centralized in the hands of big Silicon Valley corporations. Maybe it'll be OK, we thought. Maybe the concentration of money and power will result in some really cool new stuff that the older, more decentralized Internet couldn't deliver. Maybe they won't mess it up, and try to exert too much control, and abuse our privacy. Sure! Maybe!

The experiment was a failure. We can't trust big companies, working for their own profit, to make good decisions for large, online communities. The entire industry has earned and richly deserves our distrust and indignation.[34]

As a type of autonomy, free speech is worth dwelling on a bit. At its birth, social media was every bit as much devoted to free speech as the larger libertarian Internet had been. In 2012, six years after its inception, Twitter's then-CEO Dick Costolo could still say (quoting company General Counsel, Alex Macgillivray), "We are the free speech wing of the free speech party."[35] But they did not mean it, apparently. That self-description was once famous for its idealistic boldness; later it became infamous for its hypocrisy. It was a literally a joke, according to current CEO Jack Dorsey in an interview in 2018. Dorsey said,

---

[33] "Facebook Is Changing News Feed (Again) to Stop Fake News," *Wired.com*, April 10, 2019, https://bit.ly/33XQy8P.

[34] "Why I quit Quora and Medium for good," *LarrySanger.org* (blog), February 1, 2019, https://bit.ly/3kOSczZ.

[35] Emma Barnett, "Twitter chief: We will protect our users from Government," *The Telegraph*, October 18, 2011, https://bit.ly/30QuRWx.

This quote around 'free speech wing of the free speech party' was never, was never a mission of the company. It was never a descriptor of the company that we gave ourselves. It was a, it was a joke. Because of how people found themselves in the spectrum.[36]

Twitter's U.K. General Manager, Tony Chang, put it in terms of "neutrality" in 2012: "Generally, we remain neutral as to the content". Dorsey paid some lip service to neutrality even as late as 2018, although he was reduced to incoherence on the point: "we were not absolute absolutists because we [were] building a purely neutral platform versus building an impartial platform."[37]

That was the past. They cannot deny it any longer: they are trying to tell you what to think and how to vote. As with Wikipedia, this is essentially a betrayal of the fine but naïve ideals of the early Internet. It would have struck us in 2000 as an implausibly dystopian future that the likes of Google would develop from a neutral engine for finding information to, in 2020, a new kind of digital oligarchy.

Need I go on and explain how we allowed social media companies access to our personal secrets and relationships, trusting that they would, like the server administrators of yesteryear, scrupulously keep their hands off our stuff? That was perhaps the most naïve of all; of course that trust was violated.

In short, twenty years ago, we essentially made a deal with what would soon become the giants of Silicon Valley. "Sure, go ahead and host our videos, manage our social interactions, render the news we share into a usable feed, and organize our information and knowledge. What we expect, however, is the freedom to say what we want, with plenty of options for controlling how information is presented to us. We also insist

---

[36] Hank Berrien, "Twitter CEO: That Quote about Twitter Being 'The Free Speech Wing of the Free Speech Party' Was a Joke," *DailyWire.com*, October 18, 2018, https://bit.ly/2PP9uP6.
[37] *Ibid.*

on neutrality: obviously, we would not willingly place our online lives in the hands of people who will try to control the world's democracies. We will even let you use information about us, as long as you stay within reasonable limits and do not systematically violate our privacy. Of course you would never have the temerity to do *that*. Right? So if you do these things for us, we will look the other way as you get rich using our content—over which, by the way, we expect to continue to enjoy full ownership rights and control."

If that was the deal, it was certainly naïve of us to make it, because there was no way the Internet giants were going to hold up their end of the bargain and stop at mere wealth. They were always going to parlay their position into one of raw power. When they became big enough to crush any competitors, our expectations were systematically flouted. Free speech, autonomy, neutrality, privacy, data self-ownership, it all went out the window. Over a decade after we struck this Faustian bargain, in about 2018, we started waking up, rubbing our eyes, looking about ourselves in horror, and wondering what could possibly be done about the mess we, in our naïveté, had gotten ourselves into.

III. A Return to Freedom

There are no easy answers; I will propose one, but it will not be easy to implement.

Let us begin by doing a little diagnosis. In the transition from 2000 to 2020, what went wrong? There are several plausible ideas—naïveté about the importance of sociopathic executives must be part of the answer—but I want to suggest that several problems may be summed up in one word: centralization. Our online lives became collectivized, consolidated, and amalgamated. It is worth listing the ways in which this has happened.

In social media, we lost effective control over our contributions to the public discourse; Facebook and the rest basically took ownership over our data. We can export our data, to be sure, but we cannot really do anything meaningful with that data outside of Facebook's proprietary system. Unlike a blog, the value that my social media data has depends in great part on its position within a giant community. That much is acceptable; that is the nature of social media. The problem is that Facebook exclusively owns and centrally controls this community. The same goes, of course, for virtually all other social media.

So the Silicon Valley behemoths own and centrally control not just our data, but also the social software that runs our online lives. We have also lost the ability to switch easily to "enough, and as good" (in Locke's phrase[38]) competing servers, running competing software, as we still can for our email, blogs, web hosting, domain name hosting, and some other important Internet services.

All the problems listed above ultimately flow from our lack of autonomy or control, as we participate in networks of gargantuan size with single owners. Such networks possess power beyond that of many nation states, power over our privacy, speech, what we are supposed to pay attention to, and what "we all know." This is of special importance because they ultimately wield political power to rival that of the political parties and news media, power that is all out of proportion of the representation of their owners among the populace. In democracies, that is not just a matter of concern; it is dangerous.

---

[38] John Locke, *Second Treatise of Government* V.27. The relevance here is that in the state of nature, according to Locke, a person may justify an ownership claim to some property by mixing his labor with it, if there are "enough, and as good" similar claims available to others. Perhaps an argument can be mounted on Lockean grounds against digital monopolies of the sort you see in social media, and in favor of standards and protocols supporting decentralized networks, proposed further down.

How did we come to this desperate situation? Yes, we naïvely trusted in Silicon Valley geeks, but first the geeks had to empower themselves with tech.

In the late 1990s, it was already easy for geeks, who observed the widespread support of JavaScript by browsers, to imagine new systems in which web pages worked less like the static pages of a magazine and more like interactive computer programs. That would enable people to interact among themselves in real time via an attractive, user-friendly interface. It would change the Internet dramatically. A massive step forward came with AJAX and dynamically updating pages, demonstrated by Google Maps and others. Soon many modern web pages featured live updating feeds on pages. It looked like sorcery to those of us used to a static Internet.

That was enough to launch social media, but a second innovation was icing on the cake: the advent of the ubiquitous smart phone. Suddenly, in addition to desktop computers and laptop computers, professionals and students had handheld devices that all accessed the same Internet. It was necessary to sync data across three devices. But how? The solution was simple: let the professionals handle it. You upload your data to Apple's iCloud and a thousand other cloud services—every social media site was essentially a cloud service—and simply log in from any of your devices to access everything. Browsers powered by JavaScript, and AJAX-type services in particular, made it easy to do the very same things on all of your digital devices or "platforms." Unless you were a geek, you could not very well install and run your own web server, now could you? But that is what it would take if you wanted to do it yourself.

Now the geeks understood how the cloud might work. It was very exciting. There was something like a digital gold rush. The previous, "Web 1.0" software that connected people had to be installed on many different servers, software like email, IRC chat, and Usenet. Then client software had to be installed on user desktops. These services were all "social software," but not social media in the modern sense. Big centralized services like AOL and CompuServe did exist, but they were for newbies in the 1980s and 90s. They might have seemed primitive to decent, rank-and-file geeks, but such centralized systems were what the big investors kept funding. Data storage was to be centralized, and software could be managed all in one place. JavaScript and AJAX made it possible to run all the services you needed in the browser—just as we are used to today.

From that, everything else followed. The first social media systems were just new kinds of websites, ones with user accounts. There was nothing wrong with that. But the next systems were bigger, faster, slicker, attracting everybody and his grandma. Suddenly they controlled our data and the systems it ran on.

Open source activists saw what was happening, and were up in arms, but nobody listened. The investors and their CEO flacks hoped the rest of us, the nontechnical masses, would not ask too many questions. When we did, they assured us that our data would remain our own, that it would always be reasonably private, that we would be able to speak our minds just as we always had, and that we would have some control and input into what happened in these brave new virtual communities. Stupid chumps,[39] we believe them. We really *were* naïve. After about 2014, they had their hooks firmly into us and were far ahead of any plausible competition, and the mask started slipping.[40] Power had been centralized, Silicon

---

[39] Or as Mark Zuckerberg put it, "dumb f--ks." See Laura Raphael, "Mark Zuckerberg Called People Who Handed Over Their Data 'Dumb F****'," *Esquire*, March 20, 2018, https://bit.ly/34lPXOy.

[40] You might think that the recent movement against traditional free speech rights was merely a reaction against Donald Trump, but that movement started mainstreaming in 2013. It began with the campus hype about "trigger warnings." A year or two later, "hate speech" was the topic du jour, the so-called Speech Wars had begun, still before the Trump phenomenon, and it was suddenly possible to

Valley was in charge, and they did not seem to mind who knew it.

Perhaps we trusted geekdom because—"Well, you know geeks!" The popular perception of geekdom may be naïve, but it matters: "Geeks? They are smart about computers, but they do not really know anything about the messy real world, right? Sure, you can trust them with your data. They are socially clueless but, like the servers they operate, they recede into the background. They are fine. Companies started by geeks will be like that. I mean, look at these people, like Mark Zuckerberg and Jack Dorsey; they are just programmers that hit it big. They are harmless. You can trust them."

I think a lot of people thought this way. But it turned out to be grossly wrong. We did not begin to understand the power dynamics of social media and Silicon Valley until it was too late. As soon as power began to be wielded digitally, the power-mad learned to code. Investors cashed in and the Establishment, both business and government, stood up and took notice. The digital revolution, like other revolutions, was a change of power, and geeks were the new power players on the scene. If power corrupts, some geeks were certainly corrupted. They are not necessarily the nice, harmless nerds you knew in school. Many powerful ones are sociopaths. Some, doubtless, are monsters.[41]

Similar remarks apply to Wikipedia, although the dynamics were a little different. I have already discussed the naïveté of the early participants (including myself). But the naïveté of the readers mattered too. A lot of readers decided to trust

---

talk about restrictions on free speech in the United States of America.

[41] We might infer this simply from the fact that many move up to the position of CEO. Jack McCullough, "The Psychopathic CEO," *Forbes*, December 9, 2019, https://bit.ly/3gXjotR. Other geeks become powerful government contractors working for spy agencies and the military.

Wikipedia as "good enough" mostly because it featured long articles, lots of pictures, and most impressively, many footnotes. And it was written by harmless geeks, right?

But the news media was instrumental as well. I remember being surprised at how seldom I had to answer criticism and hard questions—I was very aware of all the hard questions that it was possible to ask.[42] One of the first studies, not peer reviewed, appeared in the top science journal *Nature*[43] and gave Wikipedia a glowing review according to a methodology that was shockingly poor for such a distinguished journal. For a long time I thought this gentle media treatment was due to the laudable kindness of the media, which merely wanted to encourage such a public-spirited project. But, considering how both the news media and Wikipedia evolved over the next fifteen years, I now wonder if the kid glove treatment was done because journalists understood better than I did that, in time, the project could become a particularly effective mouthpiece of the Establishment.

At any rate, as I said in the first section above, early participants naïvely assumed the project would forever be rooted in its early commitment to freedom, openness, neutrality, and egalitarianism, all features to be found in the early Internet. Meanwhile, Wikipedia's readers naïvely bought the line that you could trust a charmingly public-spirited resource that a bunch of geeks so carefully built. After all, it has so many footnotes—it must be OK! Their naïve reliance gave it a web traffic rank of #4 among all websites, according to Alexa.com.[44]

---

[42] See my version of "Wikipedia/Our Replies to Our Critics," October 11, 2001, https://bit.ly/2OBBs00.

[43] Jim Giles, "Internet encyclopaedias go head to head," *Nature* 438 (2005): 900–901, https://www.nature.com/articles/438900a.

[44] See https://www.alexa.com/siteinfo/wikipedia.org for the current ranking. Until 2019. As of this writing, the site is ranked at 14. What the drop in ranking might mean is unclear.

But let us not forget that Wikipedia is the encyclopedia that Google built: as I explained in my memoir,[45] almost from the beginning, Wikipedia search results ranked highly on Google. Of course, you can argue that this was due to the inherent merit of Wikipedia and the fact that people really are often just looking for the information contained in encyclopedia articles. But note also that Google has contributed millions to Wikipedia and makes use of Wikipedia information in its influential Knowledge Graph API. However all that is, it is certain that Google helped establish Wikipedia's undeserved popular perception of credibility.

The underlying problem is similar to that of social media: Wikipedia, too, centralizes control over our information. Rather than being spread out across many competing articles on many different servers owned by many different entities with many points of view, it is all on one server network owned by a single nonprofit organization (the Wikimedia Foundation), promulgating one article per topic, explained from a single Establishment point of view, closely guarded by aggressive participants. If you want to participate yourself, you must learn to play the game. Chances are, you will not be able to. It is the encyclopedia only a select few can *successfully* edit. The "collegial" group dynamics I described in an early promotional essay for Wikipedia[46] are long gone.

Decentralization is the answer.[47]

The entire blockchain movement agrees. However much it is motivated by the desire for filthy lucre, it has received a sympathetic ear from many of us because of the crying need for decentralizing our data, software, and systems. Perhaps

---

[45] Chapter 1 in this volume.

[46] "Britannica or Nupedia?" Chapter 2 in this volume.

[47] The following discussion of decentralization is adapted from my "Proposing a 'Declaration of Digital Independence,'" *Wired*, March 12, 2019. Cf. my "Declaration of Digital Independence," Chapter 11 in this volume.

blockchains will play a role in doing that. But many of the essential technologies of decentralization can be achieved simply through protocols and existing, coin-free decentralized networks like Torrent networks.

But what, exactly, *is* decentralization? We should ask that more. An explanation will give us a roadmap for creating a freer Internet. On my view, there are seven components to a fully decentralized, open network, whether of social media, encyclopedias, or anything else.[48]

1. *Open, common standards and protocols.* There cannot be a decentralized social media network unless there are rules that are held in common among an arbitrarily large, open group of publishers and readers—for example, standards for types of content and protocols for transmitting and displaying it. The network is defined by these standards and protocols. Email is an apt example. By contrast, Facebook is a good example of a giant network that is centralized partly because it lacks an open standard; that is why you cannot just transfer your Facebook posts to some other social media website. Wikipedia, too, publishes articles but not according to any sort of distribution standard or protocol, as they could. If they did, maybe there would be an even larger body of free encyclopedia articles that all use that standard.[49]

2. *Multiple publishers.* A wide variety of (not just one or two) completely independent websites, apps, individuals, companies, organizations, etc., should be able to publish to the network. For example, the RSS-driven "Blogosphere" extends well beyond any one blog publisher such as WordPress, Blogger, Medium, etc. This eliminates the centralized "walled

---

[48] A decentralized encyclopedia network is described in "Introducing the Encyclosphere," Chapter 10 in this volume.

[49] MediaWiki markup is not such a standard, since it concerns only how the content of the article is to be marked up, not how to organize all the metadata about an article.

gardens" of corporations like Google, Microsoft, and Apple, as well as Wikipedia.

3. *No central content repository.* Not only should there be many publishers, there should not be any "master" database of the content—for example, no central database that all copies are expected to stay consistent with. Content should be either duplicated the same everywhere (as in the case of blockchains and Usenet) or else assembled on the fly from an arbitrarily large number of sources that one subscribes to (as in the case of RSS). Twitter, among many others, fails this test. While Twitter has an API, it maintains the master copy of all tweets and will not serve tweets hosted elsewhere; although you can publish first elsewhere and make copies on Twitter, Twitter treats its copies as the canonical tweets. Similarly, Wikipedia aims to be an essentially closed and central repository of encyclopedic information. Surely the decent thing would be to support the inclusion of competing articles. I cannot imagine Wikipedia doing that, though. We need to create what would be, essentially, an open *superset* of all encyclopedia articles.

4. *Open to all publishers.* There are no special requirements, beyond strictly technical requirements, for a publisher to use the network. Anyone who wants to set up a service that distributes encyclopedia articles, microposts, pictures, videos, etc., that are published on the network can do so. Codification of living standards and protocols and technical direction by groups like ICANN and W3C is generally fine. This prevents any organization or association from taking editorial control; so there could not be any network-wide group of fact-checkers or moderators such as Facebook and others have assembled. It also prevents central coordination by a privileged group of publishers.

5. *Multiple readers; equal access to the entire network.* It should not matter which reader you use to view other people's content, and it also should not matter where the content was published. You should be able to locate all the same types of public content on all (or many) of them, just as you can use any browser to locate anything on the open Internet, and you

can use any blog reader to read any RSS blog. This eliminates reprobate closed blogging platforms like Medium. It, despite using RSS, does not (as far as I know) allow its users to incorporate blog posts from outside of its own network, not without cohosting the posts on Medium. Despite being a public resource and volunteer-driven, they even require that you have an account just to read more than a few articles.

6. *Open to all users.* You should not need any specialized skills, and participation should not require any special payments or permissions beyond minimal, well-justified ones. For example, the web is easy enough for almost anyone to use, and the only cost is the price of your Internet connection. Anyone can register a domain name, from any of zillions of domain name hosting companies, for a nominal fee. WordPress's 2018 redesigned block-based editor helped the "clueless newbies" to get into blogging a little more easily. Open protocols helps to guarantee that networks stay open to everyone, without permissions, qualifications, or abilities. This eliminates subscription services, "pay-to-play" websites and APIs (like many Google services, which are built on user contributions) and blockchains, academic or industry groups, etc. It also, in my opinion, eliminates networks that ordinary users do not have a chance of setting up. If you have to be a programmer to be able to participate in the system as an ordinary user, it is not really decentralized for that reason alone. It is centralized, or focused, in the hands of geeks.

7. *Individuals control their own content.* You should be able to fully own and control the distribution of your own content, just as you control your email, your blog, or your website. The network should empower no one to block or censor it at the network layer (or only for technical reasons). The HTTP and HTTPS protocols and the RSS standard are excellent examples. There simply should not exist any central authority or conditions that you must satisfy, other than DNS and web hosting companies, the means to pay them, and government regulations. Most social media apps fail this test, no matter how much they like to talk about how decentralized they are.

Only a standard or protocol (and things made out of them, like Torrent networks and blockchains) can credibly satisfy this requirement; only an entire network of websites, run by neutral, technical standards and protocols, can actually guarantee individual control. Of course, even extremely widespread adoption of such standards would not stop Facebook, YouTube, and Wikipedia from imposing speech restrictions on their users and readers. The difference I want to see is that speech restrictions should not prevent others, who do want to view such blocked content, from being able to view it as part of the same network.

According to these requirements, there are various ways in which social media and Wikipedia are not yet decentralized:

- The mere existence of some well-developed standard, such as the ActivityPub social networking protocol, is not enough; it must actually be in use.

- Moreover, it does not suffice that a few small websites and apps are using a standard. Until several fully independent websites are doing so, it is not a robustly open standard.

- If certain necessary tools do not support the standard by enabling content to be exported in a standards-based feed, by importing and incorporating content from different publishers, etc., decentralization still has not happened.

- If the tools for participation are usable only by people with significant technical skill, that fact prevents robust or strong decentralization.

- More generally, until many more of the billions of people toiling in the centralized digital plantations of Big Tech have switched to decentralized social media and a decentralized encyclopedia network, the Internet will remain centralized. A relatively small network can be decentralized in a perfectly good sense, to be sure, but its availability does not mean that social media in general has been decentralized.

The advantages of a more decentralized Internet should be obvious. A return to decentralization would restore many of the ideals of the original Internet. Freedom, openness, neutrality, and egalitarianism could again become the norm, because neither the data nor the systems to control it would be in the hands of powerful corporate or government authorities. They could not be, because control would be in the hands of individuals. Of course, any system can be dishonestly attacked and manipulated; but a decentralized Internet would provide fewer levers of control and structurally empower individuals, small business, and small organizations.

Free speech would reign so long as there were no mechanism for network-wide censorship, just as there is none for blogs or websites generally. Competition among many different social media and encyclopedia systems would guarantee a maximum of user autonomy. Openness—the open, accountable wielding of power—would prevail because there would be no levers of power that could be operated from behind the scenes. Neutrality might finally have a chance because the inherently tolerant nature of decentralized networks allows no particular point of view to prevail. And such networks would foster digital equality. Decentralized networks would give equal rights to all to use and propagate their information, develop tools, and innovate. They are a level playing field, with Silicon Valley elites and their powerful collaborators no longer specially privileged.

Powerful forces stand to lose political dominance and billions of dollars if we succeed. We can expect them to fight back and to use dirty tricks. We have already seen how Wikipedia was essentially occupied first by trolls, who established the insane anarchical culture, which ultimately empowered activists and shills to use Wikipedia to push their agendas. We have seen how well-funded geeks were able to build slick new tools and attract the masses, absorbing their data for profit while manipulating them for political gain.

The Establishment wrings its hands about "misinformation" and cyber-crime—meaning information that it does not control and wants to monitor. So I am concerned that new, only partly-decentralized systems would bake in a layer of editorial management and surveillance that would enable, when the next crisis hits, a new kind of top-down control similar to what we have labored under in the last decade. We must fight against that.

But it is no longer 2000. We are not quite as naïve as we were twenty years ago. We should be more aware of the importance of keeping the management of the protocols open and democratic, and out of the exclusive control of giant corporations and oppressive governments. We must ensure that the networks we use to share our digital lives and catalog our knowledge remain decentralized. They must be *provably* decentralized. That will make authoritarian and totalitarian usurpations of our rights much more difficult, if not structurally impossible. A community charter[50] for governing a decentralized network would probably not be necessary for the simple reason that there is no community to govern, no more than there is any community of website owners.

But the ultimate safeguard of free networks is the people who use them. We must not be complacent. We must educate our children about our digital rights, and think of and jealously guard them, just as we teach and think about our civil rights. As life becomes digital, our digital freedoms become every bit as important as our traditional freedoms. It is probably only in such a political context that, sometime in the future, we will indeed finally be able to rely on an "encyclopedia anybody can edit," because it is a network anybody can join. It could naturally bring out and highlight the best of our free knowledge.

---

[50] Such as one for Wikipedia, described in Chapter 1 in this volume, that I regret never getting adopted; or one for Citizendium, which we did adopt.

Origins of the Essays

All previously-published essays here are in new editions, with one exception (Chapter 11). Further notes about the essays precede each selection above.

"The Early History of Nupedia and Wikipedia" first appeared in April 2005 on *Slashdot*, a group blog devoted to technology news and opinion; it was later reprinted in Chris Dibona, Mark Stone, and Danese Cooper, *Open Sources 2.0: The Continuing Evolution* (O'Reilly, 2006).

"*Britannica* or Nupedia?" appeared in July 2001 in the now-defunct *Kuro5hin.org*, a community-edited blog and discussion site. "Wikipedia is wide open" appeared the following September on the same site.

"Wikipedia's Original Neutrality Policy" can be found buried deep in the change history of "Wikipedia:Neutral point of view". This particular version—the last I worked on—was posted January 5, 2002.

"Why Neutrality?" was commissioned by *Ballotpedia.org*, appearing on that site in December, 2015, when I was consulting for them on the neutrality policies and procedures.

"Why Wikipedia Must Jettison Its Anti-Elitism" appeared in December, 2004 on *Kuro5hin.org*.

"How the Internet Is Changing What (We Think) We Know" was a speech given at the Upper Arlington Public Library, Upper Arlington, Ohio, in 2008.

"Who Says We Know" was an invited essay, published April 2007 on the now-notorious group blog site *Edge.org*. It was notorious for connections with Jeffrey Epstein. John Brockman offered to represent me as a literary agent and landed me a book deal. I never met him, and I never finished the book.

"Individual Knowledge in the Internet Age" was an invited paper; it was made the cover article for the April 2010 issue of *EDUCAUSE Review*, a journal about technology in higher education.

"Is There a New Geek Anti-Intellectualism?" has appeared on my blog *LarrySanger.org*, in June 2011.

"Introducing the Encyclosphere" was first a speech delivered at TheNextWeb's Hard Fork Summit in Amsterdam, in October, 2019.

"Declaration of Digital Independence" was published in June, 2019, and is still freely available, on *LarrySanger.org* and elsewhere.

"The Future of the Free Internet" is a new essay.

About the Author

LARRY SANGER was born in Bellevue, Washington, and from age seven grew up in Anchorage, Alaska. He earned a B.A. in Philosophy from Reed College in 1991 and an M.A. in Philosophy from the Ohio State University in 1995. He decided against a career in academia but finished a Ph.D. in Philosophy anyway, also from Ohio State, in 2000, the same year he started Nupedia. The next year he started Wikipedia (see Chapter 1 in this volume). Both were projects for Bomis.com, the company of which Jimmy Wales was partner and CEO.

Following the early 2000s tech recession, he taught philosophy at local area colleges in central Ohio. In 2005, he started a long string of online reference and educational projects, including Citizendium, WatchKnowLearn, and Reading Bear, and consulted for such online encyclopedia projects as Ballotpedia and Everipedia. He is still an active Internet consultant and project developer with a web presence at Sanger.io. He is now building support for the Encyclosphere project (see Chapter 10 in this volume).

In his spare time, Larry helps home school his two sons, plays Irish traditional music on the fiddle, and writes on the Internet, where he has a blog, LarrySanger.org.

This is his first book.

Index

Index

Index

Index

31, 140, 146–49, 153–64, 170,
219, 246. *See also* knowledge
Oxford English Dictionary, 42, 221
Panelas, Tom, 56
participation, 8–9, 13, 18–26, 32–
35, 49–52, 55, 59, 62–65, 79,
105, 130–34, 170, 212, 224–25,
229, 233, 241–43, 246–47. *See
also* collaboration; community
partisanship, 44, 74, 75, 78, 86, 93,
116, 119, 227
peer review, 4, 7, 8, 9, 12, 13, 14,
15, 46, 47, 48, 59, 63, 66, 67, 68,
76, 162, 164, 167
Peirce, C.S., 156
Philip Cross, 228
philosophers, 144, 152
philosophy, philosophers, x, 11,
13, 16, 78–79, 83, 85, 97, 101,
105, 110, 114–115, 120, 130–31,
155–56, 169, 179–180, 192, 200,
201
Pink, Daniel, 8
Plato, 144
policy, of Internet projects and
society in general, x, 6–9, 12–
13, 20–37, 44–51, 55, 69–84, 85–
87, 91, 95, 102–7, 110, 113–15,
119–20, 123, 126, 129, 133–36,
172, 179, 206, 224, 226, 229,
233. *See also* rules
power, over people, 99, 104, 111–
12, 128, 135, 152–54, 171, 206–9,
212–15, 219, 224, 228, 235–38,
241, 248. *See also* authority
prejudice, vs. impartiality, 90, 99,
167, 178, 192
privacy, 147, 212–16, 229, 235–38
ProCon.org, 124–25
programmers, programming, 14–
20, 45, 64, 165–66, 193–94,
208, 211, 217, 221, 232, 241, 246.
See also software
propaganda, 87, 94, 96, 100, 103–
4, 112, 161. *See also* fake news

protocols. *See* standards,
technical, and protocols
pseudoscience, 80–81
publishing, iv, 6, 24, 63, 65, 85–
86, 124–27, 143, 152–53, 164,
188–89, 194, 206–8, 211, 216,
221, 244–47
Quora, 170, 235
rationality, 90, 95–101, 107–9. *See
also* objectivity; neutrality
Raymond, Eric S., 65, 167, 168
Recent Changes log, 59, 65
Reddit, 153, 170, 230–31
reference works, x, 6, 57, 156
relativism, 79, 168
reliabilism, 155
reliability, 4–5, 14, 19, 42, 49, 54,
66–68, 106–7, 129–30, 140, 147–
49, 154–58, 163, 165, 168, 215,
223–24. *See also* credibility
repository, content, 33, 42, 207–
8, 211, 216, 245
Resnikoff, Ned, 89, 227
rights, iv, 30, 53, 55, 113, 170, 171,
194, 213–16, 237, 240, 248–49
Ritchey, Jason, 14, 16
Robinson, Ken, 196, 201
RSS (Really Simple Syndication),
207–9, 244–46
rules, of Internet projects, 6, 8,
21–26, 29, 37–39, 44, 49–53,
100, 124, 223–27, 244. *See also*
policy
sapere aude (Kant apothegm), 98–
99, 108
scholars, scholarship, xi, 58, 84,
115, 119, 161, 185–86, 198. *See
also* academics (professors),
experts
Second Life, 147, 185, 230
shame, shaming, ix, 23, 43–44
Shell, Tim, 8, 12, 20
Shirky, Clay, 187–89, 195
Silicon Valley, 205, 230, 235–41,
248

Index

www.ingramcontent.com/pod-product-compliance
Lightning Source LLC
Chambersburg PA
CBHW071107050326
40690CB00008B/1141